A FEW DROPS OF WATER

The Story of The Questors Theatre
1929-1989

by Gwenan Evans and others

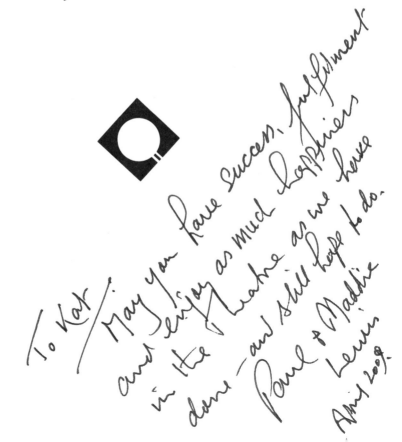

To Kat,
May you have success, fulfilment and enjoy as much happiness in the Theatre as we have done — and still hope to do.
Paul & Maddie
Lewis
April 2009.

Published by:
Mattock Press
The Questors Theatre
12 Mattock Lane
Ealing
London W5 5BQ
England

Printed in the UK by Hobbs The Printers of Southampton

(2012/89)

What have we achieved since 1929? . . . I think that perhaps the most important achievement of all is a tradition of service to the theatre. What is ahead? Many exciting things—looming large amongst them is our new theatre, only a material thing, but itself, so we hope, a contribution to the future development of the theatre, the development perhaps of new dramatists, of new actors and actresses, designers and producers; the adding of a few drops of water to the mainstream of theatre.

Alfred Emmet, October 1950

Foreword

by Dame Judi Dench, President of The Questors Theatre

The Questors Theatre has a unique story to tell. Over the 60 years of its existence it has triumphed against all the odds to become one of the best-known and most respected amateur theatre companies in the world.

It has always aspired to the highest possible artistic standards, demanding total commitment from its members. It has encouraged new playwrights, particularly through a 18-year period of annual New Plays Festivals and, most recently, through the establishment of a national Student Playwriting Competition. It has run an internationally-recognised Student Acting Course for over 40 years. And it has fostered communication between like-minded theatres, nationally through the Little Theatre Guild of Great Britain and internationally through the International Amateur Theatre Association.

The Questors has long had a world-wide reputation for innovation and experiment in styles of production, in design, in staging and in choice of plays. The Questors Playhouse, a truly adaptable theatre, the first such playhouse to be designed and still one of the very few which have been built, is a tangible monument to the vision and theatrical courage of Alfred Emmet and his band of fellow-members.

For the sake of all members of The Questors, past and present, this story deserves to be recorded for posterity, for all lovers of the theatre. That is what this book tries to do.

Judi Dench

Introduction

In compiling this history, I decided to eschew a strict chronological format, although I hope the story does flow in a fairly logical way. There are so many strings to The Questors' bow that to deal with them all on a strict year-by-year basis would have led to a totally confusing and indigestible narrative line.

Also, since I am, by Questors standards, still a 'new girl', and because there are others far more qualified than I to analyse the significance of many of the key activities, I invited a number of long-standing active members to contribute chapters on specific topics. These chapters appear in the text at what appeared to me to be the most appropriate points.

I am greatly indebted to many members of The Questors. In particular, to the conscientious Archivists of the past 20 years, Wyllie Longmore, Wilfrid Sharp, George Benn, Carol Metcalfe and Muriel Thomas, who have made my research of written archive material a relatively simple task. To others who have kept detailed records over the years, especially Martin Bowley. To Denis Robinson for his meticulous researching of the early history of Mattock Lodge. To those who willingly agreed to contribute chapters to this history, whose names appear in the appropriate places in the text. To the many members who have sat with me and talked into my tape recorder, particularly Lister Beck, George Benn, Michael Green, Kath Harrington and Rena Rice. To John Davey, Michael Green and Wilfrid Sharp, for reading and checking the manuscript in its various stages and for many helpful suggestions. And to Martin Bowley and Roger Kelly, for encouraging me to undertake the project in the first place and for all their help and support.

Most of all, however, my thanks are due to Alfred Emmet, not least for allowing me to tell what is really his story. A founder member and The Questors' first Hon. Secretary, Honorary Director for 21 years, Director of Studies of the Student Group for 38 years, member of the Committee of Management for 31 years and Vice-President since 1981, Alfred's name has been synonymous with that of The Questors for over half a century. His was the inspiration behind the whole organisation, and the reputation which The Questors enjoys in the world of the theatre is in large measure a reflection of his personal standing. Without Alfred's foresight, enthusiasm and determination, it is probable that The Questors Theatre would not exist at all; it would certainly not exist in the form it does today. It is no surprise that the entry under 'The Questors Theatre' in *The Oxford Companion to the Theatre* for many years read simply "see Emmet".

Alfred has been a constant source of encouragement and support throughout the period of the preparation of this book. Not only has he contributed three chapters and allowed me unrestricted access to the meticulously-kept records of his time as Secretary and Honorary Director, but he has patiently sat and talked into my tape recorder for hours, and spent a fair proportion of his 1988 summer holiday recording Questors reminiscences on tape with his wife Kit and John Clemow. He has also carefully read and checked the manuscript at every stage; needless to say, all his comments have been to the point and have invariably resulted in a much better and clearer narrative. I hope he feels the finished article to be satisfactory—it is as much a tribute to him as to The Questors.

Gwenan Llwyd Evans
July 1989

Contents

		page
Chapter 1	The Early Days, 1929-1939	1
Chapter 2	The War Years, 1939-1945	9
Chapter 3	The Site is Purchased, 1945-1952	15
Chapter 4	The Next Step, 1952-1954	23
Chapter 5	An Adaptable Theatre	31
Chapter 6	Towards a New Theatre, 1955-1962	35
Chapter 7	Other Activities, 1955-1960	45
Chapter 8	"This is a Beginning", 1962-1964	52
Chapter 9	Bricks and Mortar	58
Chapter 10	Making Waves, 1964-1969	67
Chapter 11	Studio Theatre at The Questors	72
Chapter 12	The Questors at School(s)	80
Chapter 13	New Plays at The Questors	87
Chapter 14	The Questors and Coarse Acting	94
Chapter 15	Organisational Nuts and Bolts, 1964-1989	102
Chapter 16	Under the Grapevine	114
Chapter 17	Playing Away	119
Chapter 18	The Questors on the Fringe	126
Chapter 19	IATWs: Some Personal Reminiscences	132
Chapter 20	An Outward Looking Theatre	146
Chapter 21	Now We Are Sixty, 1964-1989	151
Chapter 22	The Founder's Dozen	162
Chapter 23	On Being a Student	166
Appendix 1	Productions (in chronological order)	175
Appendix 2	Personnel	199
Appendix 3	Our Quest	200

Chapter 1

The Early Days,
1929-1939

On September 5th, 1929, a new theatre group was formed in Ealing, having 17 members and a bank balance of 7s.11 ½d. The group comprised half a dozen or so enthusiastic young people, who had previously acted together in various local productions, and a number of their friends who had been persuaded to join them. The aim was merely to enable the friends to act together more regularly and more often. Alfred Emmet, a founder member, recalls:

> "Actually, being all very young at the time, we had very big ideas. A dramatic society was to be only one part of a larger new local organisation, and so we solemnly christened ourselves 'The Ealing Junior Arts Club (Dramatic Section)'. This was of course a great impertinence on our part because it was done without any reference to the well-established and active Ealing Arts Club which, not unnaturally, took considerable exception. So the name had to be changed, and at an historic meeting over lunch in a Soho Restaurant one Sunday in November, it was decided, for no particular reason except that by the coffee stage no-one had thought of anything better, to change the name to 'The Questors'."

The name was actually the brainwave of Alec Payne, the group's first producer, and it came well before any policy was formulated, although the society very quickly began to live up to its name, as a perusal of this story will show.

So it was under this title that the group gave, on November 19th, 1929, the first of two performances of its first production, *The Best People* by David Grey and Avery Hopwood, at the Park Theatre in Hanwell. The names of those original 17 members of the group, most of whom were involved in this production in some capacity or other, are listed below as they appear in the first Minute Book:

Mr Alec Payne	Mr J D Ruck
Miss M R Browne	Mr A E J Emmet
Miss B Sharp	Miss I Browne

Miss H Hobson	Mr F Cockburn
Miss L Hobson	Mr P Elliott
Mr S Low	Miss R Elliott
Miss V Low	Miss Simpson
Mr G Hadley	Mr E R Emmet
Mrs Alec Payne	

Alec Payne was appointed the group's Producer, Alfred Emmet its Honorary Secretary and John Ruck its Business Manager. Again from that first Minute Book comes this reference to the plans for the first production, which will help to set the scale of the enterprise in context:

> "The Business Manager is authorised to advertise 'The Best People', save that he is not authorised to incur expenditure exceeding £1 without further reference to the Committee."

It is worth noting that the Committee eventually ratified expenditure of the princely sum of £2/19/ = !

The Questors continued to use the Park Theatre for the next two productions, the second of which, a triple bill of one-act plays, earned the following comment in the *Middlesex County Times*: "They are well named, for questing is in their blood". Alfred Emmet says of one of these plays, **The Road of Poplars** by Vernon Sylvaine, "(it) was destined to trigger an early change in the whole direction and policy of the Club". The production was entered for the 1931 British Drama League Festival; the contact with the BDL opened The Questors' eyes to the exciting new theatre movement which was just getting underway in this country. The policy of doing only plays regarded as 'worthwhile', on which The Questors has never compromised, was established in the following year.

That triple bill referred to above proved to be The Questors' last production in the Park Theatre. Despite the artistic successes, the group had been persistently losing money and a cheaper venue had to be found. Indeed, the first few years of the Club's existence were characterised not only by artistic adventure but also by a series of financial crises. The second production (Noël Coward's *I'll Leave it to You*) made a heavy loss which left the club £8 in debt and every member who had participated in the show was asked to contribute 10/ = to keep the enterprise solvent! By 1931, it had become obvious that the group could not continue losing money in this way, so productions transferred to the smaller and more rudimentary St Martin's Hall in Acton.

2

Productions still made losses however and a report on the "deplorable state of the Club's finances" was read out at the first Annual Dinner in May 1931; a surplus of 10d was managed by the end of the financial year. A year later, it was crunch time again, as reported in the series of *Historical Notes* published in the show programmes during the 1940s: "An historic meeting of the Acting Members was held on 24th May 1932, when it was decided to carry on. This meeting was an important milestone, for it was there that the policy of only doing 'worthwhile' plays became explicit, though not without opposition; from this meeting also grew the tradition of co-operation and team-work, which has helped the Club through so many difficult periods since". Financially, the Club was saved that year by "an anonymous friend who had faith in The Questors" and who donated £5.

Having declared its policy of doing only those plays it regarded as worthwhile, The Questors, in choosing Bernard Shaw's *You Never Can Tell* for the Autumn 1932 production, felt compelled to apologise in the programme for presenting such a 'commercial' piece of theatre! This led to the following review in the *West Middlesex Gazette*:

> "Here then, is a dramatic society that exercises a censorship over playwrights, producers, financiers and everyone else connected with the theatre. Arrogant? Perhaps. Bold? Yes.

> "Refreshing, too, to find a society that can give sound reasons for producing a certain play."

Four years after its foundation, with the finances still precarious, The Questors began to look around for premises of its own, and indeed opened negotiations with the local Girl Guides Association, whose Hut in Warwick Road, Ealing (which occupied part of the present site of the Ealing College of Higher Education), the group had been using occasionally for play readings. These negotiations fell through, but a much better opportunity soon presented itself. E Stuart Monro, who was District Commissioner for the Boy Scouts Association and who also had a great interest in the theatre, suggested that The Questors join the Ealing Boy Scouts in their premises at 12 Mattock Lane, to share expenses. This property was a disused Catholic church, the old St Joseph's and St Peter's, which had been built in 1896 in the grounds of a large Victorian house,

3

Mattock Lodge. By all accounts, the story of how the church came to be disused would be worth a book in itself, involving as it does disagreements between the incumbent priest, Father Richard O'Halloran, and the archdiocese of Westminster. These disagreements led in 1897 to the issue of the following official notice from Cardinal Vaughan to all Catholics in Ealing:

> "That the Rev Richard O'Halloran has been canonically sus-
> pended from the use of all ecclesiastical facilities including that
> of saying mass, that his place of worship is not recognised as a
> Catholic church or chapel and that no Catholic can frequent it
> or receive sacraments from him without sin."

However, Father O'Halloran obviously enjoyed a good deal of support from his local congregation and continued to hold services in his small 'Iron Church'. Since this church was his personal property he could not be compelled to move out and he maintained his active ministry there until his death in 1925, despite having actually been excommunicated in 1914.

The house itself had been built in the early 1850s and was the first house to be erected on the North side of Mattock Lane between Ashton House, a large manor house at the Eastern end of the road (demolished in 1901), and Dane Road a few hundred yards to the West. Its first occupant was a retired military man who had served in the Duke of Wellington's army in the Peninsular War and who named the house Peninsular Lodge. It was renamed Mattock Lodge by a subsequent owner around 1885. Father O'Halloran acquired the property in 1895 and willed it upon his death to Miss Ann Webb, daughter of his former housekeeper (the widow of an officer in the Indian Army), "for the care she has taken of me", referring particularly to her nursing him through a long and severe bout of rheumatic fever. By 1930, Mattock Lodge was occupied by Miss Webb and her twin sister Hilda, both unmarried.

In June 1933 The Questors moved into the 'Iron Church' and worked all summer to build and equip the stage, install the lighting system, hang curtains and so on, at a total cost of £75, which was partly financed by the issue of 'Founders' Shares' at £1. These were originally intended to be repaid "as and when finances permit". In fact, when finances did permit, some considerable time later, most Founders were happy to leave their money with The Questors.

In September, the following article appeared in *The Times*:

4

"The Questors have during the summer built a stage 39ft wide and 14ft deep, with a proscenium opening of 20ft. This has been done on a new method, in which metal tubes have been used as supports instead of the usual wooden construction. The members of the club are now engaged in building dressing-rooms, making curtains, and installing a cyclorama and lighting set on very modern lines.

"When completed the theatre should lend itself to dramatic experiments, in which The Questors have always been specially interested."

On October 14th 1933, the first Questors Theatre officially opened with speeches and a demonstration of the then highly advanced stage lighting system, devised by Frederick Bentham, which was revolutionary in many ways, not least in its absence of footlights. Recalling the occasion in the July 1987 issue of *Questopics*, he wrote:

"It was a matter of pleasure and pride that I was the first to stage any kind of 'show' before an audience... What did 'my' show consist of? Well, I told an audience clad in their dinner-jackets about the wonders of the new stage lighting installation; two old German Schwabe spots outfront, two baby-spots and four baby-floods behind the pros. and six cyclorama circuits. But this was not just talk; the three top cyc. circuits actually worked!"

It was lucky, by all accounts, that the three circuits referred to did work, since they were still being wired up behind the drapes while the preceding speeches were being delivered! It had been originally planned to open the theatre with a performance of a specially written Masque, but time could not be spared for rehearsals. Work on the theatre had gone on literally until the last minute, with a final non-stop spurt of 24 hours.

The first production in the Mattock Lane theatre opened on 6th December 1933 and with the choice of play, The Questors served notice of things to come—by presenting the English première of an experimental new play by Shirland Quin, **Dragons' Teeth**, "undoubtedly the most experimental work done by a London society in recent months, if not years", according to *The Amateur Theatre*. This had an elaborate and expressionistic dream sequence in the last act, involving around 70 characters, which obviously meant doubling, trebling, quadrupling and even quintupling of parts. It was not staged without some considerable difficulties; Alfred Emmet, who directed, remembers particularly

5

that two cast members, playing nine parts between them, dropped out actually on the afternoon of the first performance, necessitating furious re-rehearsal, even while the first act was in progress. There had been no time to rehearse costume changes, and several times, the actors discovered that by the time they had changed, the scene they had changed for had already finished! Despite all this, the show was very well received and is remembered by those who saw it as a most exciting production.

Over the next five years, The Questors continued at 12 Mattock Lane in association with the Boy Scouts, building up its regular audience membership to 200 or so and managing to record a small surplus at the end of each season. The 'audience membership', a class of members not wishing to act, but who paid an annual subscription in return for an entitlement to claim one free seat for each production during the year, had existed almost from the first days of The Questors.*

At this stage, the company, which numbered about 30, was presenting four shows a year, one of which was an Annual Drama Festival. These Festivals, which were internal Questors events, although an adjudicator was invited from outside, gave groups of acting members a chance to get together and put on a series of one-act plays, and the events proved enormously popular. They were also instrumental in developing The Questors' interest in, and reputation for encouraging, new plays, as will be seen later.

Throughout this period, experimentation with stage form and design continued. In 1934, for example, came the first use of entrances in front of the proscenium, for John Masefield's *The Witch* (from the Norwegian of H Wiers-Jenssen), directed by Alfred Emmet and designed by Audrey Perkins. This the *Middlesex County Times* believed was "the most perfect production they have yet staged". Alfred Emmet recalls the simplicity of the setting, which consisted of a pillar and the stained-glass window (part of the original chapel) at the back of the stage, lit from the outside, to suggest the interior of a cathedral.

In 1935, Dudley Clark's designs for F Sladen Smith's *Wonderful Zoo*, in which the scenery was all painted on sheeting hung

---

* Over the years, these members, now termed 'Club Members', have proved an enormous source of strength, not to mention steady income in advance, to the theatre, providing some guaranteed audience regardless of the choice of play.

6

on a double curtain rail around the stage, were featured in a scenic design exhibition in the West End. And as early as 1936 came the first experiment in the round, of some scenes from *Twelfth Night*. The progress of the stage form experiments from that point and their importance in shaping the thinking that eventually led to the design of the current Questors Playhouse are discussed in detail in Chapter 5.

Between 1936 and 1938, two complete seasons on a single theme were presented—to illustrate the history of drama. The cycle, combining full productions and play readings, started with Aristophanes' *The Birds* and finished with an experimental play, *A Bride for the Unicorn* by Denis Johnston, which was the most ambitious effort since *Dragons' Teeth*.

During these years, despite the hard work put into the building by the members, as a theatre 12 Mattock Lane could still perhaps best be described as basic, if not rudimentary. The building itself, which had come to be affectionately known as the Tin Hut, was made of timber, with a corrugated iron roof and interior walls of bare, stained matchboarding, which while aesthetically leaving something to be desired were acoustically magnificent— Bernard Miles, visiting many years later, likened speaking in this auditorium to being inside a 'cello. Audience comfort was a problem. Not only was the floor completely flat, but the only seating was a number of hard wooden chairs belonging to the Boy Scouts—extremely uncomfortable and apt to rock noisily on their uneven legs. Cushions, made by the membership and hired out to the audience at a penny a throw, improved matters to some extent.

However, in 1938 a further crisis occurred when the Boy Scouts pulled out of the partnership for financial reasons—and took all their chairs with them! The Questors, ever hopeful, signed the sole lease for 12 Mattock Lane and appealed for £200 to re-seat and re-equip the auditorium. This Appeal was launched by Gwen Ffrangcon-Davies, who was President of The Questors at the time, and Margaret Webster, a past-President, with the very catchy slogan "Cough up or stand up!" The gamble paid off and the money was forthcoming. A set of tip-up seats was acquired second-hand from an old cinema (at 7/6d each) and fixed on battens in groups of six; in between productions, the front seats had to be moved back to leave room to construct scenery on the floor of the auditorium. This particular job, according to several members who joined round about this time,

7

was one of the most unpleasant and back-breaking that they were ever called upon to do, either before or since. The back rows were built up for improved sightlines and those members in the know soon learnt when booking their tickets to ask for Row H, this being the first raised row and thus offering the best view. Seating capacity was now 183 and a fair degree of comfort offered, although considerable audience tolerance was required— many members recall the tendency of whole rows to tip backwards when someone stood up to let a latecomer past, to the great distress of the people in the row behind who feared they might lose their legs at any moment.

The first season as sole tenants of the building proved The Questors' most successful to date, both artistically and in terms of audience. Six productions were mounted, one of which, André Obey's *Noah*, was considered to be the peak of The Questors' pre-war artistic efforts. Production runs increased from two to three performances and all seemed set fair for the future.

8

Chapter 2

The War Years, 1939-1945

When war broke out in 1939, all theatrical activities were suspended, in accordance with a previously-agreed decision. Many of the group's key personnel were called up or evacuated, the audience membership dropped by about half and it seemed inevitable that the financial loss would be considerable. Gradually, however, after only two or three weeks of inactivity, those members left behind in Ealing came together to discuss whether there was anything of value that could still be done. "We found we had three assets", Alfred Emmet noted in the 1939/40 Annual Report, "our theatre, a tremendous keenness to do something and a strong conviction of the importance of continuing cultural work under war conditions."

So the company continued to prepare productions, taking them out to ARP depots, hospitals, factories and so on. Throughout the darkest years, the blitz, blackouts and all, rehearsals and performances went on. The Questors stuck even more firmly to its policy of undertaking only worthwhile plays during this period, believing that only work of the highest worth could be justified under the strains of the war years. Planning inevitably had to be from show to show only, depending on who was available. The first production was in fact a revue, using material that had already been prepared for a 'Surprise Night' during the previous year. Considerably more ambitious productions were undertaken, however, ranging from Bernard Shaw's *Arms and the Man* in 1940 to the British première of Ostrovsky's *It's a Family Affair* in 1943.

The 1940/41 season has been described as the nadir of The Questors' fortunes and there is little doubt that had it not been for a certain amount of luck and the determination of Alfred Emmet, then this history might well have finished here. In the early days of the blitz, just a few days before the 1940 Autumn production was due to open, the first bomb damage occurred. Two small bombs landed near the theatre, one of which cut off the gas and electricity and the other was just three feet away from causing severe, if not permanent, damage to the building itself. For many weeks afterwards, until the gas was reconnected, the only heating in the theatre was one small domestic oil stove. Rehearsals nevertheless continued, with the cast wrapped up in as many layers of clothing as possible, often having to spend the night in the basement of Mattock Lodge when all transport ceased for an air raid alert.

Inevitably, these deprivations had their biggest effect on the size of the audiences, and houses of between 30 and 40 were considered very respectable. During the months of the blitz in the winter of 1940/41, in order to present a show which allowed the audience to get home before dark, an hour-long programme of 'Shilling Shakespeare' was devised, consisting of excerpts from *Romeo and Juliet*, *All's Well that Ends Well* and *A Midsummer Night's Dream*, and given as weekend matinée performances. The audience membership for this year was down to 99 and the average audience per production run only 195 (compared with 449 in the last pre-war season). Stringent econ-omies were practised, limiting the average production budget to just £7, and the Club managed to stay solvent. The Annual Report described it as ''A year of sustained battle'', and Alfred Emmet paid tribute in the *Historical Notes* to ''the warriors of that year, (to whom) those who came after owe an immeasurable debt. Had they failed, The Questors might well have stopped. But the ground was held.''

In the same season, The Questors gave the first production of a full-length new play written specially for the company, Michael Kelly's *Icarus Preserved*. Although partly a response to the difficulties of finding suitable plays when so few actors were available, the seeds of The Questors' interest in doing and commissioning new plays had already been sown. As mentioned earlier, an Annual Drama Festival had been part of the season since 1933, these Festivals being an opportunity for the acting members to mount their own short, small-cast productions. The supply of suitable one-act plays for this purpose had soon dried up and so members had begun to write their own. Michael Kelly, who had joined The Questors to work on lighting and who was by this time Lighting Manager, began his writing career with such one-act plays. It was the success of that wartime performance of *Icarus Preserved* and other new plays (of Michael Kelly's and other authors) that were put on during the following five or six years, which led to the policy of choosing at least one new play every season and ultimately to The Questors' continuing reputation for encouraging new playwrights.

Despite the difficulties, there were lighter moments, of course. A production of the classical Chinese play *The Romance of The Western Chamber* being taken out to an anti-aircraft detachment in Essex, for example, with the cast and crew travelling to the venue on the underground, carrying the necessary staging equipment and costumes with them. The journey was interrupted by an air raid, and the train stopped at a station. Never one to waste an opportunity, Alfred Emmet got the cast out on the platform and ran an extra rehearsal, much to the amusement and surprise of the American GIs on the opposite platform. On another occasion, a production of *The Importance of Being Earnest* was taken out to a gun site at Wormwood Scrubs. The performers had to share the stage with a couple of camp cats, who behaved impeccably to begin with, sitting one on either side of the stage. As the play progressed, they began to move about and had to be accommodated in the action, one having to be removed from a chair before John Worthing could sit down!

The Questors thus, remarkably, survived the blitz and by 1942 things were beginning to look a little brighter. Audience membership climbed back to the pre-war level of 200 or so and finances were healthier. In addition to the productions which were still being taken out to other centres, special performances were staged at the Theatre for local groups, including schools, the Women's Voluntary Service and the YWCA. The Questors was not alone in expanding its activities at this time; rather this "was part of the general, nationwide upsurge of interest in cultural and artistic activities after three or four years of war". When it became possible to think more generally than merely to concentrate on day-to-day survival, preparations for the future began to be made. Again, quoting from the *Historical Notes*, "We felt it necessary and possible to look ahead and try to lay the foundations to enable The Questors to play its part in the ...renaissance which we believed would follow the war."

In 1943, a five-point policy statement, which remained central to The Questors' philosophy for many years, was issued. While the policy had really existed beforehand, nothing had been written down and it became necessary to formulate a document which could be formally approved by a General Meeting of members. This became even more urgent in the years immediately after the war because a 'palace revolution' among the membership was trying to move the theatre towards popularising the choice of plays*. Once again, Alfred Emmet's determination won through, motivating the majority of the membership to share his vision and conviction that The Questors should not compromise its guiding artistic principles, and the five-point policy statement was approved.

Much of that first hard-won policy statement, which has shaped the development of The Questors, is still policy today. It was an active policy, in that for many years, progress against each of the five points was checked and reported upon in the Annual Reports. The aims were set out in the statement as follows:

> "(1) to improve the quality of our work, largely by training schemes and fuller periods of rehearsal;
> (2) to increase the quantity of our work: more productions, giving opportunities to more people to participate;
> (3) to reach out and help other groups, especially local youth groups etc;
> (4) to increase audiences and link them more closely with the work of the theatre;
> (5) to fulfil to a greater degree the function of a Tributary Theatre (ie. tributary to the mainstream of theatre).''

To allow implementation of this programme, and also to cope with the increased administrative load created by the rapid growth in audience membership which had taken place, it was decided to appoint a full-time paid manager of the club. Fortunately, the increase in membership also meant that this was financially feasible, and the first General Manager, Betty Mercy, took up her duties on January 1st 1944.

One of the first steps taken to implement the first of the five policy points was the establishment of training classes for acting members. These were continued regularly for two or three years and developed directly into the Student Acting Course. This was set up in 1946, to train actors for work at The Questors. It was run unaided by The Questors for one year and then put on a more formal footing, and subsidised by the local education authority, from the following year. The Student Acting Course

---

* Many of the decisions taken by the Club in this period required drastic measures to achieve them, including the expulsion of some members from the Club by resolution of an Extraordinary General Meeting, committee members *en bloc* leaving the platform to speak from the floor against agreed motions, and the holding of quantities of proxy votes in readiness to overturn defeated proposals.

continues to be a mainstay of The Questors; forty uninterrupted years of its running were celebrated in July 1987. It is now a two-year course, with up to 60 applicants chasing the 20 or so places each year; Chapter 23 gives the details of its development.

Another key element in improving the quality of the work done was an experiment tried in 1943 of a very long rehearsal period, for the première production of a play by Rodney Ackland, *The Dark River*. The whole company worked on the play for a month or two before it was even cast, studying the background and the characters and being set essays on various aspects. Whatever the motivation for the experiment, it proved a great success. The author was invited to the première and agreed to attend, although he admitted in his autobiography that this was not without considerable trepidation. In the event, he was so impressed that he went backstage afterwards, introduced himself and said "I've seen my play tonight. I know I shall never see it again". The Questors performed the play again at the special request of the author, for an audience of his theatrical colleagues and as a result *The Dark River* was subsequently produced in the West End, with Peggy Ashcroft in the leading role understudied by Betty Mercy who had played the part at The Questors; the 14-year old Ronald Langdon who had played the young boy at The Questors repeated his performance in the professional production.* Rodney Ackland had been much impressed by the rain effect created by The Questors, so much so that he asked to borrow the device, which consisted of a strip of plywood roughly nailed into a circle and covered with brown paper, in which dried peas were rattled, for the West End production.

Alfred Emmet notes that "the importance of that production, however, was not so much that it led to a West End showing as that it showed us what could be done with an altogether fuller rehearsal schedule". This practice was duly built into the programme for the future, and The Questors has ever since aimed for a minimum of 100 hours of rehearsal for each production. In the opinion of many members, it is on this policy, together with the training provided by the Student Acting Course, that the reputation for high artistic standards of The Questors has been based.

Moving to the second of the five points, regarding the quantity

---

* Alfred Emmet was invited to direct the West End production, but had to decline because he was in a reserved occupation.

of the work, little could be done to increase this under war conditions while members' availability was so limited. However, in November 1945, two shows were rehearsing simultaneously for the first time and seven productions were mounted in the 1945/46 season, compared with five in the previous year.

To promote the third of the five policy points, reaching out to help local youth groups, short-term drama courses for youth groups were organised, and The Questors helped to establish the Ealing Youth Drama Festival in 1944. This ran successfully for many years. The Questors' own drama workshops for local youngsters were started a decade later, in 1954; see Chapter 4 for details.

Audience numbers had been gradually increasing since the low of 1941, and this trend continued, gathering momentum, apart from a small blip in the summer of 1944 during the period of attacks by flying bombs. In the 1942/43 season, the average audience per production was run 380; by 1945/46, this had climbed to 1,196.

As to the tributary function stated in the policy, which meant seeing its own work in the context of the theatre at large, contacts with other Little Theatres had been fostered during the last two years of the war. The contact was formalised in 1946 with the inauguration of the Little Theatre Guild, with The Questors Theatre as the first Secretary. The People's Theatre of Newcastle-upon-Tyne was the Guild's first Chair, and the other two founding members were Highbury Little Theatre (Sutton Coldfield) and the Bradford Civic Playhouse. An account of The Questors' involvement in and with the LTG is given in Chapter 20.

In 1945, another seminal production in terms of development of stage form occurred, when for the first time the action in a naturalistic play was brought out beyond the proscenium arch onto a forestage. The play was Ibsen's *A Doll's House*, which, incidentally, was actually being performed on VE Day, May 8th. According to the reviewer in the *Middlesex County Times* this was "a highly sensitive and discerning production (by Eric Voce) and the setting, designed by Honor O'Nians, in which use was made of the apron stage, striking the eye as completely right." The experiment proved successful beyond expectation, as discussed in Chapter 5. So the Club emerged from the black years of the war bloody but artistically unbowed, ready to continue and extend the policy of experimentation.

Chapter 3

The Site is Purchased, 1945–1952

The immediate post-war years saw the consolidation and development of the artistic policy. Between 1945 and 1950, for example, no fewer than seven new plays (out of a total 34 productions) were presented. The rest of the programming showed the continuing emphasis on finding a wide range of good drama, particularly works by European dramatists—including Ibsen, Chekhov, Pirandello, Ostrovsky and Jean-Jacques Bernard.*

These years are remembered with affection by those who lived through them, as a period of joint exploration, both of the plays themselves and of ways of working. Prior to joining The Questors, most members' experiences had been confined to acting in local amateur dramatic societies, church groups and so on, and the seriousness and professionalism of the approach was a revelation. Indeed, the Theatre (and more particularly, Alfred Emmet as a director) had already achieved a nationwide, if not international, reputation which attracted high-calibre active members from other Little Theatres to Ealing, when they moved to London. Not that the professionalism could prevent the occasional disaster worthy of the most Am of AmDram productions! Michael Green has memorably recorded several of these in his best-selling book, *The Art of Coarse Acting*, most of the incidents in which happened at The Questors. Two in particular dating from this period have been recounted by so many members who actually witnessed them that they must be true.

The first relates to a production of **The Thracian Horses** by Maurice Valency in July 1949, with a set design by Ernest Ives which represented a breakthrough in ways of unifying main stage and forestage areas. It was a very hot summer and the actor playing Zeus, who appeared late in the final act, was to make his entrance flown in on a cloud. He had to get into position before the act began. He was encased in plastic, a

---

* It should be remembered that at this time this represented dramatic fare which was widely at variance with the rest of the London scene; it was a rarity to see even Chekhov performed in the professional theatre during the 1940s.

material that had just been discovered by the Wardrobe, and sported a large beard. To cope with the heat under the lights, he first attempted to eat ice cream, which wouldn't go through the beard and, being deposited on the cloud beside him, proceeded to melt and drip onto the stage below. He eventually resorted to drinking bottled beer through a straw, a ruse which proved only too successful and by the time he made his entrance, Zeus was indeed a benevolent god!

The November production in the same year, of *Othello*, seemed to be particularly disaster-prone. Remembered by many as a most visually striking production (it was designed by Graham Heywood*), it is equally vividly recalled for not one, but two, separate 'accidents'. The first arose from the carefully choreographed sword-fight between the actors playing Montano and Cassio. The former was a believer in acting on the inspiration of the moment and several times in performance he departed from the rehearsed fight, cutting Cassio so badly on two occasions that the actor had to be rushed to hospital for stitches in his head. Eventually, the worm turned; one night after the combatants had left the stage, the fight was continued in the dressing room, to the mystification of the audience and of poor Iago left on stage, who could hear every crash and grunt quite clearly! Another story from this production which is often related concerns the actor playing Roderigo and the night he accidentally fell off the stage when he was 'killed'. In the blackout which immediately followed the scene, he crawled on his hands and knees all the way up the side gangway of the auditorium, the nodding feather in his hat causing a certain amount of surprise to the owners of the knees he passed on his way, and exited through the back door. The frantic Stage Manager, meanwhile, whose instructions were not to bring the lights up on the next scene until Roderigo had passed him into the wings, was convinced that he had lost an actor!

The active membership gradually returned to full strength as those who had been posted abroad came home. Several members had in fact loyally sent regular bulletins back right through the war from the exotic places in which they had been called to serve and dispatches from abroad, for example from George Benn in the Middle East, were a notable feature of the wartime

---

* Formerly Günter Heilbut, a German Jew who escaped to England during the 1930s, who was responsible for many stunning set designs and who was to play a major role in the planning of the new theatre.

16

issues of the *Members' News Bulletin*. Those who had been in the thick of the fighting were glad to return to the relative sanity and normality of The Questors and threw themselves back into the life of the Theatre with a will.

Modern technology was now beginning to creep in. The first telephone had been installed in early 1945, an enormous boon after operating in the Theatre for II years without one. And in 1946, even greater joy greeted the advent of electric light in the lavatories! These, at this time and for many years yet to come, were still 'outside', in a separate small brick building at the back of the Theatre behind some lilac bushes. There were two, one for the ladies and one for the gents, and it was not an uncommon occurrence for members of the audience to find themselves queuing up in the rain with fully costumed and made-up cast members.

Another landmark was achieved in 1946: The Questors was finally granted a catering licence, after many years of trying. Coffee and tea had been provided for audiences in the intervals, but without a catering licence, it had not been possible to buy the supplies, which were of course rationed during the war. The Theatre had therefore relied on gifts made by the members of tea, coffee, powdered milk and so on. Even in January 1946, the prospect of obtaining the licence seemed remote, as was recorded in that month's *Members' News Bulletin*: "Thanks to all those members who have recently come to the rescue with supplies of tea and dried milk. It seems strange that we still cannot get a catering licence, despite the strong personal recommendation of the Director of Education (for Ealing)". Obviously this strong personal recommendation finally paid off later in the year!

The more ambitious planning and experimentation which had become the artistic hallmark of The Questors by 1946 now extended to thoughts about the Mattock Lane premises. As the level of activity increased, so the shortage of space became acute, the more so since everything had to be done in the theatre building itself—performances, rehearsals, auditions, construction of scenery, making of costumes, committee meetings and the not inconsiderable general office administration which was now involved. Naturally, most of the space was taken up by the auditorium and stage, with a tiny kitchen and servery, and a small office which doubled as general administrative office and Box Office, at the back of the auditorium. Behind the stage there were two very small dressing rooms, or rather one dressing room divided into two compartments by a curtain, which has been described by many of the acting members who used it as little more than a corridor. Making-up had to be accomplished standing since there was little enough room to pass at the best of times and shows involving period costumes with full skirts for the ladies were dreaded by all.

The rest of the site, apart from the house itself, to whose basement The Questors had access for storage of properties and furniture (a somewhat dubious privilege, since it used to flood fairly regularly and the properties had to be rescued from floating away down Mattock Lane), and the lavatories already referred to, included a brick building at the back. This had originally been a kindergarten attached to the Catholic chapel but was by now occupied by a drinking and social club of notorious repute in the locality, known as Ye Olde Mattock Barn Club.

The Questors had for some time been trying to obtain the lease on this building; quite apart from the need for space, the noise from these rather unwelcome near-neighbours was very trying. Alfred Emmet recounted the details of the "prolonged negotiations" (as they were described in the 1946/47 Annual Report) to obtain the lease in his 1980 lecture to the Ealing Museum Art and History Society:

> "The usual procedure was that we would call on our landlady, the surviving Miss Webb, who still lived in Mattock Lodge with her parrot and an old retainer called Florrie. We would plead with Miss Webb how desperately we needed to take over the Barn Club and she would promise us that come next quarterday we could. Then the proprietress of the Barn Club would get wind of this and in her turn would visit Miss Webb. She would leave behind her a £5 note on the mantelpiece. Come quarterday Miss Webb would explain, almost with tears in her eyes, that she "hadn't the heart" to turn Mrs whatever-her-name-was out, and we had to start all over again.... at last, in 1947 we managed to obtain the desired lease, though it cost us quite a tidy sum to buy out the proprietress of the club."

Records show that this tidy sum was in fact £66/13/4d, plus three guineas in costs.

Once the lease had been obtained, the Barn Club building quickly became an indispensable part of The Questors' expanding empire, being converted into a workshop, wardrobe, rehearsal room/Green Room, with an additional lavatory and small office-cum-library at the top of the stairs. It was separated from the theatre building by a small lobby, which housed a tiny washbasin (the only washing facilities available to cast members for removal of make-up), a gas ring and a miraculous gas meter, which appeared to run for ever on a single coin. Once this coin had been inserted, the gas duly came on and the coin fell straight through, to be retrieved and used again the next time the gas ran out.

By 1947, more specific thoughts about the future were crystallising and the Club became aware that to have security of tenure and freedom to do more to the site the first step would have to be to buy the premises. Miss Webb was a life tenant, so that while she was at liberty to lease part of the property, she could not sell it. Inevitably, as she was The Questors' landlady and lived on the premises, they got to know one another over the years and there are a number of apocryphal stories told about Miss Webb and Florrie. There is no doubt that they were an extraordinary pair. Miss Webb was tiny in stature, chronically short of money and very lonely. She was also highly eccentric, becoming more so towards the end of her life, and had a habit of walking about in the garden with candles. Members have remarked that she was reminiscent in some ways of Miss Havisham in Charles Dickens's *Great Expectations*. Rena Rice, who was General Manager of the theatre for many years and who had most contact with her, remembers being obliged to take tea with Miss Webb from time to time, in the room which backed onto the lawn, "...a big lounge, with shutters, which were ceremonially opened for tea, although I used to wish they hadn't been, because the room was packed with old mattresses, piles and piles of old newspapers and tattered old Indian screens, and hung with cobwebs. The cups had rings of dust around them and we'd sit and have tea, with syrup instead of sugar, and I'd watch the little mice running around my feet." After tea, Miss Webb would often press a small gift on her visitor— an old book or a newspaper cutting, perhaps, and once, an extraordinary white satin box containing yards of old-fashioned white satin stays trimmed with pink feathers and rosebuds.

Florrie was as remarkable as her employer, if not more so, being also very small, but extremely plump and of indeterminate age. Her hair was worn long and curtained her face, and she was invariably wrapped in a shawl and wore bedroom slippers. The Questors stalwarts who spent nights avoiding air raids in the Mattock Lodge basement during the war recall the eerie sight of Florrie descending the stairs with her candle, "like a witch from Macbeth". She would often be sent into the Theatre in the evening, to ask someone to fetch "sixpenceworth of brandy for Miss Webb" from The Three Pigeons at the end of the road. The unlucky soul who was caught invariably had to dig into his own pocket, since a nip of brandy was worth a good deal more than sixpence, even in those days.

A first approach towards buying the premises outright was made to the Trustees of the estate in the autumn of 1947, with the suggestion of opening negotiations for the purchase of the site on the death of the life tenant. Following a meeting and other communications with the Trustees, The Questors was told early in 1948 that they would be prepared to sell the Mattock Lane Estate for £12,000.

An independent valuer advised The Questors that the maximum value, for the whole site including the house, was £7,000, largely because of the requirements of the new Town and Country Planning Act relating to development charges. Also because of the strict building regulations of the time, it was unlikely that an independent buyer would be prepared to offer more than £5,000. Since time appeared to be on The Questors' side, it was decided not to force negotiations. Planning permission to develop the site as a theatre was however applied for. It was found that planning permission had never previously been sought, either by the Boy Scouts or by The Questors when they first moved in, but by extreme good fortune, user rights had been established by a matter of just three or four months. Planning permission in principle was thus little more than a formality and was granted a few months later.

Whatever the outcome of the negotiations, it was obvious that money would be needed for the purchase and so a Building Fund was set up in 1948 and the first of many major fund-raising campaigns got under way. The Committee also began to take steps to make The Questors a limited company, a necessary prelude to its owning property. This move was not without significant opposition among the membership, which was eventually overcome, although there are recollections of a number of acrimonious General Meetings. The outcome, however, was that The Questors was incorporated as a company limited by guarantee on 2nd June 1949 and The Questors Limited, the name by which the company is still known, came into existence. There were eight signatories to the original Memorandum and

Articles of Association: Alfred E J Emmet, E (Eric) Voce, Francis W Smith, M E (Michael) Kelly, Wilfrid T C Sharp, Richard F Wood, J L (Lister) Beck and Betty Ogden.

An offer of £6,000 was made for the site but this was so far below the vendors' asking price that it was ignored. Negotiations then virtually ceased for almost two years and The Questors had actually started to look around for a possible alternative site to purchase—members recall in particular going to look at a disused cinema in Acton. Then, in August 1951, Miss Webb died and things started hotting up. Alfred Emmet's account of the next few months, despite being admirably succinct, gives a good indication of the brinkmanship embarked upon and the uncertainty of the final outcome:

"'...it was clear that the Trustees were now determined to sell as soon as possible at the best price they could get. We put the negotiations in the hands of a solicitor. The price came down to £10,000. Then to £8,500. We still waited, relying on our surveyor's advice. Then, on Friday 18th January 1952, we were told that an offer of £5,000 had been received for the theatre part of the site alone, and that this would be closed with unless they had a better counter offer by the following Monday. It happened that I was in Brussels that week-end for the inaugural meeting of the International Amateur Theatre Association, and moreover had left without leaving a note of where I was staying. Some neat detective work by my wife, a series of urgent telegrams, a return at lunch time on Sunday, an emergency committee meeting on Sunday afternoon authorising our representatives to negotiate and by the end of lunch on Monday we had agreed to buy the whole site for £8,500."

As the Building Fund then stood at £4,000, drastic action was needed. Efforts to raise money had been stepped up the previous September, when it became clear that the crisis point was imminent. At that point, the Fund totalled £2,350 and an urgent SOS (Save Our Stage) appeal for £5,000 had been launched with some very high profile support, as the examples of comments from leading theatrical professionals quoted below indicate:

"The Questors Theatre have a considerable value for the theatre both in the excellence of their work and in the great encouragement of new dramatists"—*Christopher Fry*

"I consider its continuance essential to the theatre life of this country"—*George Devine (Co-Director of the Old Vic and Director of the Young Vic)*

"I go often to The Questors Theatre and am always impressed by the vitality and enthusiasm on both sides of the curtain"— *Tyrone Guthrie*.

Despite all this, and an active fund-raising programme, the money had been slow to come in and the balance of £4,500 would have to be found within a few weeks. Attempts to secure a bank mortgage and financial support from the local Council were unsuccessful. The vendors were urging completion by the end of March, and the fate of the Theatre once more seemed to hang in the balance. Then, literally days before the completion date, The Questors received the totally unexpected offer of a £4,000 mortgage for 20 years at the extremely low rate of 2½% from Guinness, on condition that the company's own dramatic society could use the theatre for free for up to three weeks a year. So once again, it appeared that Lady Luck had stepped in at the last minute to save the Theatre.

Completion was actually delayed by a month, but on April 25th 1952, The Questors became proud owners of the whole 12 Mattock Lane site. George Benn, who was then Chairman, wrote in his Statement in the 1951/52 Annual Report that "the theatre purchase is the end of a chapter, but not the end of the book". The SOS appeal had by then raised a total of £10,290, including the mortgage, so that the Club was left, after payment of legal and conveyancing charges, with slightly in excess of £1,400 for repairs and alterations to Mattock Lodge. It had been decided to convert the house into apartments to let, to bring in revenue, while keeping two rooms for use as a Club Lounge. Planning permission was required for the latter, as it was technically a change of use. This, although initially turned down by the Ealing Borough Council, was granted on appeal to the Minister and the first Lounge opened in the following year; in a nice ironic twist, the Town Clerk, chief executive of the Council (who also happened to be a member of The Questors), was invited to perform the opening ceremony, and did so.

Chapter 4

The Next Step,
1952–1954

As indicated in the previous chapter, the purchase of the site
had been viewed very much as the first essential step in the
development of the plans for a theatre complex that had begun
to crystallise. Eventually, it would be necessary to build a new
theatre, if only because the Tin Hut was already in poor repair
and beginning to leak like the proverbial sieve. So a resolution
was put to the Annual General Meeting in October 1952, and
approved, authorising the Committee of Management to proceed
with the preparation of plans for a scheme for the development
of the whole site. In the following extract from the December
1952 edition of *Forestage* (the first Club magazine which had
replaced the broadsheet-style *Members' News Bulletin* in 1949),
Alfred Emmet outlined the rationale behind the planning:

"...The present auditorium is too small for growing audiences;
we are increasingly handicapped by lack of space for all the
theatre's activities; it is doubtful whether the present
building...can be kept in good condition for more than a limited
number of years. But I think the most exciting reason of all is
the opportunity to experiment in theatre design.

"...The Questors...are in an almost unique position to venture.
The economics of building a non-commercial theatre are very
different from those of a commercial theatre. The difficulties of a
building licence would be less, partly because we could build by
instalments over a period of years, partly because we may be
able to use much voluntary labour, getting licences for materials
only. Licensing regulations are much easier for a small theatre...
Moreover, we have an ideal site, and are near enough to London
for such a project to excite considerable interest."

It was hoped, and subsequently confirmed, that much interest
and support could be generated among eminent theatrical professionals. No new theatre had been built in the United Kingdom

for over 20 years and although there was a great deal of keen debate on the subject of theatre architecture, there was at this time precious little opportunity for theories to be put into practice. So, The Questors believed, if the new theatre could genuinely be an experiment, or pilot scheme, for the theatre as a whole, support and, it was hoped, funds could be forthcoming on a nationwide basis.

There was no intention, however, of waiting until all the necessary money had been raised. After all, The Questors had never yet made the assurance of funding a criterion for taking important decisions, either before taking over the sole lease on the theatre at 12 Mattock Lane or before agreeing to purchase the site. Again from *Forestage*: "We envisage rather a stage-by-stage development by annual instalments, perhaps first building on to our existing theatre additions which will form part of the eventual new theatre. It must be accomplished without any important interruption in our play-producing activities. It must be done bit by bit over a period during which we will have the excitement of seeing it grow."

A New Theatre Committee of four—George Benn, Alfred Emmet, Graham Heywood and Ernest Ives—was charged with the responsibility of producing an architect's brief. They were greatly assisted by a New Theatre Advisory Panel of eminent professionals, including John Allen, Frederick Bentham, E Martin Browne, Muriel St Clare Byrne, George Devine, Tyrone Guthrie, Michael MacOwan, Norman Marshall, Bernard Miles, Michel St Denis, Glen Byam Shaw, Richard Southern, André van Gyseghem and Michael Warre. They were also fortunate in that the architect appointed, Norman Branson, was a member of The Questors and one of its leading stage designers, who also had experience as an actor and director, so that he understood perfectly the requirements from an artistic point of view of the building he was commissioned to design. The nature and detail of the New Theatre Committee's discussions are covered in the next chapter. Here it will be sufficient to state merely that the outcome of the deliberations was that a small-scale adaptable playhouse should be built, in which various stage forms and arrangements could be used, and the architect's brief then prepared. For the record, four sets of plans were drawn up and duly torn up, but the fifth version, representing a consensus of the views of the active members of the time, was put before the general membership.

24

It was by no means plain sailing from then on; there were several factions among the membership who felt quite strongly that it was absolutely crazy to attempt to build a completely new theatre and that even if it happened it would be 'the death of The Questors', or at least the loss of the close-knit company spirit which had so characterised the first 25 years. However, the Honorary Director (and, in fairness, several other members as well) was determined and with his usual persistence set about convincing the doubters. By no means all of them came round immediately, but gradually enough of the membership became infected with his enthusiasm and realised that it might after all be feasible to build a new theatre complex using voluntary labour, while continuing to stage a full programme of productions in the old theatre, for the plans to be approved at an Extraordinary General Meeting in January 1955.

Then came the problem of getting the design accepted by the relevant public planning authorities. George Benn, in a later account of the period, noted:

> "At a meeting with the Middlesex County Council Theatre Licensing Committee at which the architect explained the scheme, the committee room had been hung with blow-ups of classic theatre disasters*: that day was lost before it started! There was a marked reluctance to give planning consent... Our principal witness was a member of one of the most eminent firms of consultants in London at the time (and he came without charging us a fee). We got our own way in the end".

While all these deliberations had been proceeding, developments had already taken place on the site. Mattock Lodge was now up and running as a full part of the theatre, with a library and a Club Lounge where all the catering, from Sunday Teas for rehearsing casts and crews to after-show parties, was done. The General Manager (as the Theatre Manager was termed in those days), Rena Rice, was now living on the premises, having moved into a self-contained flat (without bathroom) on the first floor in 1953. The rest of the Lodge was converted into six bed-

---

* These were photographs of several devastating theatre fires; the Local Authority officers' objections largely rested upon The Questors' desire to dispense with the conventional safety curtain to achieve the open stage.

sitting rooms, which were let out to Questors members. *Forestage* recorded for posterity in September 1953 that the first tenants of Mattock Lodge were Margaret Popham, Fred Crosby (although he was almost immediately replaced by Michael Green, who went on to become the longest tenant), George Johnson and Gerald Rawling. Many very active Questors members over the years lodged in these bedsitters which, with rent at £2 a week, were much sought after; a strange reluctance by the former tenants to recount any stories for the record probably gives as good an indication as any of the sorts of goings-on which were the norm! Michael Green did, however, consent to give an expurgated account of his time in the Lodge:

"Living in Mattock Lodge as a tenant was near-Paradise in some ways. The theatre and rehearsals were about 30 seconds' journey and most of the bed-sitters were occupied by active Questors members who gathered for long sessions over coffee and drinks after rehearsals and particularly on Sunday mornings when we would discuss the theatre reviews in the Sunday papers. When playing a part it was possible to make up in the privacy of one's room and stroll over to the Theatre, perhaps coming back between appearances to have a rest or even a meal!

"However, there was the disadvantage of being on the spot and tenants were liable to be roped in whenever an emergency arose, be it heavy lifting, serving teas or replacing dropped-out cast members. I remember being cast as the priest in John Whiting's *Morning Song* as a result of a stone being thrown at my window by a desperate director when someone dropped out at the dress rehearsal."

The Questors during this period had a total membership of between 1,000 and 1,300, with average audience per production around 1,500 and total audience for the season around 10,000. Eight productions a year were staged, including the by now well-established two Student Group productions of a programme of one-act plays in February and a full-length play in July. Because the capacity of the house was only 183, production runs had been increased to ten, usually opening on a Saturday and closing a week and a half later, on a Wednesday. The public discussion of each production, which had been a feature of The

26

Questors' programme for many years, was held in the Theatre on the following night , as was the traditional after-show party. The latter events usually included an irreverent skit on the production just gone; over the years, Wilf Sharp and Vincent McQueen, among others, have proved themselves past masters at barbed, witty and highly amusing take-offs. Possibly the greatest triumph in this context was Wilf's reduction of the entire plot of *Hamlet* to ten minutes, in a version which contained the immortal line, "let's get dirty, Gerty".

Artistically, programming continued to be adventurous, with at least one new play per season and three English premières between 1950 and 1953. The production of Thornton Wilder's *The Merchant of Yonkers* (fore-runner of *The Matchmaker* and subsequently *Hello, Dolly*) is remembered for a freak occurrence during the Sunday matinée. Barbara Emmet (Alfred's wife, who is universally known as Kit), who played in it, recalls that she and Ted Scrivener "were standing one on either side of the table having this terrible argument, and he had to take off his hat and dash it down on the table. The brim struck the table and the hat bounced into my hands. So I threw it back on the table and it did the same thing, landing neatly in Ted's hands. The audience thought it was a carefully rehearsed piece of business and it was a complete and utter fluke!"

Especially disaster-prone seems to have been the April 1953 production of Jean-Paul Sartre's *Crime Passionnel*, in a translation by Kitty Black, remembered as a text of astounding quality. The production, however, had its moments; a particularly difficult technical sequence involved an off-stage explosion causing among other things a window to fall in, narrowly missing the target of the assassination attempt. On one occasion, the window fell in several minutes before the explosion happened, before the actor playing Hugo (John Clemow) had received his cue to move, and he calmly propped the window up against his desk and carried on. On another night, the bottle of brandy

---

* These discussions, known among the production teams as 'inquests', had been a key element in the attempt to bring active and audience membership of The Questors together to think and talk constructively about theatre in general and about the work of The Questors in particular. They were extremely well attended in those days and it is a matter of regret that they have over the years become less popular with audiences, to the extent that they were finally discontinued, at least on a regular basis, in 1986.

which was a vital property for the rest of the scene (Hugo's response to his narrow escape being to get extremely drunk) was nowhere to be found. The actor sidled to the wings to ask where the bottle was and was told that one of the other actors, fearing the bottle would get damaged in the explosion, had thoughtfully placed it under the table. Later in the run, having successfully got drunk, Hugo hurled his glass so hard that it went through the scenery. And to cap it all, this unfortunate actor, rushing off stage for a 5-second costume alteration for the transformation scene right at the end of the play, found himself helped into an inside-out raincoat by a wardrobe assistant who immediately vanished leaving him struggling to get the buttons done up!

Interesting recollections, for more curious reasons, surround one of the new plays of this period, *Poor Man's Miracle* by Marian Hemar. This was another landmark of sorts, being the first time that the action of the play was not confined to the established acting area but spilled out into the auditorium, with actors in the aisles and gangways. The production was attended, on two consecutive nights, by the delegates to a BDL Conference, and a discussion of the play, led by Norman Marshall, was held subsequently in the West End. It became clear during the discussion that there were two totally opposing opinions and it was discovered that all the people who were against the play had attended the first of the two performances, while all those who had enjoyed it had seen the second. The members of the cast had been unaware of any differences between the two performances, although they had realised that the audience reactions on the two evenings had been very different. This was attributed to the fact that on the first night the curtain had to be held while delegates found their way across London and so the show started late. The members of the audience who were punctual were getting impatient while those who were late were flustered. An interesting experience of audience psychology. The leader of the discussion, incidentally, was so late that he did not see the first act at all!

Experimentation with staging of course continued, the most influential production of these few years undoubtedly being Alfred Emmet's production of *King John*, with set design by Graham Heywood, in January 1954. Apart from the—for those times—quite revolutionary use of a thrust stage, this production was also intended to be played without an interval; although the Committee of Management in prudent mood would not allow more than one performance of that particularly experimental notion. King John was played by Albert Hooper, who is remembered for many bravura performances as the Questors 'Shakespeare heavy', Constance by Colette King who was to become one of the leading directors in the transition from the old to the new theatre, and the Bastard by Pat Bowley, an extremely talented Australian actor who left an indelible stamp on many Questors productions. The rest of the large cast included virtually all the male acting membership, plus a few hopefuls who were auditioned at around that time and who, if they are to be believed, were accepted for acting membership more on the basis of their capacity for spear-carrying than their acting ability!

Although individual productions like *King John*, with hindsight, are singled out as being particularly important in these terms, experimentation of one kind or another was continuous. Other examples, from that same 1953/54 season, include *Clérambard* (the English première of the play by Marcel Aymé), in which the cast sat at knitting machines for much of the play and which was seen by Clive Brook and then produced by him in the West End, and Barbara Emmet's production of Susannah Centilivre's *A Bold Stroke for a Wife*, in which boxes for the audience were built on the stage, to simulate the original Restoration staging.

And then came 1954—the 25th anniversary year of the founding of The Questors. The Silver Jubilee itself was celebrated in true adventurous Questors style, with a complete season of New Plays; the justification for this was summed up in *Forestage*: "New plays are the life blood of the theatre. Were the supply to dry up, the theatre would dry indeed". This decision was not taken, however, without opposition and a degree of pessimism as to whether the audiences would express their fear of the unknown by voting with their feet. In the event, the 1954/55 Annual Report admitted that the Jubilee season had the predictable effect on audience numbers, but that the falling-off had been only small; the average audience per production for that season was 1,335, compared with 1,425 during the previous year.

Indicating The Questors' continuing commitment to youth work, the Silver Jubilee year saw the formation of the Young Questors. The Student Group had been gaining in popularity, with stiff competition for the relatively few places, and several applicants each year were being turned away on the grounds of

29

their youth. It was therefore decided to establish the Young Questors, under the direction of Rena Rice, for promising young people who were too young for the Student Group proper. There were soon five groups running, covering a number of age ranges, and several 'graduates' of Young Questors went on to progress through the Student Group and into the main acting member-ship, where they remain to this day—Dorothy Boyd Taylor, Monyene Kane, Gillian Kerswell, Robin Ingram, John Turner and Michael Langridge being a few names of those who are still particularly active on the Questors stage.*

---

* Gradually, the range of classes offered has increased to include Drama Playgroups for 5–9 year-olds, Stage 2 groups for 10–14 year-olds and Junior Drama Workshops for 14–17 year-olds, so that all children of school age can be catered for. By the middle of the 1980s, at which point the most recent 'baby boom' seemed to have peaked, in Ealing at any rate, a total of five Drama Playgroups, six Stage 2 groups and four Junior Drama Workshop groups were running, all taught on a voluntary basis by Questors members, and upwards of 250 young people were coming to The Questors each week for classes.

Chapter 5

An Adaptable Theatre

by Alfred Emmet*

When, in 1933, we converted the old chapel in Mattock Lane to be our first theatre, we had (as mentioned in Chapter 1) the great advantage of advice on the stage lighting installation by Frederick Bentham, then a young enthusiast carrying out experiments in a model theatre in a back bedroom of his parents' house in Willesden, but later to become the doyen of stage lighting in the British Theatre. At his instigation we installed a simple cyclorama, and also dispensed with footlights, an almost unheard-of step at that time. Although it was not the intention, the latter innovation led directly to the possibility of experiment in the use of a forestage.

As we recorded in a note to the members of the New Theatre Advisory Panel:

"It was probably the small size of our stage that induced us in 1935 to build a forestage and come out of the proscenium arch (this was for *The Taming of the Shrew*). At first its use was confined to Shakespeare and such plays as 18th century comedies and Aristophanes. Then we found that we could use it to advantage for such modern, non-naturalistic plays as *A Bride for the Unicorn* (1938) and *Noah* (1939).

"Naturalistic plays were in the main always kept strictly within the picture frame until 1945, when the producer (sic) of *A Doll's House* used a forestage, bringing much of the action down onto it with furniture placed in front of the tabs. This was so successful and satisfying that we were soon using some form of forestage for practically every show, including...plays that one would not normally think of bringing outside the picture frame.

"We found that it worked".

---

* Alfred Emmet OBE was one of the original 17 founder members of The Questors and the first Hon. Secretary. He was Honorary Director from 1949 to 1969 and a member of the Committee of Management for over 30 years. He founded the Student Group and was Director of Studies for 38 years. He has been a Vice-President since he retired from the Committee of Management in 1981.

31

We had long been consciously experimenting with alternative theatre forms: in 1936 there was a tentative but rather abortive attempt at 'in the round' with scenes from *Twelfth Night* (as the entire audience was less than a dozen, there were hardly enough of them to go all the way round anyway); in 1950 we even tried putting the play (*Christmas in the Market Place*) on the floor of the auditorium and some of the audience on the stage, though that did not teach us much except about the problems of sightlines. In the main, however, we were exploring the problems of spilling out of the proscenium onto a forestage, such problems as the differences in actor-audience relationship, the use of scenery on the forestage, ways of unifying the main stage and forestage areas, the use, or rather non-use, of the front curtain, and so on.

When in the 1950s we were beginning to think quite seriously about a new theatre, though as yet only in general terms, all we were sure about was that it would not be a picture-frame theatre. Over the years The Questors had probably had more experience of breaking away from the 'prison' (as it was often called) of the picture-frame stage than almost any other theatre group, so we were well placed to progress further. At that time, there was much discussion generally in theatrical circles about 'What kind of theatre for the post-war period?' and naturally, we were getting tuned in to this thinking. When we bought the site in 1952, however, the question became a particular and immediate one.

There was no question but that we were going to build a new theatre, but the question was, as elsewhere, what kind of theatre. So we set up a Committee (of course!), charged with the task of preparing plans. Its prime function was the fundamental one of defining the relationship between acting area and auditorium. This New Theatre Committee, consisting of George Benn (Civil Engineer, Scene Designer and Stage Manager), Graham Heywood (Commercial Artist and Scene Designer), Ernest Ives (Architect and Scene Designer) and Alfred Emmet (Hon. Director of The Questors), being aware of the danger of compromise between various views, deliberately refused to start by asking each other's opinions, but began instead by exploring together certain basic principles. In this we were much assisted by our very eminent Advisory Panel, who had agreed to help us with occasional advice as we progressed.

Together we examined such questions as the choice between

Evolution or Revolution (there were many tempting revolutionary ideas for theatre floating about at the time; on the other
hand, if thinking in terms of evolution, our own starting point
would be, not the conventional proscenium theatre, but our own
development from it); the true nature of Theatrical Illusion (an
illusion of reality created in the enclosed stage space and presented to the audience, or an illusion created in the imagination
of the audience, therefore requiring a greater sharing); on
what does 'Intimacy' in the theatre depend (the shape and
arrangement of the audience seating in relation to the actor, for
instance); the case for an Adaptable Theatre (should we not
rather be looking for a contemporary form of playhouse which
is right for its period, as for instance the Georgian playhouse
was right for its period?)

These discussions and consultations were of course accompanied by other research and by further experiments in the
theatre, notably the production of *King John* in 1954, for which
a thrust stage was built well out into the auditorium with rows
of seats on each side; this, in particular, greatly influenced our
thinking. Then came the exciting day when, after many months
of work, we discovered that all the members of the Committee
had arrived quite independently at the same conclusion: it was
to be a flexible, or adaptable, theatre.

The case for the adaptable theatre was put in an article in
New Theatre Magazine a few years later:

"An adaptable theatre may be justified on one or other of two
grounds:

1. That no one kind of playhouse can be suitable for all kinds of
play and, therefore, a theatre planning (as does The Questors) a
repertoire including classical plays of all periods as well as
contemporary and new plays must be adaptable;
or
2. That due to the absence of theatre building and the lack of
normal development in theatre architecture, no one can be sure
today what kind of playhouse really best meets contemporary
needs and therefore adaptable theatres must be built to find out.

"...This brings us precisely to the purpose of The Questors'
adaptable theatre, for it was the second of the above arguments
which finally swung them in favour of this form. In other words,
The Questors are setting up a small scale pilot experiment from
which to learn. It is a piece of living and vital theatre research
such as has not been previously attempted.''

Chiefly due to the war and its aftermath of severe building restrictions, there had been no new theatre building for some 20 years. Moreover the restrictions of the theatre licensing regulations, which required a solid proscenium wall and the provision of a safety curtain, had resulted in a total stagnation of the architectural form of theatre. There was a widespread desire for a fresh approach to the question of what a playhouse should be. The Questors hoped to make some contribution, on the small scale of its project, to finding the answer.

Norman Branson ARIBA (a member of The Questors, designer, actor and director) was appointed architect and the New Theatre Committee prepared his brief. Recognising the problems of complete flexibility, we posited that a degree of compromise would be accepted in respect of picture-frame stage use, which we reckoned would seldom be required. We could also accept some measure of improvisation in respect of theatre in the round on the assumption that the theatre could be readily adapted to a permanent theatre in the round should that be the development ultimately desired. After several schemes had been submitted, discussed and rejected, Scheme No. 5 was regarded as coming near to solving the problems. Further consultation with the Panel in October 1954 resulted in some minor modifications and early in 1955 a revised scheme was submitted to a general meeting of The Questors and approved. Thus we became committed.

The architect's approved scheme was for the whole theatre complex, including what are now known as the Bernard Shaw Room and the Constantin Stanislavsky Room. Over the next few years, while these ancillary buildings were gradually being constructed by Questors volunteer labour, the plans for the Playhouse itself, though without any change in the basic principle, were constantly refined and improved, partly as a result of further experiments both in the old theatre and in productions in the Stanislavsky Room. The architect's brief in 1954 had specified that the plan should allow completion of the project by stages "within, say, 10 years." It was in 1964 that the Playhouse was opened in the presence of HM the Queen Mother.

This we described as 'The Beginning'.

Chapter 6

Towards a New Theatre, 1955–1962

Following approval of the plans for the exciting new theatre complex by the membership, the venture was launched at a press conference held at the Arts Council headquarters in St James's Square on 10th May 1955. It generated much high-profile publicity, both nationally and internationally. The *Evening News* reported that "London's liveliest amateur drama group—The Questors of Ealing—is to build a theatre that will break away from the 'picture frame' type of stage. Its projected 'three dimensional and living' theatre will enable it to give conventional, forestage, open-stage, arena-stage and space-stage productions." The plans were the subject of papers read, followed by searching question and answer sessions, at the Royal Society of Arts, the Royal Institution of British Architects, the London Congress of the International Association of Theatre Technicians, the Society for Theatre Research and numerous other organisations. Articles appeared in journals and magazines the world over, including *The Architect's Journal*, *Architectural Review*, *World Theatre*, *International Lighting Review* and *The Builder*, and The Questors was included in two significant books published in the following year (Peter Coates's *A Handbook for the Amateur Theatre* and Stephen Joseph's *Theatre in the Round*). A model of the proposed new theatre also featured prominently in an exhibition of 'Changing London' at The Building Centre in Central London (an exhibition which also featured models of London Airport, the BBC television studios and the Crystal Palace development scheme).

A meeting was held at the Garrick Club, attended by many influential theatre professionals and addressed by Felix Aylmer and Ellen Pollock. As The Questors had anticipated, a new theatre was hot news in 1955—a new kind of theatre even more so. Luck was again on their side in the choice of slogan; one of the newer crazes of the time was the so-called '3D cinema'. The phrase '3D theatre' was tentatively put forward as a shorthand explanation of the Questors design and it captured the imagination, not least of the headline writers:

"WORK TO START ON 3-D THEATRE" (*Middlesex County Times*)
"3-D theatre" (*Manchester Evening News*)
The original cost estimate for the project was £50,000 and the Building Fund stood at a little under £8,000 at the end of 1954. Major fund-raising would obviously be needed. On 11th May 1955, the evening following the official launch of the scheme, the New Theatre Appeal was launched at a public meeting at Ealing Town Hall. Chaired by the Mayor of Ealing, Alderman W J Gooderham, this meeting was attended by more than 700 people; indeed, Alderman Gooderham commented that he had never seen such a well-attended meeting in the Town Hall. The principal speakers were Angus Maude MP, E Martin Browne and Alec Guinness; the last-named giving an address which has lingered long in the memory. It was during this speech that he uttered the sentence which has since often been quoted, describing the Questors plans as "The most exciting theatrical venture to be launched in this country." Long-standing active member Kath Harrington, in charge of the hospitality suite on that evening, recalls that Alec Guinness also disclosed that he had once attended a performance at The Questors way back in 1933, on the night before he decided to become a professional actor.

Norman Branson's plans were, of course, not for the Playhouse alone, but for the entire site. The elements were to be (listed anti-clockwise starting in the South-East corner): a meeting room seating 100, with kitchen; cloakrooms; rehearsal room; workshop; dressing room and wardrobe; playhouse; Mattock Lodge. The Tin Hut, in which it was hoped to continue to stage productions right through the transition phase, sat squarely in the middle of the eventual, vaguely horseshoe-shaped, complex envisaged. Of the buildings, only Mattock Lodge and the workshop already existed, and it was intended at this stage that Mattock Lodge should form the main entrance of the theatre. Indeed, the first Appeal leaflet published, with a cover designed by Osbert Lancaster, shows a taxi drawing up outside Mattock Lodge and the audience entering through its front door.

It was planned to start with the ancillary areas on the principle that it would be easier to raise money for the Playhouse after the lavatories were built rather than the other way round. The rate of progress would obviously depend on the rate at which the money was raised. Another key factor was that as much of the work as possible was to be done by The Questors' own voluntary labour. Two weeks after the Appeal meeting, work started on digging the foundations of the meeting room, after an informal ceremony during which Marius Goring cut the first turf. The *Middlesex County Times* recorded that shortly afterwards, the loudspeaker began belting out "a well known tune from 'Snow White', urging that 'We dig, dig, dig, dig, dig, dig, dig...' Then several leading members of the theatre took their cue from this and started to work with picks and shovels".

In the early days of heady enthusiasm, the building labour force was considerable and the foundation-digging proceeded quickly. That first autumn, for example, although this was more of a publicity stunt than anything else, teams continued to dig by floodlight while the show was performing. The ruse served its purpose; on September 19th, *The Times*, no less, reviewing The Questors' production of the English première of Gunther Weisenborn's *The Three Honourable Gentlemen*, began thus:

> "The Questors are in the front line of the amateur theatre in this country, and that is more or less where the audience arriving for the first night of the new season on Saturday found them. A night shift of volunteers was busy with picks and shovels digging trenches for the foundations ... on the site where it is hoped to erect what will be one of the most adaptable theatres in the world."

George Benn noted in *Forestage* in October 1955 that the digging of the foundations by members' own labour had saved an estimated £58. The Shaw Room project, he wrote, "is by way of being a guinea-pig in as much as it will enable us to assess how much we can reasonably expect to do ourselves". Professionals were called in to fill in and level the foundations but once the bricklaying got under way, it was over to The Questors again, under the leadership initially of Eric Voce and then of John Clemow when the former had to retire because of ill health. Lister Beck quickly became foreman of the bricklaying team, which included 20 to 30 members at the outset, both male and female in true egalitarian Questors style. None of them had any idea at all of how to go about building, but they soon taught themselves and many who had hitherto believed themselves to be no good with their hands found a surprising aptitude for bricklaying. They were fortunate in that one of the professional team who had helped with the foundations, a man called Tom Parker, was so taken with the spirit of the project that he stayed on for some time to instruct the Questors workers voluntarily. In fact, had it not been for his tuition, the corners might well have defeated the volunteer gang who, although they managed the straight lines well enough, had a few problems with the tricky bits!

It may be invidious to name names but in this context, more than any other perhaps, tribute needs to be paid to the few loyal stalwarts who persevered with the building of what are now known as the Bernard Shaw and Constantin Stanislavsky Rooms for a total of five and a half years. These members were, in addition to the three named above, Tom Boyd, Denis Robinson, Bob Anderson, Ruth Howard, Martin Carr, George Benn, Alfred Emmet and Tony Shipley. Of course, many others participated when they could and special squads were recruited for particular tasks—the tenants of the bedsitters, for example, were regularly rousted out of bed by Lister Beck at 9 o'clock on Saturday mornings to help unload a lorry-load of bricks or carry heavy girders!

At the beginning, when enthusiasm was still high, many members would go straight from work down to the Theatre and put in two or three hours bricklaying before rehearsal. Inevitably, it became impossible to maintain the early momentum and the posse of builders slowly dwindled to the hard core. There were some bad patches, those members recall, when the work seemed to be going forward very slowly, particularly in the Winter when it was snowing and work was really confined to weekends. From time to time, appeals would be issued to the membership for help and, considering how long the enterprise went on, the response was extremely good.

However, despite the publicity and messages of support which accompanied the launch, the money had been depressingly slow to come in. By the time the 1955/56 Annual Report was published, only £9,205 of the estimated £50,000 required had been forthcoming. Big money was needed from outside, and the efforts were redoubled. Letters were written to every conceivable source and as much publicity as possible sought; the new theatre project was featured twice by the BBC and once by ITV in news items during the 1955/56 season and was the subject of a full-page report in the *Evening Standard*.

An excellent 'photo-opportunity' was dreamed up for the topping-out of the Shaw Room, when the roof had been completed. On 3rd October 1956, the last night of Ibsen's *The Master*

38

Builder (an appropriate choice of play—as was commented at the time, it was performed with real feeling), Dame Sybil Thorndike officiated at the ceremonial hanging of a garland on the Shaw Room roof, using the wreath which Master Builder Solness had used for the same traditional ceremony in the play. The Questors architect, Norman Branson, was persuaded to do the honours; fortunately without the dramatic outcome which Solness suffered.

The entire Shaw Room block, including kitchen and cloak-rooms, was completed and officially opened on 5th July 1958, by (Sir) Michael Redgrave, who had become President of The Questors in the same year; the ceremony was also attended by several other influential theatre professionals, including (Sir) Michael Hordern, George Benson and Benn Levy. *The Times* reported the following day: "Mr Redgrave received the key of the Bernard Shaw Room from the president of the Shaw Society, Miss Ellen Pollock." According to the *Sheffield Telegraph*, Michael Redgrave said that "The Questors Theatre has a social value for the whole of the country" and the *Thames Valley Times* recorded his comment that the project was "the most remarkable communal centre that any city or borough could have." In appealing for £7,000 urgently, he announced the endowment scheme—£100 for a seat in the new theatre to be endowed in the name of the donor.

Work on the next phase, the rehearsal room which it had been decided to call the Stanislavsky Room, was by then already under way, following a ceremony to lay the foundation stone. This, on 7th June 1958, had been performed by Victor Stanitsyn and other members of the Moscow Art Theatre on their first visit to London after the war. The inscription on the stone itself reads:

> "Constantin Stanislavsky who loved the theatre. This stone was laid by members of the Moscow Art Theatre company, 7th June 1958".

A most moving ceremony, those who attended recall, and certainly newsworthy—part of the proceedings were relayed live by BBC Radio. At the reception and party afterwards, members of The Questors were able to communicate their gratitude to the visitors, through "just the right number of interpreters".

The work of building the Stanislavsky Room seemed even harder than building the Shaw Room had been, as the team of

39

bricklayers was now pretty small and the specifications had demanded a room at least 18ft high—it was intended that it should be possible to run rehearsals with full sets. However, there were to be no windows and the builders were grateful for small mercies. An International Voluntary Service camp helped during the summer of 1959 and this certainly generated more widespread publicity through BBC television coverage which was networked in France, Spain, the USA and by the general BBC Overseas Service. It was not until 1st October 1960, however, two and a half years after the laying of the foundation stone and nearly 10,000 bricks later, that the Stanislavsky Room was officially opened by Dame Edith Evans, who said: "It is one of the most adventurous things I have known. It is the answer to those who say the theatre is going down." A performance of the last scene from *The Three Sisters* was given and film shown of the opening of the Shaw Room and the laying of the foundation stone.

Meanwhile, the fund-raisers were still hard at it. The Appeal Sub-committee had set up an elaborate appeals index, divided into categories. Literally thousands of letters were sent: to past, present and potential members of the Questors; to 'theatre people' and playwrights; to 'important local residents' and 'important interested individuals'. Members dreamed up the usual, the not-so usual and ever more imaginative ways of persuading people to part with their money. Special perform-ances were organised—one particularly successful innovation, which subsequently became a long-running Questors tradition, was a Christmas melodrama, the first being *Sweeney Todd* in 1956 (directed by Michael Green)*. Because of the need for economy, *Sweeney Todd* was done on a shoestring, the major item of expenditure being 7/6d (37½p) on red toothpaste—for blood.

Among the most popular events which swelled the New Theatre Fund were the Variety Concerts, held sporadically in the Tin Hut and invariably sold out. These were arranged and usually compèred by Wilfrid Sharp, who managed to persuade various professional artistes to contribute 'turns' to the pro-

---

* These 'Special Performances', for which both members and guests had to pay for their tickets, gradually became a standard feature of season programming, representing as they did a source of considerable revenue and by the 1970s, each season typically contained four 'All Pay' shows.

grammes. Their names, of course, were valuable for publicity purposes. They were usually backed up by groups or individuals from The Questors, with Eric Kirby as accompanist or pianist-compère. Among the professional artistes who generously gave their services on such occasions were (Sir) Bernard Miles doing his rustic act, Harry Locke (himself one of the earliest members of The Questors) with a delightful one-man French film act, the Sadler's Wells baritone Denis Dowling and Winifred Copperwheat the distinguished viola player. Help was also given from time to time by other amateur dramatic societies such as The Court Drama Group and schools, especially Latymer Upper, The Godolphin and Latymer Girls and St Paul's High.

Talent contests also proved popular fund-raising events, particularly when celebrities were persuaded to act as judges; the actress Sylvia Sims performed this duty on one occasion. Indeed the talent contests, together with the melodramas, probably represented the beginnings of Coarse Acting (of which more later). Alan Drake, who was one of the most prominent of fund-raisers at the time and who was described some years later in *Questopics* as a "grand master of the art of cajoling people into doing those things that in their right minds they would not even contemplate", recalls some of the techniques employed in persuading audiences to part with further money:

"I think my active participation in fund-raising began around 1956. I'd joined The Questors a year or so earlier and following a minor appearance in Kit Emmet's production of **Hamlet** and several days in the Emmets' flat in Haven Green Court being nursed through Asian flu, I became one of Alfred's dedicated 'yes-men' in fund-raising ventures. I was working quite close to his office in the City; an invitation to lunch meant only one thing—he had thought of something else for me to do. We needed to appeal directly to our audiences.

"By that time, I was heavily involved in Michael Green's Christmas melodramas. My style of acting and slightly passé appearance lent themselves perfectly to the playing of juvenile leads and the audience learnt to cheer whenever I appeared on stage, no matter what I was playing. I was very rarely cast in a serious role as a consequence. But a happy rapport with the audience was necessary if one was going to ask for money. Deeds of covenant were what we wanted and I usually placed a couple of people in the audience (loss leaders, in marketing terms) who had agreed in advance to sign. Once a couple of people signed, others inevitably followed.

"Another highly successful practice was used during Alan Chambers' production of *Twelfth Night* in 1962, in which I played Sir Andrew Aguecheek. At the final curtain, I fished Deed of Covenant forms out of my painted hessian drawers; an essential element in getting money from an audience is to get them to laugh!"

Another popular fund-raising event, which was repeated several times during this period, was the Garden Party held in the theatre grounds. It is worth digressing slightly at this point to describe the gardens themselves. During the 1950s Mattock Lane, with its large houses set in spacious grounds, still had a very countrified atmosphere. The road was still lit by gas and carried little traffic. Mattock Lodge had a particularly large and pleasant garden, with lawns at the front, daffodils in Spring and several lime and walnut trees; the wonderful smell of the limes would greet members on their approach along the Lane. At the back, apart from the lilac bushes which hid the infamous outside lavatories, was another lawn and a few trees. Members would naturally use the garden for recreation, especially the Sunday Teas which have been a Questors tradition practically from the very beginning.

So the Garden Parties were events into which the active members threw themselves with gusto. Organisers included Barbara Emmet, Diana Benn and Pamela Richards—indeed Barbara Emmet believes that her enthusiastic organisation of the 1950 Garden Party was responsible for the premature birth of her son David three days later! Apocryphal tales abound. Of the fortune-telling tent, for example, featuring Vincent McQueen and John Clemow conning an unsuspecting populace into believing they were gypsies. The booth was advertised by a coffin outside with a gloved human hand hanging out under the lid. Pony rides and sideshows were set up in the next-door garden, the two gardens being linked by a bridge built from rostra. Some years later, several highly successful barbecues (a phenomenon just introduced from the USA) were also held in the garden, thanks to a contact with the US Air Force base at Ruislip.

Despite the best efforts of the membership, progress towards the £50,000 target remained painfully slow: at June 1957, the

New Theatre Fund stood at £13,483; June 1958, £16,058; June 1959, £19,990. George Benn, who was Chairman from 1953 to 1957 (and again from 1962 to 1972), recalls: "Fund-raising was of course the main headache for some 12 years. Our membership was in the region of 1,300. It is as well to remember that there was no Grapevine Club to make large annual donations and no profitable letting of buildings. It was before the days of the fund-raising profession. The new theatre sub-committee poured forth a spate of ideas ranging from snowball teas, through autographed bricks to endowment of seats; so much so, that one minute in the file is annotated 'really, one day this committee will burst'." He recorded later that, by 1959, "many of us began to feel that we should never raise the necessary money." The appeal was going stale. Even the arch-optimist himself, Alfred Emmet, confessed many years later: "Even the most confident among us were beginning to be assailed by doubts... though we would certainly none of us admit it."

The turning point came in December 1959 when, encouraged by the news that The Questors' old LTG friend and colleague the People's Theatre had been unanimously awarded a grant of £10,000 by the Newcastle-upon-Tyne Council, an application was made to Ealing Council for a grant. Alfred Emmet takes up the story in his 1981 lecture to the Society for Theatre Research:

"A careful case was prepared and representatives of The Questors attended a meeting of the General Purposes Committee to answer questions. The Councillor who, as Mayor, had chaired that big meeting at the Town Hall (to launch the Appeal), took up the cudgels on our behalf. When we thronged into the public gallery for a meeting of the Council on 16th February, 1960, we learned that the General Purposes Committee's recommendation was to make a grant of £7,250, being about a quarter of the balance of the sum required, when the Council could be assured that we had guarantors for a further £14,500. In Ealing, there was no question of unanimous approval, as in Newcastle. The proposal met very strong opposition and the debate seemed to continue interminably. At last a vote was called on a motion to refer the recommendation back, and the Mayor... announced the result, for... 26; against ... 27. By one vote the theatre was saved, for I truly believe if that help had not been forthcoming at that time, it is more than probable that the scheme would have foundered. Once again, a friend had rescued us."

In order to impress the Council with the strength of members' support and determination, George Benn had organised a rally of Questors members and some 20 or 30 sat in the public gallery, from which frequent background murmurs of surprise, disagreement or pleasure emanated as appropriate, which no doubt had some effect upon the outcome!

That conditional grant inspired the members to redouble their own fund-raising efforts. They were greatly encouraged in July 1960 by the award of a £3,000 grant by the Calouste Gulbenkian Foundation. Having taken nearly five years to raise the first £20,000, the £14,500 needed to claim the Council's £7,250 was raised in 18 months and by June 1961, the New Theatre Fund at £46,709 was finally approaching the original target. The November Annual General Meeting of members that year instructed the Committee of Management to proceed with the contract for building the Playhouse itself, it being recognised by everyone that this would be beyond the DIY capabilities of the members. Discussions opened with Taylor Woodrow as contractors. And then came the next shock. Even after making a number of modifications to the original design to cut the cost (described in detail in Chapters 8 and 9), the contractors' estimate was still significantly higher than that estimated seven years previously.

So began another frantic search for financial guarantees, around £30,000 being needed before Taylor Woodrow would be prepared to start. After three fruitless months of targeting financiers and companies, especially those with charitable reputations or known interests in the theatre, in June 1962 the Midland Bank agreed to give The Questors overdraft facilities on mortgage of up to £23,000. Taylor Woodrow were then instructed to proceed with detailed estimates and plans. In March of the same year, the Leche Charity had offered a grant of £5,000, conditional upon The Questors' managing to raise an additional £10,000 by the end of the year. This was achieved—just—the last few pounds being collected as a result of dramatic appeals from the stage on the last night of the last production of the year! So at last the building of the Playhouse could proceed, although this was by no means the end of the money-raising; when it was completed in 1964, it was with a debt of nearly £20,000 outstanding.

Chapter 7

Other Activities, 1955-1960

During all the years of building and fund-raising, which could so easily have sapped all available creative energy, one thing The Questors certainly did not do was to compromise on the development of its central five-point policy, which had come to be known as 'The Quest'. Throughout the 1950s, experimentation continued, not just with stage form but also with design, technical aspects, lights, sound and styles of production.

Examples which members have picked out from those years, for a variety of reasons, are given in the following paragraphs:

Gilgamesh (1956) was another new play by Michael Kelly, directed by Colette King and designed by Norman Branson. The open staging of this production anticipated, in the restricted conditions, much of the open stage work subsequently developed in the new playhouse. Scene changes were effected by the use of mobile periaktoi (or prisms), each powered by a concealed stage hand who, torch in hand, followed a course marked by lines on the stage to achieve a series of abstract arrangements, the movements choreographed to coincide with the thematic development. In the latter respect, The Questors was once more mirroring experiments going on elsewhere; mobile scenery was being used, for example, in the Shakespeare Memorial Theatre's *King Lear* with John Gielgud. At one memorable performance of *Gilgamesh*, smoke was seen emerging from the top of one of the cavorting periaktoi; investigation revealed the source to be the pipe tobacco of one Michael Green!

Ibsen's *The Master Builder* (1956), already referred to for the first night ceremony, was important in that it was the first experiment in bringing a traditionally naturalistic 'picture-frame' play out onto an improvised thrust stage, with the audience on three sides. This demonstrated the value of being able to rid the stage of the realistic clutter usually associated with Ibsen productions and to focus attention on the characters and their relationships.

On a lighter note, 1955 saw the production of *Fratricide Punished*, a seldom-produced anonymous play translated back into English from a German version of *Hamlet*, supposedly put together by a travelling company of English players early in the

45

17th century. The play is well-known to scholars but not known at all to present-day audiences. No doubt intended seriously, the result is quite hilarious, particularly in The Questors' production presented only a few days after Barbara Emmet's production of *Hamlet* and played by the same company taking each other's parts; an event claimed to be entirely unique in the history of theatre.

The River Line by Charles Morgan was directed in 1957 by John Clemow. The design by Edward Mendelsohn featured a movable wall, which opened up on the stage like a book to reveal a second scene, the first time that such a technique had been tried.

And then in October 1957, Alfred Emmet's production of Shakespeare's *Henry V* was memorable for many reasons. Firstly, it used not just a thrust stage, but the whole theatre. By this time, a raised box had been constructed at the back of the auditorium for the sound operators (although most sound effects were still done live in these pre-tape recorder days), and this was used for the scene at Harfleur, so that the exchange between Henry and the Herald took place over the heads of the audience. An exit through the auditorium, the newly-cut emergency exit in fact, was used for the first time, when the British Army entered the gates of Harfleur. Another feature of the production was the treatment of the Chorus (played by Pat Bowley) who was dressed in jeans and sneakers, in contrast with the historical costume of the rest of the cast. The shock of the opening moment of the play when out of the darkness a spotlight suddenly revealed this unexpected figure commanded immediate attention. Michael Green recalls that this worked tremendously well, not only distancing the Chorus from the actors but also from the audience (this was still the time when people would dress up to go to the theatre, of course), so that he became what Shakespeare intended him to be, a neutral commentator on the action.

However, it is for completely different reasons that Michael has written, most amusingly, about this production in *The Art of Coarse Acting*:

> "I shall not easily forget a production of Henry V which coincided with an influenza epidemic. We were always one player short, in any case. It was a sort of floating gap, filled each night by whomever could get into the messenger's costume in time...
>
> "The epidemic, however, made things much worse. No one

knew what part he would have to play next. Mysterious messages would be left at the office during the day ('Mr Green, someone rang to say you are Lord Scroop tonight. Does that make sense?').

"Worse still, you would turn up at the theatre all unsuspecting, and be making-up as Bardolph or some such harmless role, when the stage manager would approach, thrust a heap of armour into your arms and say: 'Bert's ill. You're doubling the Earl of Essex tonight.'

"Since there was no time to learn the appropriate lines, one came on stage, usually from the wrong side, groping about in ill-fitting armour and trying to read from the script at the same time. It is hardly surprising that as a result I died after a sword fight which I should have won...

"The climax came when even with everyone doubling two or three parts there just weren't enough men to go round. The only thing left to do was to cut the play as we went along, omitting those on the sick list.

"It was the quickest performance of Henry V on record. Whole episodes of English history vanished. The French court was reduced to one man. I don't think the Battle of Agincourt ever took place. In the end we discovered we had done it in five minutes over the hour, which as far as I know is a world record."

Whether that is an exaggeration or not, it certainly makes a good story, and there is no doubt that there is more than an element of truth—many people, when asked about *Henry V*, say "oh, yes, the famous Asian flu one". Yet another curious coincidence relating to this production concerns the actor Michael Williams, Vice-President of The Questors since 1986. In 1957, he was a young student at RADA, living with his aunt and uncle in Ealing, and he clearly recalls coming to the Tin Hut to see *Henry V*. Whether or not he coincided with one of the worst Asian flu nights is not known!

In Barbara Emmet's 1958 production of *The Long Spoon*, a new play by Alexandra Mikellatos who was another of the Questors members who started writing for the company, the stage was roughly divided into two halves, lit separately for alternate scenes. At the final dress rehearsal, before an audience of old-age pensioners, the lighting operator, who was of necessity (the wings were extremely small) positioned so that he couldn't

47

see the stage, got one cue out so that the wrong half was lit*. After two or three lighting cues, with the actors frantically chasing the pools of light around the stage, the director realised that the poor operator had no idea he was out, so the performance was stopped and the situation righted, to the delight of the audience, who really felt they were getting ''a view of the works''.

Also in 1958 came Colette King's production of some passages from James Joyce's *Finnegan's Wake*, adapted by Mary Manning under the title **The Voice of Shem**. This English première utterly confused the audiences, who found Joyce's text, even in its adapted form, quite incomprehensible. Nevertheless, it is remembered for a stunning and innovative setting, in which a flight of forestage steps from stage to auditorium floor level was used as a major acting area, giving an enhanced actor-audience relationship. Another first and a device which has subsequently been much used in the commercial theatre.

In November 1960, Alfred Emmet's production of **The Glass Menagerie** by Tennessee Williams was notable for two reasons. Firstly, it was the inaugural production in the recently-opened Stanislavsky Room. This was something of an opportunist move—it was realised when this rehearsal room was finished that a space had been created which it would be stimulating to use for the production of plays, something that had never been envisaged during the planning. That first production was such a success that it was decided to alternate productions in the theatre and the Stanislavsky Room and later to stage all the productions in the Stanislavsky Room in the period between

---

* The lighting arrangements in the Tin Hut deserve a mention, particularly the famous dimmers which have been described in a mixture of awe and fondness by several members. These were not, it is quickly asserted, exactly 'state-of-the-art' but were a cheap home-made set which just happened to do the job extremely effectively. They were made from drainpipes, six of them, the bottom being sealed with concrete in which was embedded a metal plate. A matching plate was fixed to a rod suspended by cord over a series of pulleys and so could be raised or lowered through the solution of salt in the drainpipe to vary the electrical resistance and so the intensity of light. The principle was impeccable, the practice less so. For one thing, the liquid might evaporate during the run, upsetting carefully plotted dimmer settings; over-enthusiastic operation would result in audible splashing noises. Worst of all was a tendency for the dimmers to get over-heated and boil, with disturbing effect. As the relationship between distance between plates and light intensity was not arithmetic, the system required extremely careful and expert handling; tribute has been paid by many to the skill of Gerry Isenthal in their operation.

48

demolishing the Tin Hut and opening the new theatre (of which more later). *The Glass Menagerie* was also the first truly in-the-round production that The Questors had ever been able to mount; despite all the experimentation, the layout of the stage in the Tin Hut was just not suitable. The totally empty space of the Stanislavsky Room was seized upon with gusto.

Social facilities for club members were not forgotten in all the flurry of planning and building. The Club Lounge, as mentioned already, had opened soon after Mattock Lodge was taken over but, with the completion of the Shaw Room in 1958, it was decided to use that room as the coffee lounge during show intervals, connecting it to the theatre with a temporary covered way. This made possible consideration of opening a club bar in Mattock Lodge. The lack of a bar on the premises was keenly felt by many members; the nearest source of liquid refreshment, other than coffee and tea, was The Three Pigeons, about 200 yards away and late rehearsals or shows which came down near closing time meant a mad dash down the road to try to catch 'last orders'. Catering for last night parties meant ordering drink in advance and bringing it in.

There remained considerable opposition, however; doubts were expressed that the presence of a bar might attract the wrong people to join The Questors—members who were more interested in drinking than in seeing plays—who might gradually take over control and change The Questors' policy. Great care had to be taken lest running a bar, which would hardly be regarded as a charitable activity, might imperil the Theatre's enormously important status as an educational charity* (and the fiscal advantages that that implied). Eventually the doubters were persuaded on financial grounds—it was undeniable that having a bar on the premises would bring in money, desperately needed to build the new theatre. By establishing an independent club to run the bar, the status of the Theatre itself would be protected. The trading profit was tax-free because it arose from the members trading with themselves; a clause was inserted in the constitution that spare profits should be donated to The Questors. So in 1958, Arthur Boyd Taylor was asked to organise

---

* The Questors has been registered as an educational charity since 1931. Originally little more than a formality, it meant that the Theatre was exempted from paying entertainments duty. Following the passing of the Charities Act in the early 1950s, an official application for registration of the company as a charity was made and granted.

the establishment of the bar and the Grapevine Club was quickly formed. Michael Green recalls that the bar opened for a dummy run on the dress rehearsal night of a revue called *Questrionics*, and remembers the director, Barbara Emmet, giving the historic instruction after the rehearsal: "OK everyone, notes in the new bar". The official opening was on the following evening. That too was a fairly low-key affair in view of the fact that in those days "drink was like dynamite" and the licensing laws were very strict. In the ensuing 30 years, however, this Club has become one of the mainstays of The Questors, in more senses than one, providing not only congenial surroundings for socialising with like-minded people and informal discussions of past, present and future productions, but also upwards of £250,000 of additional income. A more detailed history of the Grapevine Club is given in Chapter 16.

A discussion of the development of The Questors from 1955-60 would not be complete without reference to two other important innovations, both of which met unequivocally requirements of 'The Quest' and both of which are subjects of separate contributed chapters in this book. The first was the extension of the Theatre's youth work in 1959, when a company was formed to tour local schools. This activity was continued for 12 years, and was the forerunner of Questabout, the Theatre-in-Education team which was established in 1972. Chapter 12 fills in the details.

The Questors also continued to place emphasis on attracting new plays; indeed, more formal recognition of the importance of new plays to the company was made in the 1959/60 season, when the first New Plays Festival was held. This included *The House of Cowards* by Dannie Abse which won that year's Charles Henry Foyle New Play Award, and three short plays by James Saunders, the first production by The Questors of this author's work. The New Plays Festival duly became another Questors tradition, and a total of 18 such Festivals, with three new plays playing in repertory over a week, were held, the last one being in 1977. In 1969 Alfred Emmet wrote as follows:

> "We are often asked 'Why do you have a New Plays Festival?', 'Why three plays?', 'Why not find one new play and put it on for a run?'

> "Such questions miss the whole point of the Festival, which is to create an opportunity of presenting new plays in an attractive and acceptable context. The fact that The Questors hold this

annual Festival and have done so now for ten years, means that playwrights, knowing this opportunity exists, are encouraged to send us their plays. It means that at times we are able to commission new plays, which is the case with all three plays in this year's Festival... a number of (plays included in previous Festivals), including some of the most successful, would never have been written if it had not been for the Festival. We feel that it provides a real and positive encouragement to new writing for the theatre.''

Chapter 13, while covering the general subject of New Plays at The Questors, comments particularly on these Festivals and their importance.

Chapter 8

"This is a Beginning" 1962-1964

As discussed in Chapter 6, sufficient funding, or promises of funding, had been secured early in 1963 for detailed planning of the Playhouse to begin, and the contract with Taylor Woodrow was signed on 16th March 1963. Work actually started two days later and proceeded quickly. After the gruelling years of bricklaying and struggling to raise pound after weary pound, it was tremendously exciting and stimulating for the members finally to see the shell of the auditorium taking shape before their eyes. But it was sad to see the lovely garden of Mattock Lodge turned into a muddy desert, the daffodils which used to spatter the grass bravely struggling to bloom amid the bricks and girders. The foundation stone of the Playhouse was laid by the President of The Questors, Sir Michael Redgrave, on 13th July 1963; greetings from many of the country's leading theatres, both amateur and professional, were read out at the ceremony. In addition to the two quoted below, theatres which sent messages included: The Royal Court; The Belgrade, Coventry; The Vanbrugh; The People's, Newcastle; The Yvonne Arnaud, Guildford; and The Chichester Festival Theatre, the last-mentioned in the form of a personal message from Sir Laurence Olivier, its Artistic Director.

Bernard Miles wrote, on behalf of the Mermaid Theatre:

"Every new theatre enterprise in London is of immense value to all the enterprises already operating, so Good Luck to The Questors from the Mermaid, may you stimulate new audience interest in theatre-going and continue to contribute to the competitive spirit of adventure which is the lifeblood of all theatrical endeavour."

The Theatre Royal, Stratford-upon-Avon, sent an outstandingly generous and heart-warming message which was printed in full in issue number 13 of *Quest News* (the broadsheet-style active members' newsletter which was published occasionally between 1961 and 1965), although only part of it could be read out at the ceremony:

"In the long and distinguished history of The Questors Theatre, there can have been no prouder day than this one. The Stone which is laid today is the culmination of a vast effort which stretches back through the years and rests on the enthusiasm, skill and vigour of countless people. The Questors has not been emulated for productions of merit and courage, for its training schemes, for its festivals, and for the importance of its position in the whole field of contemporary theatre. Indeed, its standards and its vision transcend the arbitrary division of the theatre into the body amateur and the body professional. There can hardly be a greater witness to belief in the paramount importance of Theatre and Drama than the construction, literally by one's own labours, of a new theatre. When that theatre is also devoted to new forms, concepts and principles, then it becomes a signal and splendid achievement. The Royal Shakespeare Theatre is not a little envious of the glowing opportunities which your new theatre will offer you, but we know that you have magnificently earned them. We offer you our respect and our good wishes. All honour to you."

A whole year before this splendid occasion, on June 29th 1962, the last official production in the old Theatre had been staged— *The Children of Saturn* by Lydia Ragosin, one of the plays in that year's New Plays Festival. The Tin Hut however, was celebrated in a nostalgic entertainment entitled *Going, Going*, arranged by Wilf Sharp with music by Eric Kirby and performed by them and the other stalwarts of the many previous Questors revues on 29th September 1962. It was billed as "Positively the last performance of any kind to be given in the old Questors Theatre before it is demolished to make way for the new" and tickets were priced at 10/6d. Issue number 7 of *Quest News* describes the occasion thus:

"I do not think there can have been so many people in the theatre at any time since the permanent seating was put in in 1938. Everyone seemed to share the sense of occasion ... Though much of the evening was naturally nostalgic in tone, the final emphasis was on the future. As the programme note said 'The new theatre is the inheritance of the young in heart'. Incidentally the Grapevine Bar (despite the exhortations of the Temperance Quartet*) took a record total of £64 during the evening."

The evening ended with a most appropriate, and totally unre-hearsed, finale. At the end of the performance, the atmosphere

* See footnote on next page

was electric and the audience demanded curtain call after curtain call. The perspiring Stage Manager did sterling service closing and opening the curtain, which ran along a track behind the proscenium pelmet, parting in the middle. Eventually, the poor curtain track could take no more—as the curtain halves slowly advanced towards the centre for the umpteenth time, there was a loud crack and the curtain refused to budge any further. After nearly 30 years of faultless operation, the track had broken, occasioning a characteristic observation from George Benn to the effect that in any well-designed structure all the components should fail at the same time. (It is claimed that he was then left to lock up in case the roof also caved in.)

After the final curtain call, with all the cast still gathered on stage, Alfred Emmet stepped forward. Most people expected a nostalgic speech, harking back to the good old times in the Tin Hut. They should have known him better; all Alfred said was "At six o'clock this evening, the New Theatre Fund stood at . . .", gave the exact figure and walked off. A striking way of reminding everyone to start looking forward, not back.

Work started on stripping out the old Theatre immediately, together with the allied conversion of Workshop to Green Room and Dressing Room to Workshop. One of the first tasks was to take down the old chapel bell from the little belfry on the roof of the Theatre, very carefully—it was a large and most impressive-looking bell which had been cast in 1896, according to the date inscribed upon it. The rather quixotic intention was to preserve it and remount it at the top of the stairway to the Playhouse, for use as an interval bell. Unfortunately, disaster struck in the weeks following its removal from its original position, during which time it had been standing in the grounds. One foggy day (London in those days was still subject to the thick 'peasoupers' associated with films of Jack the Ripper and other such melo-dramatic themes), members arrived to discover that the bell had vanished. Doubtless, it had been stolen by scrap dealers, for the valuable bell-metal, but it was a great blow and also an

---

* The Temperance Quartet was an offshoot of one of Michael Green's Christmas melodramas. It first appeared in the classic American temperance melodrama *The Drunkard* and was so popular that it performed on numerous other occasions, singing original 19th Century temperance songs such as 'Please Sell No More Drink To My Father'. The original members of the group were John Howard, Kit Emmet, Dorothy Boyd Taylor and Arthur Boyd Taylor. Ironically, Arthur was the Grapevine Club's first Chairman.

unpleasant sign of the times—security was beginning to be a consideration in a way that hitherto had not been necessary.

All productions in the 18 months or so from September 1962 to the opening of the Playhouse were mounted in the Stanislavsky Room; a full programme continued to be presented and a virtue made of necessity in exploring different forms of presentation, to the limits of the excitingly empty space which the Stanislavsky Room offered. Productions ranged from Anouilh's *Traveller Without Luggage*, through Shakespeare (*Twelfth Night*), Shaw (*The Devil's Disciple*) and Mrs Henry Wood (*East Lynne*), to Colley Cibber's *The Comical Lovers* and *Long Day's Journey into Night* by Eugene O'Neill. The whole of the Fourth New Plays Festival, a total of seven plays (six one-acters), was also presented in the Stanislavsky Room, as were the now-traditional Christmas melodramas, which broke new ground with *Bulldog Drummond Strikes Back*.

Meanwhile, the building was proceeding well and a mere six months after the foundation stone was laid, the contractors completed the shell of the building. By April 1964 the Playhouse was ready. A Gala opening performance of Ibsen's *Brand* took place on April 22nd in the presence of Her Majesty Queen Elizabeth the Queen Mother—a night often referred to as 'The Beginning'. Indeed, the phrase 'This is a Beginning' became something of a motif (much as 'Towards the New Theatre' had done in the years leading up to it) and was the title of the second of two films made by a member of The Questors, Fred Pateman, to record for posterity the historic events leading up to, and including, the opening of the Playhouse.

The Gala itself, also attended by the Norwegian Ambassador and several other celebrities, is an occasion etched in the memories of all the Questors members who were there. Several members who were involved in the hard work of building in the years that led up to it have remarked that that night made it all worth while. Her Majesty obviously enjoyed the occasion too; she was quoted in the press the following day as having commented that "It's all so wonderful'. Careful research and preparation had gone into ensuring that the entertainment of the Royal visitor would go smoothly, including the removal (temporarily, of course) of an entire row of the beautiful new red plush seats, for comfort and security reasons. George Benn had earlier gone to Kensington Palace to ascertain from Her Majesty's aides what kind of hospitality would be appropriate; champagne was

55

duly acquired. The members who were to sit next to the distinguished guest were also chosen with care—and varied between acts! A congratulatory message was received soon afterwards:

> "I am commanded by Queen Elizabeth to write and tell you how much she enjoyed visiting The Questors Theatre. Her Majesty was most impressed, not only by the very high standard of acting, but by the tremendous enthusiasm shown by all members of The Questors."

The play chosen to open the Playhouse, the first English performance of James Forsyth's translation of **Brand**, "perfectly demonstrates (The Questors') dramatic courage", according to one critic. It was directed by Alfred Emmet, with sets by Tadeusz Orlowicz and costumes by Margaret Reichlin, and the cast included Ray Moss as Brand, Ffrangcon Whelan as Agnes, Hugh Forsyth as Einar and Jan Kenny as Gerd. The Gala performance was preceded by a prologue, specially written by Patric Dickinson and spoken by Gwen Ffrangcon-Davies; the following extract from the text was printed in the souvenir brochure marking the occasion:

> We are here to praise the fruits of an
> endeavour
> A great endeavour marvellously achieved—
> What oft was thought, now seen to be believed!—
> A double triumph: here and now, and for ever.
> Praise be. You know what theatre you are in.
> On stage you actors! Let the world begin!

Possibly the last word about this momentous occasion should go to the reviewer who wrote the following day in the *Thames Valley Times*, neatly summarising the feelings of the Questors membership: "Above all, the occasion was a just reward for Alfred Emmet, director of The Questors, to whose inspiration and unflinching zeal the new theatre is a lasting monument".

This chapter is perhaps best completed by summarising some of the technical details involved in the revolutionary Playhouse of which The Questors now found itself the proud owner. George Benn, Chairman of The Questors for a total of 14 years and one of the four members of the New Theatre Committee, wrote the following in 1983:

> "*A New Concept in Theatre Design* was the title of a paper read to a meeting of the Royal Society of Arts on 29th February 1956 by

56

Norman Branson, ARIBA, with Sir Kenneth Barnes, lately Principal of the Royal Academy of Dramatic Art, in the chair. The architect drew attention to the lack of significant change in the architectural form of the theatre during the last hundred years. This stagnation could be due to the restrictions of the theatre licensing regulations which required a solid proscenium wall and the provision of a safety curtain. There had been virtually no new theatre building for some twenty years. A fresh approach to the question of what a playhouse should be was required, and this is the ground broken by The Questors. Branson's design of the theatre breaks away from the picture frame stage and enables the available space to be unified by giving two playing areas— the main stage and the forestage—between which the action could alternate as desired. This gave, said Branson, a flow of the play and resulted in a very pleasing and easy relationship between the actor and the audience.

"The work that the planning committee put into the architect's brief for an adaptable plan can be summarised as follows:

a) costs - every penny has to be raised and therefore the emphasis is on economical construction;
b) stage and auditorium arrangements should achieve flexibility without being tied to traditional stage forms. We require a picture frame stage, a proscenium stage with forestage, an open stage and an arena stage;
c) if financial constraints dictate and flexibility over the whole range cannot be achieved, some compromise in respect of the picture frame stage, and some measure of improvisation in respect of the arena stage, can be accepted. But a flexible proscenium plus forestage and open stage is however required;
d) the scene dock must give ready access to the stage; it should be insulated from the workshop; no transference of scenery to and from the dock during performances is anticipated, but the use of scenery on the forestage should be envisaged."

In the next chapter, Tony Shipley gives details of the stages between the planning and the execution of the new, functional, adaptable theatre.

Chapter 9

Bricks and Mortar

by Tony Shipley*

In July 1955, the international journal *World Theatre* carried an article entitled 'Plans for a New Theatre to be built by The Questors Theatre, Ealing, London'. There may have been snappier titles but the article set out some revolutionary ideas in twentieth century theatre building. It described, in the name of the architect, a project "for a small permanent playhouse seating about 350 persons". All ancillary accommodation was "separated from the main theatre building by efficient fire-breaks. This arrangement, together with the very large number of emergency exits leading directly to the open air, should give a safety factor above that of the traditional theatre despite the absence of a permanent proscenium and safety curtain". It may seem strange that this herald of theatrical free-thinking should choose an almost apologetic air on safety for the opening notes, but it does remind us of the attitudes of the time. Theatres had to have proscenium arches and iron safety curtains to obtain their licences; only a club theatre could think of building anything else.

The theatre described in the article is not quite the same as the one we know today. The playhouse itself was a 15-sided structure encompassing a seating and acting area which was distinctly oval in shape. Five staging variations were described; the picture frame, with wagon stages and a fixed cyclorama; the proscenium stage with adjustable forestage; the open, or thrust, stage; the arena, or in-the-round, stage; and the space stage, for which the proscenium was opened out and the cyclorama extended to produce a semi-circular acting area of 30 feet radius. There was a trapped basement below the forestage pit, from which the actors could reach the stage by means of stairways, and audience circulation within the auditorium, behind the back row of seats. This row was partly enclosed to give an impression of boxes. The arrangement of the gangways was also somewhat

---

* Tony Shipley joined The Questors in 1959 and was Stage Director from 1962 to 1971. A member of the Committee of Management from 1962–71 and from 1974–83, he has been House Engineer since 1971.

58

different to that adopted in the final design. There was a balcony with three rows of seats and above that a cantilevered lighting gallery which later gave way to the present simpler and more flexible grid system.

Lighting was to be all-important in this adaptable and experimental theatre. In the larger stage forms, particularly the space stage, with a presumption of minimal scenery of an architectural nature, the definition of the acting areas and the accentuation of the action was to be achieved by light. Artist's impressions tended to show sharp-edged cones of light illuminating the actors and conveniently stopping without casting either spill or shadow. To lighting designers trained in proscenium theatres where there was always a convenient wing or scenic piece to hide the less happy consequences of geometrical optics, this concept was somewhat alarming.

It was nonetheless a concept which greatly excited theatre designers, as we shall see later. They were searching for the theatrical equivalent of the television director's ability to point up the action in live drama, by pointing the camera. Liberation from the proscenium arch and the choice of playing space offered by a flexible theatre were not just whims of a group of amateurs.

In June 1961, the third biennial congress of the Association Internationale des Techniciens de Théâtre was due to be held in London. There was no United Kingdom society of theatre technicians which could sponsor and organise such a congress and a series of informal meetings initiated by Richard Pilbrow and others in the professional theatre led to the creation of the Association of British Theatre Technicians. The ABTT duly organised the congress, which took place in the National Film Theatre; the chosen theme was 'The Planning of Adaptable Theatres'. Stephen Joseph edited the proceedings and remarked that "Delegates came from all over the world. The subject of the congress had a special relevance in this country. It was a rare opportunity and a valuable experience".

It was to emerge in the course of the congress that the two theatres with the greatest flexibility were the Loeb Drama Centre at Harvard and The Questors Theatre; both designed for amateur use. Others, such as the Nottingham Playhouse and Cannon Hill had only limited flexibility because of a combination of machinery costs (to achieve adaptability without high manpower demands) and fire regulations. Still others were not adaptable at all but were considered worthy of inclusion in the proceedings because they had dispensed with the proscenium stage.

Norman Branson spoke about The Questors Theatre. He described the original design and the considerations which had led to the changes resulting in the present form. The balcony was thought to introduce a divisive element; it was removed so that the entire audience could share a single space. For similar reasons, the boxes in the back row were done away with. Experience with in-the-round staging in the Stanislavsky Room had aroused great interest in the potential of this stage form and it was realised that the proposed arena stage was far too large. A more compact stage area was designed and various combinations of acting and audience areas delineated, to achieve the desired seating capacity after removal of the balcony. At this stage of the planning, five vomitories were introduced, to provide stage access for actors from beneath the audience.

Externally, the changes were even more apparent. The cost of constructing the roof for the original polygonal shape was prohibitive, so the idea of enclosing the whole in glass based on a lattice girder framework was devised. This also allowed space for a small foyer at the Southern end. The changes were widely regarded as enhancing the appearance and utility of the building while enabling the construction costs to be reduced.

Two quotations from Norman Branson's paper at that 1961 AITT Congress sum up the quest: "The case for an adaptable playhouse is that, at this moment, when the theatre is in a state of flux, it is not yet possible to determine with certainty what kind of playhouse is wanted, what kind of arrangement suits the contemporary mood". "The Questors and I have not attempted to choose for the theatre but we have tried to take a step towards restoring to the theatre a freedom of choice".

While some of the professionals of the world theatre were clearly enthused at this prospect of freedom, it was not invariably the case. Herbert Marshall, who had just had a fairly fierce difference of opinion with Alfred Emmet on the role of amateurs in theatre, described the new Questors Theatre as having much in common with the ancient Hindu theatre and one suspects that he was being not entirely complimentary. He went on to carry the standard for the bulk of professional theatre activity all over the world "which relied upon and required the proscenium theatre". Sean Kenny on the other hand did not want to see the theatre continue writing and acting in a sort of baroque box.

He wanted to see the flexible space, with simple scenery working with good lighting in a magical manner. This was one of the occasions when Sean would expound his demand for '1000 watt bullets of light', with which he could pick out his target with clear precision.

Those six days in the National Film Theatre in 1961 showed beyond doubt that The Questors (in Ealing) was making waves that were sending ripples around the world. The number of visitors who were to call in at Mattock Lane over the next few years, from every continent, proved that over and over again.

To move from a set of general plans and artist's impressions to the detailed drawings and specifications needed for a contract is a major task. To be sure, most of the work goes on in the architect's office, but in a project such as this there is the closest collaboration between the architect and the client. The Questors planning team had plenty to consider. A considerable amount of the fitting-out work was to be done by Questors labour and this had to be organised well in advance. Stage lighting, sound and stage management control systems were to be installed by members; also, although this had not been originally intended, the heating in the auditorium. Power supplies, cable routes, access points all had to be planned and stipulated before any concrete was poured. Few members had worked in a theatre of the size of the new Playhouse and just to get the feel of how it might work, how it could be made flexible and how it would be controlled, needed much thought and imagination.

On the whole, few mistakes were made but we did have one particularly lucky escape. (It is the author's firm belief that the fates shine benignly upon The Questors, otherwise the Tin Hut should have caught fire ten times over.) While the planning of the building and its fitting out was proceeding, so was the preparation for the opening production. For the intending possessor of a splendid and adaptable theatre, what better opening could there be than a double bill, using two different stage forms? Colette King was to direct a production which would start in one form, break for a 45 minute supper interval, and resume with the audience entering the theatre to find it reset in an entirely different actor/audience relationship. Colette unfortunately became ill and could not proceed; the theatre opened with Alfred Emmet's production of **Brand**. When, some weeks later, we came to try to change the stage form the task took not 45 minutes but three days!

The contractors had virtually completed their tasks by January 1964 and the Questors building team moved in. Stage lighting equipment had to be installed and wired, the stage manager's desk (prefabricated earlier) moved in and its umbilical cord connected up, cue-lights and telephones wired through the conduits which had been specified a year previously. Seats had to be assembled, the dressing rooms had to be fitted out and there was much painting to do. The sound equipment arrived at the last moment and caused some of us to work all night to trace and eradicate 'hum loops'.

The set for **Brand** was being constructed at the same time. It was an extensive structure, known irreverently as 'The Ealing Flyover', and it was not immediately distinguishable from the more permanent parts of the theatre. Of the latter, it was the forestage assembly that gave the most trouble. Various options for the mechanics of the variable height and shape of the forestage had been considered, but when Stephen Joseph visited in 1961 with his Studio Theatre Company, we were most impressed with the flexibility of his system of folding wooden rostra. It was decided to use a similar system for the forestage levels and for the on-stage seating for the arena stage. What no-one had foreseen was that most of the forestage units are confined within a concrete pit and that timber is not noted for its dimensional stability. The rostra arrived from the joiners and were put into the pit with little trouble. Until, that is, it was necessary to get them out for the second production, **Dandy Dick**, which was played on a proscenium stage. Four weeks exposed to the dampness of a drying-out building had expanded the timber so much that it was only by unscrewing the hinges that the rostra could be removed. No matter how carefully the units were trimmed to size and marked to show their exact positions, they never seemed to fit in the same way on successive changes. Within a few years they were replaced with the steel frames with which the Questors House Services heavy mob got their regular weight-lifting practice*.

The arrangement of rostra to form flexible stage areas was of course very different from the trapped sub-stage basement which Norman Branson had been describing even in 1961. A late attempt to reduce the construction costs led to the elimination of the basement and the removal of two of the five vomitories.

---

* See footnote on next page

62

Only by this means, or so it appeared, could the estimated building cost be kept in line with our expected availability of funds. But when the contractors came to start excavating for the foundations, they were to discover site conditions which, had they been discovered much earlier, might have allowed the stage basement to be retained.

In the first half of the last century, before the coming of the railway caused Ealing's development into the 'Queen of the Suburbs', the area of Ealing Dean was essentially rural. The Victorian houses and gardens of Mattock Lane were built over fertile orchard land which, thanks to the geology of the Thames Basin, enjoyed a particularly good water supply. If water was needed anywhere, the farmer had only to sink a well to obtain it in abundance. Taylor Woodrow were to come across this reminder of rural Middlesex in the shape of a well shaft, under what is now the prompt side wing, and several pockets of deep top soil. The well, as Stage Managers may be relieved to note, was filled in with concrete; the top soil had to be excavated to such a depth that the theatre could almost have had its basement.

The 1955 article in *World Theatre* had made reference to "efficient fire breaks". The Middlesex County Council took these very seriously indeed: the separation of the Playhouse from the other buildings had to be not less than 15 feet. When the steel structure of the theatre had been erected it became clear that, due to some slight error in marking out, the distance between it and Mattock Lodge would be less than the minimum demanded. The discrepancy was less that one inch but the dimension of 15 feet was sacrosanct. The fixing bolts of the steel

---

* An indication of what is actually involved in changing the stage form can be gained from the following description published in *Questopics* in 1975: "The apron, made of 18 steel and block board modules, each 6in by 6in, can be raised or lowered to form a variety of stage shapes". More evocative, perhaps, is this piece, also taken from *Questopics*; the author was Geoff Webb, for many years Head of House Services, later Artistic Director:

> "Theoretically all these unique custom-built items switch without effort from one position to another. This may have been true on the drawing board and it may even be true now, if the system was in the hands of trained engineers. Sadly it is not; the hammer is more in evidence than the micrometer and the chisel than the scalpel...

> "The crew which does this work is easily recognisable by its repulsive appearance and by its yellow T-shirts bearing their title—the Select Committee for Removal and Erection of Workable Units—in acrostic form."

stanchions had to be cut away and, by means of winches and hawsers, the whole steelwork structure was then pulled across its foundation pads until honour was satisfied. For a very short while, the adaptable theatre was also mobile.

Construction of the Playhouse was already in progress before a decision was reached on how to heat it. Various proposals for using electric radiant panels had been put forward and rejected; a large underfloor duct had been provided under the centre vomitory in case we could afford an air-handling system (but never used except to store office stationery); discussions with the consultant engineers were leading nowhere, as no system we could afford seemed operationally acceptable. Eventually Bob Anderson designed a system using large wall heaters which he built into ducts. Working on an off-peak tariff, these would come on at 7pm boosting a total 120kW into a cold theatre. By curtain time, the theatre was warm enough to allow reduction of the power to 40kW, which also reduced the noise to acceptable levels. On cold nights, the boost would be run again during the interval. This system cost about £500 and, although designed as a temporary expedient (in the sense that it was the best that could be managed within the cost constraints and completion deadline), it worked for some 20 years. It was replaced in 1983 with a much more elaborate system that cost over half as much as the Playhouse itself had in 1964.

The major technical facilities of the theatre were to present problems of choice. In the early 1960s, the design of theatre technical equipment was entering a period of change so enormous that it is difficult, even in retrospect, to realise what were the options. By the end of the decade, transistorised equipment was universally available; in 1964 it was not. Some suppliers were entering the market with new technology, which was not always reliable, and the elegance of control systems had yet to be developed to exhibit the potential of the new devices.

For the stage lighting system there was a guide at hand. Strand Electric still reigned supreme and, with an old friend and ally, Frederick Bentham, The Questors was assured of help and advice. There were many changes in lighting control; solid state thyristor dimmers were making an expensive and unreliable debut. Large theatre practice still centered on motor driven dimmers. Smaller houses used saturable reactors (chokes). To The Questors, having used liquid dimmers in the old theatre and still using resistance dimmers in the Stanislavsky Room, the choice was critical and difficult—on grounds of both operational flexibility and cost.

With Fred's advice, we settled on an improved form of choke board with pre-set facilities, known as System LC. (This was allegedly an abbreviation for 'Len's Choke', after its inventor. Strand Electrics' system of equipment designation was inherently idiosyncratic.) Although the control desk was large enough to accommodate 72 circuits, it was originally equipped with 48. The chance to extend it to its full capacity came some five years later when some Portuguese stevedores inadvertently dropped one of Strand's exports into Lisbon harbour. When the recovered remains were returned to this country as a write-off, The Questors contrived to rescue and recondition sufficient parts to complete our own installation.

The choice of control was not the only critical lighting decision. The layout of the installation would determine where designers could put their lights and power them; mistakes would mean that the Theatre would soon acquire a mess of scaffolding and cable as additional lighting positions were needed. Twenty-five years later, very few extra lighting bars have been added—proof enough of the endurance of the scheme produced by Bob Anderson and the lighting department.

The sound installation was less successful. Fixed sound systems in theatres tended to be rudimentary at that time, with special effects bought in as needed—hardly a suitable scheme for a repertoire theatre operating on a tight budget. Also, transistors had not yet replaced valves in high-quality amplifiers. Richard Collins and his colleagues in the sound department had to settle for a specification which was less than they would have wished for and the equipment was redesigned (more than once) in the following years.

That period from January to April 1964 was frantically busy, with Questors members—too numerous to mention individually—making devoted efforts to convert an empty shell into a working theatre. No-one who took part will ever forget the experience. After a final rush of preparation, painting and cleaning up, the theatre opened on 18th April 1964 for the first performance of *Brand*. It was very much a members' night, on which those who had dreamed, contributed, laid bricks, supported or just joined to see what was this new venture in Ealing, could quietly enjoy the fruits of this endeavour. The Royal Gala opening was to be the following week but there was more excitement to come before that.

On Monday, 20th April, the new television channel BBC2 was due to go on the air. Early that evening a fire broke out in the Battersea Power Station, causing it to be shut down. The loss of power at the height of the evening peak led to a spectacular, and fortunately rare, phenomenon known as 'cumulative tripping'. The national power grid became overloaded section by section and the switches opened automatically to protect the system. By the time the engineers had regained control, all the lights were out from the South of London to St Albans. At The Questors Theatre, the emergency lighting system was put to its first test and the audience had to wait in the gloom until 8.30, when power was restored and the performance could start.

The Gala performance on Wednesday 22nd April has already been described in Chapter 8. The following day, Thursday 24th, was the 400th anniversary of Shakespeare's birth. It passed quietly in Mattock Lane.

Chapter 10
Making Waves, 1964-1969

The five years immediately after the opening of the Playhouse are widely remembered as a tremendously exciting period. Now that all the planning and theorising had actually been realised, the experiments which had been widely talked about could be put into practice. It was a period of joint exploration and of fruitful collaboration, with a sense of the company as whole making significant theatrical discoveries.

Over the years of planning and in the first years of using the Playhouse, there was an active Production Study Group of directors and designers. Not only did the group meet every few months to discuss past and forthcoming productions in a constructive and supportive atmosphere, but regular Sunday morning workshops were held in the Playhouse itself to explore practically many questions of playing styles, directing techniques and other matters pertinent to developing the collective expertise in the use of the different stage forms.

In 1965, regular internal post-production discussions were inaugurated, held on the Sunday morning immediately after the 'Get-out' of each show. These were totally separate from the public discussions, mentioned in an earlier chapter, which were open to all audience members and held a few evenings after the close of the production. The intention of the new discussion format, as Alfred Emmet explained at the time, was to be severely, but unemotionally, self-critical, "in the hope that we can more quickly learn from our mistakes in the new theatre". These sessions quickly became known, not totally affectionately, as 'Alfred's little chats' and were the subject of several vitriolic articles in the early issues of *Questopics* in 1966. The Honorary Director, however, was adamant about "the need to preserve a critical attitude to our own work ... Such a critical attitude must be based upon standards drawn from outside our own circle ... Our view of our work must always be related to something higher than our own achievement". He continued: "I would always make my starting point, 'This could have been better— how?' That, to my mind, is the question that must always be asked and, if possible, answered".

Originally led by the Honorary Director, later by the Director of Productions, and then the Artistic Director, these discussion sessions, involving the whole company which has been working on the show just finished, have continued. They still have their dissenters—it is incredibly difficult to be objectively critical about a show one has been personally committed to for eight weeks, and equally difficult to be cast in the role of critic on these occasions—but there is no doubt that this tradition has instilled in The Questors a continuing sense of the importance of self-examination and of the quest for better and higher standards of performance.

Two years after the Playhouse opened, Alfred Emmet wrote a detailed article for the theatre magazine *Tabs*, describing the experience of, and the lessons learned from, the 29 productions which had been presented in the new theatre from April 1964 to December 1966, "of which 22 have been on some form of open stage (ie. excluding end-stage productions)". He noted:

> "The first, and greatest, difficulty that we have experienced has been to get directors and designers to think sculpturally—three-dimensionally, instead of picture-wise—two-dimensionally. Most directors and virtually all designers think in terms of visual images. Such images are almost invariably seen from one viewpoint, and that viewpoint is practically always from centre front. This is a deeply ingrained habit of mind which it is most difficult to overcome. The first attempt to do so usually only succeeds in substituting some other fixed viewpoint, say from one side instead of from the front, or an effort to run round the perimeter, either in imagination or in fact, to see that it 'looks all right' from all sides.
>
> "This difficulty does not exist for the actor, who usually, once he has surrendered himself to the feeling of being surrounded or nearly surrounded by his audience, finds great imaginative stimulus from the freedom to play directly to his fellows instead of having to present a false continuous face to the audience, as in the proscenium stage convention."

One of the first lessons learned was that 'representational scenery' is of little or no use on an open stage. "Indeed, experience at The Questors Theatre does suggest that the open stage may be most effective when scenery in the accepted sense is reduced to an absolute minimum or even dispensed with entirely. The effect of the spatial relationship between, for example, a number of well chosen and carefully placed items of furniture can be most evocative, provided that the audience can see the whole of the stage floor and is, therefore, aware of such relationship.''

By this time, also, the company had come to the tentative conclusions that the acting area should not be too large, that it needed to be well-defined in some way and definitely separate from the audience space; interestingly, the conclusion had been drawn that if acting and audience spaces were not physically separated (by a floor cloth of a different colour from the auditorium floor, for example), alienation and embarrassment of the audience, rather than greater intimacy, seemed to result.

Despite some limitations of the open stage in terms of maintaining direct contact between the actor and sections of his audience, on the whole The Questors had already concluded that any such limitations were far less of a problem than those of a proscenium stage. ''The great strength of the open stage'', noted Alfred Emmet, ''is that it enables the actors fully to play in to each other, to the great gain of their performances and to the greater involvement of the audience ... who are drawn more strongly into the play.''

It may well be that the foregoing these days seems 'old hat' and blindingly obvious, but it cannot be stressed too often that 25 years ago, there was very little collective theatrical experience in appropriate styles of production for stage forms other than proscenium—there were no other stage forms. The Questors' trailblazing was acknowledged in the most distinguished circles, as evidenced by the following comment from *The Times* of March 20th, 1967:

> ''The Questors are fortunate in being able to work in what Peter Hall has recently described as 'one of the most exciting laboratory theatres in the country'. With its adaptable stage and intimate auditorium, it would be the envy of many professional repertory companies and will obviously serve as a useful model for the future.''

And many years later, Alan Ayckbourn commented, following a visit to The Questors to address an International Workshop on Directing for Theatre in the Round, ''it really is a theatre after my own heart''. Vindication, if such were needed, of the single-minded determination which had got the Playhouse built, and the dedicated efforts of the whole Questors team to provide the necessary framework to continue what was believed to be essential research into the fundamental elements needed to create a vibrant theatre.

By 1969, five years after the Playhouse opened, the practical experience of over 70 productions had changed and refined the theoretical view of the four acting arrangements included in the architect's brief. The following appraisal appeared in a souvenir booklet published to mark The Questors' fortieth birthday:

"The essential distinction seems to be between single view (some form of end-staging) and multi-view (thrust or arena). Some argue that the 'pure proscenium' form does not work well in this building but others reply that it has so far been tried only rarely— a reflection perhaps of Questors predilections. What is certain is that other types of end-staging offer many possibilities still to be explored.

"The theatre comes into its own with the thrust stage arrangement. The fixed seating is related most directly to this form; though the reactions of different producers naturally vary, the impression at times is that the three-sided pattern is the spontaneous assumption in this building, though there are often good reasons for narrowing the range of viewpoints to end-staging or extending it to the complete circle."

This analysis, which defines the Playhouse as "A space for drama to be created in", also gives a series of sample questions which the five years of experimentation with the new space had thrown up. These are worth repeating here since many are still just as valid and continue to challenge every director who comes to the said space anew.

For the thrust stage, with the audience on three sides of the acting area in roughly a semi-circle:

Where is the strongest point?

How do you address the audience, or take an aside?

How are scene changes handled, or should there perhaps not be changes?

Should the stage be lit while the audience is arriving?

For the end-stage format:

If there is no framing at the sides, does the top need masking or should the theatre's bridges and roof structure remain exposed?

Can part of the thrust stage be used as a forestage?

Where does the dangerous territory begin between single-aspect and multi-aspect theatre?

For the arena stage (in the round) with the audience encircling the acting area:

How do you make a quick entrance when it involves a long walk?

How do you cope with the fact that some of the audience sees an actor coming a long time before others?

Must actors who would otherwise be revealed by a rising curtain come on in a blackout, or is it possible to establish some new convention such as a marked change in the lighting?

How long can you happily go on looking at the back of an actor's head?

The new Playhouse provided a spur to all kinds of developments—including a significant increase in audience membership. More importantly, new creative talent was drawn in from all over the country, which brought new thinking to The Questors and extended its horizons. Tony Shipley, in a retrospective article in *Questopics* in 1983, noted that "the attraction of the new theatre with its unconventional stage forms and a company with a reputation for enterprise was bringing new talent to Mattock Lane and, since it was before the days of the professional fringe, a number of aspiring directors came to us to practice their craft." He listed as examples Alan Clarke, Peter Jeffries, Kenneth Ives, Ronnie Wilson, Michael Custance, Cecil Hayter and Stephen Hollis. In conclusion, said Tony Shipley, in a sentiment echoed by many other long-standing members of The Questors, the period between **Brand** and **Peer Gynt** (the fortieth birthday production in November 1969) was "the greatest in my years at The Questors and I am privileged to have been able to play a part in it."

Chapter II

Studio Theatre at
The Questors

by John Davey*

The Studio is an idea, not a place. All very well, but ask <u>where</u>
the Studio is at The Questors and everyone will tell you—the
Stanislavsky Room, with which Studio productions are now
inextricably linked. Ask <u>what</u> Studio Theatre is and the answer
may not be so forthcoming.

The production which is often hailed as the first 'Studio'
production (although it was not called such) and one which
undoubtedly became the benchmark for much that was to
follow was James Saunders's *Hans Kohlhaas*, directed by Bill
McLaughlin (1972). This production, evolved from scratch over
a period of six months by writer, director and cast, working
through improvisations towards a script, with its clear Brechtian
style and its examination of man in conflict with the society of
his time, seemed to epitomise what Studio theatre was all about.
After this, the Questors Studio movement was unstoppable.

Of course, that production did not emerge from thin air.
There had been a considerable background of activity which had
led up to it. The Stanislavsky Room had been used for productions almost from the moment that it was built, a few of the
directors having quickly realised that it would be an exciting
and flexible space in which to put on plays. In 1960, Alfred
Emmet had directed the first full in-the-round production there
(*The Glass Menagerie*). It was followed later in the same season
by *Waiting for Godot* and the first visit from Stephen Joseph's
Studio Theatre Company with three plays also presented in the
round. Producers' Shop Windows (as they then were) had
regularly taken place there. So successful were these that productions were soon alternating between the Stanislavsky Room
and the Tin Hut, and it was an easy decision, when the Tin
Hut had been demolished and while the new theatre was being

* John Davey has been a member since 1971, when he joined the Student
Group. An actor and director, John was Artistic Director from 1981 to 1986
and has been on the Committee of Management since 1979.

built, for all productions to take place in the Stanislavsky Room. It's interesting to note that the Chairman (George Benn) in the Annual Report for 1963 stated:

> "During the past year we have laboured under difficulties producing plays in the cramped mock-up conditions in the Constantin Stanislavsky Room. Such conditions may well stimulate the artist and technician to overcome the many obstacles in the way, but it has been hard on the audience and the Theatre staff."

Many audience members, in fact, found these productions very stimulating; the March 1963 production of *Long Day's Journey Into Night* is remembered as a particularly impressive example. Of course, nobody had conceived of these as Studio productions, but the Stanislavsky Room had been established as a flexible alternative playing space even before the Playhouse was built.

After the opening of the Playhouse in 1964 few 'bona fide' productions were mounted in the Stanislavsky Room for several years, although it was constantly in use—for rehearsed readings, for example. A number of one-off performances, perhaps best described as opportunist productions, were also mounted. One of these, in 1964, followed a Playwrights' Symposium in Berlin which had been attended by a group of Questors actors and was billed as 'Five Plays from Berlin'. This, remarkably, included the first production of the one-act version of Tom Stoppard's *Rosencrantz and Guildernstern Are Dead* (then entitled *Guildernstern and Rosencrantz*), directed by Peter Whelan. Experimental productions of one kind or another were also staged, including an all-male version of Genet's *The Maids*. By the end of the Sixties the real stirrings of the Studio movement began to be felt. Those stirrings were related to changes in society generally, and specifically to the growth of Fringe Theatre. Heady days, the Sixties; a time when society tried to shock itself into finding out what it was, when no convention could go unchallenged and 'experiment' was the watchword. In 1971 *Questopics* quoted an eavesdropping from a lady in Mattock Lane just before a Fringe Festival Production: "I know it's experimental, but we don't have to undress, do we?" Apocryphal or not (and it probably is) it chimes nicely with the spirit of the times. And she didn't have to wait too long before at least the cast started taking off their clothes!

The strong desire for theatrical experiment found expression at The Questors in a programme of Workshops, not initially intended for public performance. Writing in January 1969, Peter Whelan defined its purpose: "... to explore any kind of work relevant to the theatre—short of actually producing a play." He went on to add: "The accent is always on doing things rather than talking about doing things; on experiencing rather than theorising... The Studio Theatre dives into any aspect of theatre—though some people say it doesn't dive deeply enough ... Eventually, it must get deeper and begin to influence the main work of The Questors." Some chords are struck there which continue to reverberate even now. The opportunist productions continued, however, and included in 1969 a one-night stand of *Jens* by David Mowat, directed by Peter Whelan, a play which The Questors had come upon through the usual new play system but whose original style had much in common with the Workshop ethos. This was followed in 1970 by a three-night run of David Mowat's own production of his *Inuit*, again in the Stanislavsky Room. And in July 1970 a 'Studio Production' of James Saunders's *After Liverpool* also ran for three nights.

Activity continued and by November 1970 Cecil Hayter was leading the 'Studio Theatre Workshop Group'—not a revolutionary cell within the movement, but simply a different title. And so to 1972 and *Hans Kohlhaas*. This was actually one of the productions in that year's New Plays Festival and was presented in the Stanislavsky Room at the request of the author. Subsequently, there was a gradual move to mount regular full productions in the Stanislavsky Room and the first 'Workshop' production duly arrived in October 1972—*Narrow Road to the Deep North* by Edward Bond, directed by Roberta Hornstein in a traverse production along the length of the Stanislavsky Room. This was accompanied by an explanation in *Questopics* of Workshop's *raison d'être*, in the words of Alan Chambers:

"For some time, we have felt that there should be more room in the programme... for plays that represent the mood of contemporary theatre. This not only means putting on the work of modern playwrights but also exploring techniques and skills that are widening the approach of theatre, such as multi-media activities or improvised play-making involving movement as an art or new ways of using actors' voices."

The Annual Report for 1972/73 recorded that "for the first time, a number of Workshop productions, given in the Stanislavsky Room, were performed during the year", while the 1973/1974

Annual Report records the decision to develop the Stanislavsky Room as a Studio Theatre. In September 1974 the newly-formed Artistic Directorate included a Studio Theatre Director (Spencer Butler) who was to be responsible for ''... staging in the Stanislavsky Room a programme of Studio productions and of Producers' Shop Windows''. And it was in mid-1974 that the name 'The Studio' was first adopted, although none of that season's productions had been so described in the programmes. In the 1974/75 season there were 22 performances and the total Studio audience topped 2,000; the usual Studio run then was three performances and the usual rehearsal period four weeks. (Figures for 1987/88 were: 87 performances, 5,215 audience, usual run eight performances, rehearsal period six weeks.)

With the provision of a properly equipped space and the appointment of its own Director the Studio came into its own. The first main phase of development occurred between 1975 and 1977 when seating rostra, a lighting and sound system and a very small dressing-room (subsequently found to be inadequate) were provided. The second phase occurred in 1986/87, creating a new (and adequate) dressing-room and a new entrance and wing-space in the North-West corner.

To date, there have been seven Studio Directors: Spencer Butler (with Richard Halberstadt as Deputy), Norman Wilkinson, Geoff Webb, David Fletcher, John Wilson, Helen Walker and Paddy O'Connor. Each has approached the job with different priorities and, to an extent, different principles. Perhaps the extreme poles are best represented by Norman Wilkinson, who was appointed to carry out his declared '*laissez-faire*' policy—that is, that the Studio was a space to be used by anyone with a good idea—and David Fletcher, the only Studio Director to have produced a written policy (1983) which, as well as laying down 'Guiding Principles', actually specified the 'Types of Plays and Projects' best suited to The Studio. It is worth quoting this list (with some points slightly abridged) as it draws together most of the essential strands of 'Studio' thinking:

1) New Plays
2) Second productions of plays seen on the Fringe circuit and elsewhere
3) Playmaking
4) Classics, including Shakespeare (with the emphasis on concentrating on the text)
5) Complementing the Playhouse programme

6) Exploring the space
7) Developing new methods of working
8) Plays which are not suitable in scale or content for the Playhouse. They must, of course, be suitable for the Studio in scale and content.

It is made clear that this list is not exclusive, but it is clearly quite comprehensive. Also worth quoting are the four "key questions" which a director "must be able to answer in the positive":

1) Is this a production which would not be better realised in the Playhouse, even if the opportunity existed?
2) Are there elements of development, rather than just additional experience, to be gained from this project?
3) Can this production be mounted with a minimal amount of sets, props and costumes?
4) Does the production build on the particular character of the Studio? How?

Some very trenchant and important questions! The article of faith enshrined in question three was for many years reinforced by a maximum production budget of £30, later raised to £50, still officially in force. This had the effect of concentrating the mind wonderfully! The essence of Studio, it has been said, is the positive benefit of making do.

So how successful has the Studio been in carrying out its particular role at The Questors? And which are the productions which deserve to be remembered and celebrated?

We have presented a surprisingly small number of new plays and British premières in the Studio. Of these the most notable have been the four plays by Sebastian Baczkiewicz—*Shoeshop* (1980), *The Whirler* (1981), *Harry* (1985) and *The Man Who Shot the Tiger* (1987). Of these, *Harry* (directed by David Emmet) was outstanding in its creation of atmosphere, through both the text and the splendid set by Norman Barwick (earth-covered floor with a lean-to roof against one wall). The two Questors New Writers Studios of 1980 and 1982 also gave members a chance to demonstrate their talents, as did David Pearson's *Dancing Naked* (1984). *The Brick* by Nigel Swain (1987) was one of the very few new 'political' plays to come our way and was strikingly effective.

Several shows have been evolved by directors and casts—often an exciting experience for them and, with luck, for an audience as well. Among these can be numbered: John Wilson's *Dimension* (1976) and *Into Another Dimension* (1977) with their excellent movement work; my own *Martin Guerre* (1979) starting with an idea but no text; Geoff Webb's *Long Way Away* (1984) and *Fair Play* (which became *Foul Play* in Edinburgh) (1985), worked up entirely through improvisation; and David Emmet's extraordinarily adventurous *ESP* (1983), which pushed both theatre and audiences to their limits! David Fletcher's *Eleventh Hour Theatre* pieces (1976/77), improvised at the last moment on a contemporary issue and presented as late-night shows were also a new and exciting, if short-lived development.

'Classic' texts have received some illuminating productions. Etched in the memory are: Mike Moriarty's *Macbeth* (1976) played greatly cut and in masks; David Emmet's concentrated version of Goethe's *Faust* (1978); Brecht's *Man is Man* (1977), directed by Alan Chambers and later revived for a second Studio run; Sue Solomon's role-reversing version of Congreve's *Love for Love*; David Fletcher's small-cast *Julius Caesar* (1984); and Steve Fitzpatrick's version of Aristophanes' *Wealth* (1986).

Even more impressive, perhaps, has been the Studio's record in bringing recently-performed 'minority' plays to a Questors audience. Of a long list, a few which linger in the memory are *The Foursome* by E A Whitehead (1976), *A Mad World, My Masters* by Barrie Keefe (1978), *Glass Houses* by Stephen Lowe (1982) and the double-bill of Barrie Keefe's *Gotcha!* and Peter Barnes's *Leonardo's Last Supper* (1983).

Exploration of the Studio space has been rather haphazard. True, we have used a wide range of seating-forms; in-the-round, L-shaped, against the long wall, traverse, thrust and a few promenade productions. The end-stage format has become depressingly familiar however, often signalling the fact that, however good the production in other ways, it has not used the Studio space as its stimulation and starting-point. It is perhaps ironic that the more the original concept of making do with minimal budgets has given way to more elaborate sets and technical effects, the less seems to be the desire to experiment with the space itself.

Programming links with the Playhouse have proved difficult to achieve. I can think of only four occasions when such links have been effectively made: in 1983 between *The Accrington Pals* and the specially-devised *Anthem for Doomed Youth*; in the same year when *A Dream of Passion* was devised to accompany

Hamlet; in 1985 when D H Lawrence's *The Daughter-in-Law* was accompanied by James Hepburn's adaptations of three of Lawrence's short stories under the title *Men and Women*; and in 1988 when *The Bedbug* had strong links with *Futurists*. Whatever the difficulties are, when these links are achieved there is always the interest in seeing theatre work in the context of other theatre work—in the same style, by the same author, of the same period, and so on.

Although many Studio sets have been too 'heavy', there have been some excellently inventive designs: Norman Barwick's work on Sebastian Baczkiewicz's plays has already been noted; Roger Harris's striking use of stained glass in *Martin Guerre* deserves mention. John Stacey (master of the 'set *trouvé*') succeeded in designing an effective and atmospheric set to deal with the complexities of *The Brick*. With light and sound there has been less obvious experiment, although several effective designs, especially in lighting, have been achieved, by Ian Briggs, Tim Hayward and Pete Walters, for example.

So what has the Studio achieved? A great deal, I would say, although perhaps it has not lived up to its early promise, nor fulfilled the hopes of its early torch-bearers. In May 1974, Bill McLaughlin in reviewing the first ten years of the new Playhouse was saying of the 'Workshops': "So far, few opportunities for experiment have been taken." A year later David Emmet reviewed the progress of Studio Theatre, asking "But why have we seen no experimentation?" One of our problems has always been working out what experiment means for us and in formulating any kind of structured approach to it. If we are still interested in that Studio watchword (and, like 'the right to fail', 'experiment' has long been a banner waved before our eyes) then we need to plan our areas of experiment and work with some degree of commitment in them.

And finally—"What," I hear you ask, "would you say was the best Studio production you've seen at The Questors?" Out of many happy theatrical memories, I actually have no doubt about the one I'd pick: Tony Hill's superb production of *Moonshipt* by James Hepburn (1977). For my money, this had it all—a simple but striking set by Roger Harris; a new text about a significant political issue (just how and why America got to the moon); an original cast-audience relationship; inventive direction; original (live) music by Michael Carver—a highly entertaining evening. Every so often a production comes along

78

that leaves you thanking whichever deity you subscribe to for the existence of the Studio. Long may it continue to give us evenings like this!

Chapter 12

The Questors at School(s)

by Vincent McQueen*

The bus conductor strode purposefully into the canteen and ordered an apple turnover with custard. The succulent dish was placed before him. He took a hungry bite—and found himself eating custard with meat-patty. He turned to his driver-companion. "This turnover's delicious", he said and continued to devour steak and kidney pie and custard with every appearance of relish.

150 pairs of young eyes followed his every move with concentration, convinced that he was enjoying the apple turnover he had ordered (and had indeed expected!). For the canteen was, in fact, a school hall and the occasion was a performance in the Schools Tour of 1963.

It was in 1959 that the Education Officer of Ealing, John Wilkinson, himself a keen member of The Questors, visited me at my school to discuss what The Questors could do to interest the pupils of the borough's Secondary Modern Schools (this being, of course, before the days of comprehensive education in Ealing) in theatre. School parties were already invited to suitable performances at The Questors, but this attracted pupils who already showed some interest in drama and we both felt the net needed casting more widely. Television was beginning to establish its strong claim as the primary source of entertainment and soon there would be widespread colour television to increase its attraction.

We needed to go out and <u>sell</u> live theatre. We needed something flexible that could easily be taken (in the first instance) to the 14 widely-spread sec. mod. schools in the borough. We needed something that would not defeat the attention-span of young teenagers of widely varying abilities. We decided to eschew the performance of a complete play, even a one-acter,

---

* Vincent McQueen joined The Questors in 1953 as an actor. He was a member of the Committee of Management from 1954 to 1957 and was director of the first Questors Schools Touring Company. He has written many original entertainments for The Questors and is currently Editor of *Questopics*.

and to compile a programme of dramatised excerpts centred on a theme which might capture their imagination. In this way, we could present several kinds of play to our young audiences in one evening. A cast of half a dozen actors would have the stimulus of playing a variety of parts and the whole would be joined by a narrator in a fairly light-hearted manner.

Since school halls come in a variety of shapes and sizes, we decided to present the programme in the body of the hall, with our audience sitting round in a semi-circle. The lighting was pretty basic—four spotlights on two stands—but it gave a certain flexibility and atmosphere. Three six-foot high reversible screens were our only setting. However, we went to town on the costume and were glad we did, because our audiences were very critical. They would accept the shortcomings of the setting and the lighting but the acting and the dress had to be utterly convincing.

We were certainly lucky in both. Our Wardrobe Department members, as ever, gave their all to ensure that the costumes were not only attractive but also authentic. Woe betide the actor who went on a Schools Tour with safety-pin-secured tights! And equal woe betide the actress who failed to wear appropriate corsets under her Edwardian gown! As to the acting, it was gratifying to find that our acting membership was evidently aware of the importance of our mission, despite the discomforts which it promised. Auditions each year were well attended, enabling us to field strong casts.

One wonders if the demands of the tours were in fact more rigorous than anticipated since many of the actors have since moved away! However, among those who have stayed the course are Tony Barber, Neville Bradbury, Dorothy Boyd Taylor, Martin Bowley, Alan Chambers, Alan Drake, Kay Eldridge, Kit Emmet, Sylvia Estop, Carla Field, Mike Green, Peter Healy, Sandra Healy, Bill Rudderham, Stella Waraker and Dorothy Wood. Mary Jones, Betty Ogden and Philip Wright are stalwarts who have sadly since died, as has Pat Ferriday who was our unflappable Stage Manager. Iris Phelps was another irreplaceable member of the stage team as was Ken Lake who was always on lights.

And as for the Tours themselves, the memories are strong and happy and they come thick and fast...

Like the time the actress playing Kate Hardcastle in **She Stoops to Conquer** was locked out between entrances. She had made a stylish exit and, having two minutes before her next entrance, decided to get a handkerchief from the dressing room. This entailed leaving the school hall and crossing a quadrangle to the classroom which served as our dressing room, a return journey which she should easily have accomplished in 30 seconds. Unfortunately, an over-zealous caretaker had decided that once the show was underway he would lock all the exit doors from the hall (we were not, you will gather, subject to county council fire safety regulations!), "to make sure the little beggars don't sneak out". Something less than a compliment to our powers of holding an audience, it also ensured that one of our little beggars couldn't sneak back in! There followed much hissing and door-rattling and a spell of positively brilliant improvised dialogue from a frantic Marlow and Hardcastle marooned on stage. The actress eventually rescued them by making a less-than-stylish entrance, clambering through a delighted audience of teenage boys via the only door which could be speedily unlocked—naturally the one furthest from the stage.

Then there was the time during the tour of James Saunders's *Double Double* (also the source of the bus-depot story at the beginning of this chapter), when a particularly strict and widely-feared headmistress strode onto the stage just before the performance began. She announced in stentorian tones: "Will the girl who is eating fish and chips please present herself outside my room immediately." A shame-faced Stage Manager, Pat Ferriday, had to own up that she had been the source of the smell, while frying the properties for that night's show. We never found out whether she had to take detention or not.

Finding the schools in the first instance was often something of a hazard. Ealing is London's second-largest borough and might be justifiably termed 'far-flung.' The Secondary Schools of Ealing seemed not only to have been flung far but to have landed in particularly inaccessible corners. As our team was almost invariably coming straight from work, the members were pressed to make a 7.30pm start. Add to that pressure a mystery tour and you can imagine that there was often some fairly agitated pacing by the producer, with contingency stand-in casting being argued by those of the cast who had managed to get there. Almost always, a harassed and perspiring actor would arrive in the nick of time to make the customary cool, calm and collected entrance expected of the true Questor, with aims and objectives firmly marshalled!

Such hassle was part of the excitement of touring schools and added its own special flavour. That it was worthwhile could be gauged not only by the repeated requests to return again soon but also by requests from schools outside the borough to be included, so that our 14 schools grew to 20. We also received gratifying letters from our young audiences. These may well have been the outcome of a class English lesson but something more than the standard 'thank you letter' would often come through.

Some of these I kept—"You turned our hall into a real place of confusion" (did he mean the lovers' scene from *A Midsummer Night's Dream* which we had been presenting?) "I think your actors were very good at remembering their lines" (that can't have been the night Kate Hardcastle got locked out). "I really felt I was going through a terrible experience" (it could have been the performance, but we liked to think she was identifying with the Anne Frank we had presented).

That extract from *The Diary of Anne Frank* was part of a programme on comic relief in drama, which had been suggested by the English department of a school we visited. We usually presented four excerpts in an evening, chosen to contrast in period and style. The other three excerpts in Comic Relief were from *Macbeth* (the Porter's scene, what else!), *St Joan* and *Maria Marten*. Another series, the first, was built round Mistaken Identity as a theme. The scenes chosen were from *Henry V*, *Pygmalion*, *The River Line* by Charles Morgan and *She Stoops to Conquer*; two comedies, a history and a 'straight' play, from four very different periods. It seemed to work well and was the pattern we followed for several years.

Some of the other programmes included, under their various themes:

Styles of Acting—*Henry V*, *The Way of the World*, *East Lynne*, *The Importance of Being Earnest* and *Roots*;

Ambition—*Twelfth Night*, *Lady Audley's Secret*, *The Skin Game* and *Le Bourgeois Gentilhomme* (not in French!);

The Plays of Shakespeare—*Macbeth*, *Richard III*, *The Merry Wives of Windsor* and *A Midsummer Night's Dream*;

Irish Playwrights—*Playboy of the Western World*, *O'Flaherty VC*, *The Shadow of a Gunman* and *Juno and the Paycock*.

In 1966, a second schools-touring company was set up to present a slightly more serious aspect of theatre, doing short plays like *The Bald Prima-Donna* (Ionesco), *The Sandbox* (Albee), *The Workout* (Bermel), *The Proposal* (Chekhov), *A Phoenix Too*

Frequent (Fry) and *Charlie* (Mrozek). These performances were followed by a discussion of the play between the pupils and the cast and producer. Notes on the plays were circulated to the schools in advance of the visit. Although the programmes were directed in the first instance at Grammar School 5th and 6th Forms, the demand quickly grew from the Secondary Modern Schools as well; in fact, of the nine Ealing schools who hosted the 1967 tour, only three were Grammar Schools. This second company continued alongside the first for a couple of years and gradually took over altogether.

News of the dramatic 'lollipops' being enjoyed by the Secondary Schools in Ealing made the Primary sector envious and in 1971 a trial scheme was run for younger pupils. Here there was a more direct need for audience involvement and, indeed, the concept of Theatre-in-Education as opposed to 'Theatre for Children' was just beginning to be popular, demanding a more participatory approach to all our work. A presentation was evolved based on Lord Shaftesbury's work in putting an end to child labour in the 19th century. This proved to be an exciting and stimulating topic and one into which our young audiences threw themselves with a will.

Each member of the touring company became a leader for up to ten children in the audience. The School Hall was ingeniously transformed by the clever disposition of school chairs and acres (so it seemed) of black plastic into the subterranean workings of a coalmine. The children were the child labourers and the Questors actors were the adults in their lives—mine managers, foremen, parents. The actors would first discuss with their groups the pattern the 'play' would take, the children being encouraged to contribute to the story. The play would then proceed, a mixture of loosely-scripted drama by the leaders and improvisation from the children. Questabout had arrived!

Gerry Blake, then Director of Youth Activities at The Questors, described the format of Questabout in *Questopics* in April 1972:

> "Most of the work being done at present begins in the group's training sessions, as improvisations on an agreed theme; but by the time each programme is ready to tour, its framework is fully structured. Its underlying idea is to provide an exciting experience which allows a high level of active participation, and which will provide a stimulus for a whole variety of creative activities. The programmes... call for careful preparatory and follow-up work."

84

Teachers had already played their part in these proceedings by including the historical background in their classwork. The performance was therefore reinforcing the children's experience at several levels. It must be recorded that there were often tears in the eyes of the watching teachers, sometimes, admittedly, occasioned by laughter at the children's antics, although not infrequently caused by the sensitivity and emotion the young performers brought to the playing of their roles.

This pilot run was deemed a success and the Local Education Authority agreed to fund a scheme with a professional director; John Wright was appointed and Questabout gradually took over all the schools touring activities. In 1973, the company played 72 performances, an enormous undertaking for amateur actors who were doing their normal jobs of work during the day. Gerry Blake again: "It was hair-raising. At 6.45 four or five cars would arrive at the theatre—filled with settings, props and people— and tear off to the outskirts of Ealing. In order to fulfil the quota (required by the LEA) the company sometimes played three or four different programmes a week and at weekends we had to stocktake to sort out the circus from the coalmine!" By this stage there were three main programmes, each aimed at a different age group—*Circuses* for 6-8 year olds, *Lord Shaftesbury and the Mines* for 9-11 year olds, and a *Lord of the Flies* workshop for GCE pupils. All proved enormously popular; *Circuses* went on to become The Questors' longest runner ever, with over 90 performances, and was still booking well when it was finally dropped from the repertoire because "we just couldn't bear another performance".

Throughout the first two years, the company was never larger than 12 and often dropped down to seven or eight. In 1974, Questabout was the largest TIE (Theatre-in-Education) team in England and the one carrying the most extensive repertoire. The team already included many teachers (as does the general membership of The Questors) and it was decided to ease the load with some daytime performances using seconded Ealing teachers where this was possible. Primary Schools, in any case, preferred daytime performances as this opened the experience to even younger children.

Questabout went from strength to strength through the 1970s and early 1980s, with Glynn Caren, Michael Davies and then Glynn Caren again succeeding John Wright as director. Glynn Caren later established a professional TIE company, known as

The Salamander Theatre Company, and for some years the two companies, Questabout and Salamander, complemented one another, with Salamander performing during school hours while Questabout visited other schools in the evenings.

Since the mid-1980s, however, Questabout has been inactive. It gradually became more and more difficult to go into schools to give evening performances and the teachers' industrial action in 1984/5 virtually wiped out the Questabout activity for that year. Local Education Authority funding was also a factor; while Ray Moss was Drama and English Adviser to the Borough of Ealing, The Questors had an enthusiastic advocate. In later years, following his retirement, it became increasingly difficult to justify the operation of two inter-dependent TIE groups in Ealing.

The Questors continues to invite schools parties to many of its productions and arranges study days on appropriate plays (principally Shakespeares), which involve the parties of pupils and accompanying teachers coming to the theatre for a day-long seminar and discussion with the cast and director of the play they will see in the evening. Plays for children have also been presented over a period of many years, including productions by visiting specialist Children's Theatre Companies such as the Polka Theatre Company and Kovari the Magician, and The Questors' own productions, specifically at Christmas, several of which have been written by members (details of these may be found in Chapter 13).

Let me end this chapter and encapsulate my thoughts on the Schools Touring Companies of The Questors by quoting yet another of the unsolicited testimonials received from a member of one of the audiences we were fortunate enough to catch in his or her (the writer signed formally with an initial) salad days. "It was all very intresting and exiting and you was all wunderfull"(sic). 'Green in judgement'? We like to think not!

Chapter 13

New Plays at The Questors

by Wilfrid Sharp*

The name of our Company, The Questors, implies that we are involved in a quest or adventure, a search for something praiseworthy, just as The Quest was once the name given to a medieval knight's noble pursuit, whether of a fair lady or The Holy Grail.

Our particular quest covers a variety of objectives and among them, of course, is the quest for new and worthwhile plays. In 1965, Alfred Emmet wrote: "It is important that a theatre such as ours should present new plays, and moreover new plays by unknown and young writers...There are not, and never can be, enough masterpieces to go round, and unless someone is prepared to do the promising plays, the promising playwrights will never go on to write the masterpieces that some of them at least may have it in them to write. And this is where a theatre such as The Questors comes in...At the same time, it must be admitted that audiences are slow to venture to unknown plays, and Questors members are no exception to this; they hang back from a new play they know nothing about until someone has told them it is good." In 1988, Max Stafford-Clark, the director of the Royal Court Theatre, wrote (*The Sunday Times*, October 2nd): "Of course it's true that new work is always vulnerable and that occasionally houses will plummet. This unfashionable term has now been replaced by more modish phrases such as market viability and incentive funding. But to equate immediate box office success with value to posterity can be a mistake".

In other words, putting on a new and unknown play is to take a financial risk, a risk that The Questors has always been willing to take, albeit perhaps more willingly in the past than

---

* Wilfrid Sharp has been an acting member since 1947. He was a member of the Committee of Management from 1949 to 1951 and was one of the original signatories to the Memorandum and Articles of Association of The Questors Ltd. Wilf has written and directed many original revues and entertainments and was the Theatre's Archivist through the late 1970s and early 1980s.

in the present. From the Club's inauguration in 1929 to the first New Plays Festival in 1960, we presented over 30 new plays, most of which were full-length plays, ie. approximately one new play each year. Bearing in mind that the early seasons consisted of only three to six productions in all, this, it may be readily seen, represents a very high proportion of new work. Indeed, the very first play presented in the Mattock Lane theatre (known affectionately as The Old Tin Hut) was an English première— *Dragon's Teeth* by Shirland Quin, although it had been previously performed in the USA. The Silver Jubilee season of 1954/55 was a complete season of new plays and it had been a matter of policy from 1948 onwards that at least one new play be included in each season's programme. The final tally of full-length new plays presented by The Questors between 1929 and 1989 is well over 100, and this figure does not include plays given their first production in England at The Questors, but already seen in other countries. If we include such plays, as well as new one-act plays, our final tally would surely be approaching 200, which is no mean achievement for the first 60 years of our existence and one of which we should be proud. Of course, by no means all of these were artistic triumphs and it has remained true that attendances tend to drop for 'unknown' work.

In the early years, certain playwrights began to emerge as the chief begetters of new plays having their first airing at The Questors, although the routes by which they were 'discovered' varied considerably. Among these was Rodney Ackland, three of whose plays were first performed by The Questors (although the first had been published and the author was already a highly successful professional playwright)—*The Dark River* (1943), *The Diary of a Scoundrel* (adapted from Ostrovsky, 1946)* and *The Other Palace* (1952). Michael Kelly, as mentioned in an earlier chapter, actually started his writing career with one-act plays for The Questors and was very much part of the scenery in the early years of the Tin Hut. We have put on no fewer than five of Michael Kelly's full-length plays (the first, *Icarus Preserved* in 1941, being the first full-length new play specially written for The Questors), as well as eight of his one-acters. Lydia Ragosin, another of the authors premièred several times at The Questors (and the daughter of the famous ballerina, Lydia Kyasht), was

---

* This play was revived at the Old Vic Theatre in 1988 under the title *Too Clever by Half.*

successfully writing radio plays and sent in a play in 1950 (*The Tinsel of Athens*), which was put on by The Questors and was the start of a long relationship which culminated in the commissioning of a stage version of *The Corruptible Crown*, two plays about Richard III and Henry VII which played in repertoire in 1967. And also deserving mention in this context is Alexandra Mikellatos, an acting member of The Questors. Two plays of hers were premièred: *Testament of Cresseid* in 1952, which was runner-up in the first year of the Charles Henry Foyle New Play Award; and *The Long Spoon* in 1958.

Then, in 1960 with the first New Plays Festival, a new group of playwrights emerged to carry on the tradition of writing for The Questors. These Festivals, which ran annually for 18 years, involved playing three full-length new plays in repertoire for a week. Most notable among writers featured in the Festivals were James Saunders, Dannie Abse and David Mowat. The most well-known of these is James Saunders and so far we have presented eight of his full-length plays (of which five were premières) and eight (seven premières) of his one-act plays, from *Next Time I'll Sing to You* in 1962, which was commissioned by The Questors and went on to a West End production and to win the Evening Standard New Play Award, to *Bodies* (not premièred at The Questors) in 1984.

Dannie Abse, better known perhaps as a poet, is a frequent visitor to the Theatre, both as spectator and as reader of his own work. Four of his full-length plays have had their first production at The Questors, as have two shorter plays (*Gone* and *The Joker*). *House of Cowards*, produced in the first New Plays Festival, won the Charles Henry Foyle New Play Award for 1960.

The first new play by David Mowat, *Jens* was produced in the Stanislavsky Room in 1969. Several more followed, including productions in the 1970, 1971 and 1973 New Plays Festivals; he was for a time 'resident playwright' at The Questors Theatre. The most recent David Mowat play premièred at The Questors, *The Almas*, was directed by the author in 1989 as part of the Diamond Jubilee season. This represented the sixth of his plays to be performed here.

Space does not permit detailed mention of foreign plays first introduced to English audiences by our Theatre, but it is worth recording that among these are such famous titles as James Joyce's *Finnegan's Wake*, *The Cave Dwellers* by William

Saroyan, *Clérambard* by Marcel Aymé, *Onkel Onkel* by Günther Grass and two plays by Michel Tremblay, *Sisters* and *Bonjour là, Bonjour* (both in 1982). *Sisters* attracted quite a number of West-End critics, and it is worth quoting two of these notices, as proof of the brave shots we have made at presenting plays new to English audiences. Michael Billington in *The Guardian* wrote: "Very ingeniously staged and sparklingly acted...It is good to see the far-from-foolish Questors rushing in where our own commercial angels fear to tread". And in *The Times*, Ned Chaillet wrote: "A production well worth crossing London to see... An amateur cast altogether unusual in its dedication to a demanding and fascinating work". Normally, of course, the professional critic does not consider it worth crossing London to see an amateur performance, unless, as in this case, it is of a play that has already achieved some fame outside England.

Fortunately, despite the demise of the New Plays Festival in 1977, our tradition of encouraging new playwrights has continued. Memorable plays which have been performed first at The Questors in recent years include several by Sebastian Baczkiewicz (*Shoeshop*, 1980, *The Whirler*, 1982, *Harry*, 1984, *The Man Who Shot the Tiger*, 1987), and others by Jimmie Chinn (*Albert, Make Us Laugh*, 1986), Steve Fitzpatrick (*The Story of Aesop*, 1987) and Jane Dewey (*Wilfrid and the Wizard Hunt*, 1982, *Waldo and the Wonderful Web*, 1983, *Micromania*, 1985). Many members, however, regret the passing of the New Plays Festivals, especially as they contributed much to the vitality of the Theatre, more than just the presentation of three new plays in a week—discussions, poetry readings, concerts of new music, late-night entertainments (nothing more risqué than a topical revue!), jazz recitals, painting exhibitions, folk songs and so on.

These 'fringe' benefits varied from year to year, but a constant ingredient was the discussion which took place every evening after the show and to which the audience was invited. The author, director and cast were all present, coffee and light refreshments were on hand and a lively, informative, argumentative discussion nearly always ensued. Also invited was a figure of some standing in the theatrical world to lead the discussion, and the following list of discussion leaders (by no means exclusive) may give some indication of the importance attached to this event; Martin Esslin, André van Gyseghem, John Allen, James Forsyth, John Mortimer, Michael Billington, E Martin Browne, John Russell Taylor, Robert Gittings, Frank Marcus, Clifford

Williams, Patricia Burke, Michael MacOwan, Kitty Black and Olwen Wymark.

A roll-call of poets who gave readings from their own works is almost as distinguished! It includes Dannie Abse, Bernard Kops, Thomas Blackburn, George MacBeth, Vernon Scannell, Patric Dickinson, Alan Sillitoe and our own Alan Chambers. Home-grown entertainments were also frequently mounted, such as Mini-Music Hall, revues, an evening with Gilbert and Sullivan and so on, often directed by Vincent McQueen with help from Michael Green. Two extra-mural events proved particularly successful. *Steam*, a railway revue compiled by Alan Chambers and Michael Green and directed by Alan Chambers, was revived twice by popular demand and toured to several different locations, while David Pearson's revue *The Gentle Art of Seduction*, originally seen during a New Plays Festival, was revived and taken to the Edinburgh Festival Fringe in 1980. So, a Questor who came to all the plays in the New Plays Festival was assured of a variegated and lively evening with plenty of 'audience participation'.

Since the last Festival in 1977, 15 full-length new plays have been presented with varying degrees of success, as far as audience numbers are concerned. (It is no easy task to decide whether or not a new play will be both an artistic and a financial success; the professional theatre is littered with plays that at first were far from being great triumphs. *Journey's End* and *Look Back in Anger* are notable examples.) In 1986, The Questors took another step towards encouraging new playwrights when Michael Green initiated the Student Playwriting Competition, now well on the way to becoming an annual event. This carries a first prize of £1,000 and a guaranteed production at The Questors Theatre. The competition, with generous commercial sponsorship, has aroused considerable interest in universities, colleges of further education and, of course, drama schools. We have been fortunate to have as judges to make the final selection our President, Dame Judi Dench, and Vice-Presidents, Roger Rees and Michael Williams. The winning play is included in the season's programme; 1987 saw the world première of *The Death of Joe Hill* by John Fay, while in 1988, the winning play, *State of the Art* by B F Herst, was produced. In 1987, the runner-up in the competition, *The Brick*, by Nigel Swain, was also presented and this play formed part of the Questors touring programme at the Edinburgh Festival Fringe in 1988. Two plays won jointly in

1989—*The Mind Forest* by R D Steadman-Jones and *War Street Serenade* by Katy Louise Dean.

Another way of promoting a new play of merit is to give a rehearsed reading before an audience, and this The Questors has always done. Hopefully, one can then judge from the audience reaction as to whether or not the play would merit a full-scale production, especially if time is allowed after the reading for a discussion with the audience. This then gives the author the opportunity to cut, amend or rewrite sections prior to full performance. Examples of plays which were first given as rehearsed readings and then, after some reworking, as full Questors productions include *The Tuscan Artist* by Michael Kelly, Alexandra Mikellatos' *Testament of Cresseid* (originally read under the title *A Sop of Sorrow*) and Dannie Abse's *The Joker*.

A large number of original plays is submitted (unsolicited) to The Questors every year, which is in itself a tribute to our reputation. They are all read and the process of selecting from them plays for possible production has varied over the years. The most recent procedure is as follows: Every play submitted is read on average by three different readers, chosen by the New Plays Adviser for their experience, judgment, conscientiousness and so on. These readers will have no knowledge at all of each other's opinions. Their reports are read by the New Plays Adviser who forwards those plays with consistently favourable reports to the Artistic Director and the Studio Director. These two officers make a final selection of any plays which they consider should be given a full production, either in the Playhouse or the Studio, or scheduled for a rehearsed reading.

The attitude of playwrights to the new play service that an organisation such as The Questors can offer is perhaps best summarised by the following quotations:

From a letter to The Questors by Alan Ayckbourn:

"I am resigned to the fact that one either has a play done well by a company like your own with little financial reward, or has the script massacred and so-called commercialised to financial profit by a well-known management".

From a programme note by James Saunders for the New Plays Festival of 1967:

"It isn't difficult to convince a playwright that his new, or first, play is great stuff; convincing him that it could have been better

92

or could have been reworked or is a load of old cobblers is trickier. Tell him and he'll write you off as a know-nothing...Put the play on for him and he'll blame the production. But give half a dozen performances, each followed by a public discussion at which comments range so wide between home-spun common sense and intellectual space travel, between profound insight and pig-faced idiocy that one wonders how such diversity can come from one humanity—then, unless he's a Roman Catholic or something, he'll begin to wonder, not necessarily until later, whether some of the criticism might not be, for the wrong reason of course, right.

"Not that playwrights should be pandered to. The best thing to do with a load of old cobblers is to tie it round the author's neck and sink it. After all the talk, the only real reason for putting on a play is that it is recreational. This is the basis on which an audience should, and usually does, judge a play and on which most playwrights, I think, would wish it to be judged".

Whether or not one agrees with James Saunders's conclusions, it must surely be conceded that presenting new plays and encouraging new playwrights should be an essential part of any worthwhile amateur company's policy. It is a kind of blood transfusion as important to the continuing life of amateur theatre as it is to the human spirit.

Chapter 14

The Questors and Coarse Acting

by Michael Green*

For better or for worse, The Questors has been closely associated
with Coarse Acting ever since the phrase was first coined. On
the whole, I think it's for the better.

It all began with the publication in 1964 of my book *The Art
of Coarse Acting*, which, as might be deduced from its sub-title of
'How to Destroy an Amateur Dramatic Society', was a modest
spoof about the amateur theatre movement in general and
disasters that can happen on stage. What couldn't have been
anticipated at the time was that Coarse Acting would eventually
become an accepted term, not only for exaggerated or misplaced
performances, but for stage disaster generally. As *The Sunday
Times* said of Peter O'Toole's notorious Macbeth at The Old
Vic a few years ago, it was "more suitable for a Coarse Acting
contest".

So, although at first sight it might seem a dubious honour to
be closely linked with Coarse Acting, it has not turned out so,
and The Questors has been part of the creation of a theatrical
genre. The book is dedicated to The Questors and not only did
I draw upon experiences at Mattock Lane, but acting members
also posed for the photographs. The cover of the original
edition featured Laurence Nixon, then Treasurer, and Bill Wall,
Grapevine Secretary (both of them since sadly passed away) in
chainmail made of knitted string; Carla Field and Bill Rudderham, both still active members, were on the cover of the first
paperback edition. The book, incidentally, is still in print after
25 years, although the covers have changed.

The idea of deliberately staging Coarse Acting dates from
1970, when The Questors held an Open Day. Alfred Emmet

---

* Michael Green has been an acting member of The Questors since 1953 and
has also directed many productions, in particular the first series of Christmas
melodramas in the 1960s and the Coarse Acting shows, of which he was also
chief author. Michael was the inspiration behind the establishment in 1986 of
the Questors Student Playwriting Competition.

suggested a Coarse Acting competition as part of the activities and asked me to organise it. The idea was to put on short pieces depicting some form of Coarse Acting—either a disaster, such as the scenery collapsing, or incompetence (perhaps an actor reading his lines from inside his hat). It proved so amusing and popular that another contest was held in 1972, this time a more sophisticated version with better facilities and more preparation, billed as The World Coarse Acting Championship.

There were some half-a-dozen entries and it was one of the funniest evenings staged at the Theatre. Two or three visiting teams included The Maskers, from Southampton, who delighted the audience with a portrayal of the ghost scene from **Hamlet** in which nothing could be seen but smoke and the occasional spear. The ghost, however, could be heard as he trailed a long length of chain behind him. Like all the best Coarse Acting entries, this piece had an element of truth. Those were the days when directors would fill a stage with dry-ice smoke at the least excuse and many a West End Shakespeare production apparently took place in a dense fog.

But the high spot of the evening was the entry from the Royal Shakespeare Company, Stratford-upon-Avon, which featured Tony Pedley and Roger Rees, who brought the house down with their interpretation of the death of Caesar as performed by the Hanwell Amateur Dramatic Society. In this Caesar (Roger Rees) lost his temper, reversed the normal procedure and tried to stab Brutus (Tony Pedley). Brutus very sensibly fled and Caesar, spurting blood from half-a-dozen wounds, pursued him round the auditorium until he escaped through an exit door.

The event was adjudicated by Richard Gordon, author of *Doctor in the House*, who awarded the trophy (a decorated chamber pot) to the Bunny Langridge Players, from The Questors, for their Agatha Christie spoof, **Streuth**. This was notable for starting twice and also for having no end, as the characters got hopelessly entangled with their lines and went round and round in circles.

Thanks to Denys Nelson, a former Questors House Manager living in the New Forest, two competitions were held at the famous Salisbury Playhouse. The first, to raise money for their new building appeal, was almost the last show in the old Salisbury theatre, and the second was held in the new building. The Bunny Langridge Players entered a team for each contest and won the second tournament with a new play, **A Collier's Tuesday Tea**, a D H Lawrence pastiche. There were also entries from our old friends The Maskers and from the professional Salisbury company itself, as well as other local companies and even the National Theatre. In the NT entry, the butler aged ten years each time he appeared starting off about 30 and ending up a senile idiot.

A Collier's Tuesday Tea is worth describing for anyone who has difficulty visualising what a Coarse play is like. It portrayed a typically grim, Lawrence-style situation in a miner's house early in the century, with a dominant father clashing with the rest of the family. The acting was grim and intense. It's a mistake to think that Coarse Acting plays simply consist of hamming it up. The humour comes from the predicament of a group of actors fighting disaster. On this occasion the disaster was the collapse of the table round which the family was sitting for high tea, a situation largely brought about by members of the cast thumping their fists on it when they spoke. The table had to be supported by the cast with their hands, which led to terrible embarrassment over simple situations such as passing the jam. But worse was to come. A miner and a policeman burst in with the news that there had been a disaster at the pit. The men were needed immediately. For a few minutes the cast desperately improvised a new plot to cover this awkward situation, since they couldn't abandon the table, and in the end solved it by carrying off the table with them, leaving the rest of the cast to finish the play as best they could.

Then, in 1977, came a dramatic development. It began with a casual conversation in the Grapevine Bar, with Richard Broadhurst saying how impressed he'd been with a cod version of *Macbeth* performed at the 1976 Edinburgh Festival Fringe by Entertainment Machine.

"Cod Macbeth!" I exclaimed, "that's poaching on Coarse Acting!" There and then I made the decision to take a complete Coarse Acting Show to the 1977 Edinburgh Festival. Two pieces were already written—*Streuth* and *A Collier's Tuesday Tea*, both compiled by the company. To these were added two more written by myself: *Il Fornicazione*, a spoof opera in which the orchestra fails to arrive, and a mock Shakespeare comedy, *All's Well That Ends As You Like It*, which featured most of Shakespeare's comic ideas all rolled into one and included the most dreadfully unfunny clown. Most of the original Bunny Langridge Players formed the hard core of the company and for a venue a share was taken in The Cathedral Hall with Clive

Wolfe and a company from his Sunday Times National Student Drama Festival.

The Committee of Management gave its consent rather guardedly. It was suggested that the company describe itself as "from The Questors", rather than as an official expedition (this suggestion was tactfully ignored). Although rehearsal and other facilities were willingly granted, no money was forthcoming. To finance itself, the company opened a bank account in Chard, Somerset, where the manager was a former treasurer of The Questors, Gerald Rawling, and he granted an immediate overdraft of £1,500, personally guaranteed by Michael Langridge, Richard Johnson and myself.

Things looked ominous when the company reached Edinburgh. Everybody was dubious as to how the Festival would react to Coarse Acting, which it had never seen before. All very well as a local joke in Ealing, but Edinburgh might demand something more classy. And these fears seemed confirmed at the Sunday dress rehearsal when police marched into the hall and stopped the rehearsal halfway through, because of complaints about the noise from neighbours (it was then 11 pm). The second half had to be run through in mime. As we had already been warned that Hinge and Bracket (then unknown) had opened at the same hall the previous year to an audience of precisely six, it was a depressed company which departed for bed.

There were one or two enquiries but few bookings next day and the company gathered apprehensively in the evening in the basement which served as a dressing-room. This had a grating giving access to the pavement outside and about half an hour before curtain-up, Michael Langridge noticed dozens of pedestrians standing around near the grating.

"There must have been a car crash or something", he said. "Just look at those people".

Someone investigated and found that the feet belonged to people queuing to get in. That first night was a triumph, played to a full house, and there was not an empty seat during the entire fortnight's run.

The Press poured praise on the show. According to Miles Kington in *Punch*, it was "the hit of the Festival". Timothy West and Prunella Scales came along and congratulated the cast afterwards. Scottish TV filmed a ten-minute excerpt. The company returned to Ealing flushed with success and with a large profit.

Two years later, in 1979, it was decided to repeat the operation, under the overall title *Coarse Acting Two*. Once again four plays were taken. There were three specially-written pieces: *Last Call for Breakfast* (a Samuel Beckett pastiche by Michael Langridge and Richard Gaunt); *The Cherry Sisters*, a Chekhovian spoof by myself and the company; and another of my cod Shakespeares, *Henry the Tenth, Part Seven*. The fourth piece was *Moby Dick*, adapted from a version performed by The Maskers of Southampton in a Coarse Acting competition. *The Cherry Sisters* featured a leaking samovar which completely destroyed the tenderest moments of the play while *Moby Dick* was noteworthy for the actual appearance of the huge whale on stage. Operated by a team of three people, it rolled its eye and spurted realistically until unfortunately it came apart and the two halves blundered wildly about the stage looking for each other.

Again it was a great success. This time the group took the large George Square Theatre, with 600 seats, and succeeded in filling it nearly every night (by the end of the Festival people were queuing for returns). On the first night there was a genuine Coarse Acting incident, when the scenery teetered and threatened to collapse and had to be held up by the cast. Fortunately, the audience thought it was part of the show and a local radio station commented that the sagging set was "an inspired piece of comic invention". The seal was finally placed on the whole thing when Brian Rix came to see the show and chose it for transfer to the Shaftesbury Theatre, London, as part of the Lunatic Fringe, the four best Fringe shows running in repertory.

This was the first time a Questors show had transferred complete with original cast to a major London theatre and it was a great honour. Fortunately we were well received by public and Press. *The Daily Mail* called it "an inspired spoof". For three months during that autumn of 1979, the cast slaved away, starring in the West End some three times a week after doing a day's work. When the run finished in November, Brian Rix singled out The Questors and asked if another run, of *Coarse Acting Two* alone, could be restarted in the New Year. This time it was just not possible; everybody had to get on with ordinary life.

Among those who came to see *Coarse Acting Two* at the Shaftesbury was HRH Prince Charles, who came privately and at short notice with a group of half-a-dozen friends and sat in the stalls, where he almost fell out of his seat with laughter at one point; in fact, the point at which Henry the Tenth's throne collapsed as he sat in it, trapping him in the wreckage. Afterwards he came on stage and talked to the company and revealed that he is a fan of Coarse Acting.

About six months later, in 1980, another Coarse Acting competition was held at The Questors, and among the guests were our old friends The Maskers and Salisbury Playhouse. The winning entry was *Public Deaths*, a Noël Coward take-off by Jane Dewey, a long-standing acting member of The Questors, which had the novel theme that the chief character accidentally cut his wrist during the action and slowly bled into unconsciousness, bringing the play to a premature conclusion. The prize for the best script, presented by Curtis Brown, the literary agents, was won by David Pearson, a Questors director and actor, with *A Fish in her Kettle*. This was a French farce in which the doors jammed, so nobody could get off-stage, and was performed by the Bunny Langridge Players, those veterans of Coarse Acting.

The adjudicator was Timothy West and a week later the Press was full of a strange coincidence. While appearing in his one-man show *Beecham*, exactly the same thing happened to him as happened to the leading man in Jane Dewey's Coarse Acting winner—he cut his hand on a broken glass and had to be taken to hospital halfway through the show, which was abandoned for the night.

That wasn't the last seen of the two winning plays. They resurfaced in 1984 as part of *The Third Great Coarse Acting Show*, the first time there had been a major coarse acting production in the Playhouse at The Questors, the other shows having been competitions or Edinburgh previews. The rest of the show comprised a gorgeous amateur operatic spoof, *The Student King* by Simon Brett, the novelist and TV writer and once a Questor; and two new pieces by myself. The first, *Stalag 69*, one of the very few plays ever written to be performed twice (the scenery was upside down the first time); the second was another in the Coarse Shakespeare series, *Julius and Cleopatra*.

In 1987 the original Coarse Acting Show was revived and given the full treatment in the Playhouse (its only previous appearance in Ealing had been previews in the Stanislavsky Room). No fewer than eight of the original cast from that first Edinburgh trip in 1977 took part, along with two technical staff, Sue Kendrick and Colin Horne. Strangely enough, two others in the company, Pete Walters (lighting designer) and John

Stacey (designer), had also been at the Cathedral Hall in 1977, but with another company.

Once again The Questors was honoured by Coarse Acting's most important fan, HRH Prince Charles, who came to see the show with some friends, thus keeping up the royal link established when HRH Queen Elizabeth the Queen Mother, his grand-mother, opened the New Playhouse in 1964. HRH came back-stage and talked to the cast and crew and his last words were "You must ask me again next time".

That looked like the end, but then came the Edinburgh tour of 1988. Something was needed to guarantee good houses and bring in the customers and shield us financially. What better than Coarse Acting? So up went two of the old originals from 1977 and 1979, *A Collier's Tuesday Tea* and *The Cherry Sisters*, under the overall title *Coarse Acting Strikes Back*. And, as before, they opened to a full house. Edinburgh still loved it and Radio Forth commented "Performed with consummate skill, it's a joy to experience—catch it if you can". Remarkably, the company contained six survivors from the 1972 contests 16 years previously: Michael Langridge, David Pearson, Sonia Pearson, John Turner, Margaret Turner and Lorna Duval, all of whom had also been in the first Edinburgh tour in 1977. Another 1977 veteran in the cast was Robin Duval.

The effects of that first Coarse Acting competition in 1970 have now spread far and wide. All three shows were published by Samuel French and have been performed by professionals and amateurs all over the world, from New Zealand to Zimbabwe, from Berlin to Singapore, from Cookham to New York. Hund-reds of different companies have put on Coarse Acting and continue to do so. Tony Worth, a member of the company, was in New York a few years back and, glancing idly through the *New York Times* to see what was on that evening, he saw to his astonishment *Coarse Acting Two* advertised at an off-Broadway theatre. Naturally he went to see it and when he revealed his identity as one of the original English cast, they shone a spotlight and introduced him to the audience, who applauded generously.

What is astonishing is the way the older plays have lasted. *Streuth*, originally put on as an improvised spoof in 1972, is still one of the most popular to be performed and draws audiences worldwide. Naturally, full credit is given to The Questors in the published version (including details of the original performances and casts) and thus Coarse Acting remains a significant instrument in keeping the name of The Questors in front of the theatrical world in this country and abroad. This is helped by the fact that the original book and the plays are now recommended reading at many universities, colleges and drama schools, and even used as set books in examinations.

Chapter 15

Organisational Nuts and Bolts, 1964-1989

Development of the site continued gradually over the next quarter century, as and when improvements became financially viable. The overdraft taken on to supplement the New Theatre Fund to help pay for the Playhouse was paid off in the 1966/67 season. In the following season, part of Mattock Lodge was converted; the bedsitters gave way to the Michael Redgrave Room, an additional rehearsal room (opened in 1968), with a new general office below. This freed the Portakabin which had served as both General Manager's office and Box Office since the demolition of the Tin Hut for sole use as a Box Office, a situation which continued for some time. Although a temporary covered way was constructed to protect audiences from the worst of the elements, both when collecting tickets and when crossing from the auditorium to the Shaw Room for interval refreshments, a certain amount of discomfort had to be endured, to say the least. Members recall a popular skit, performed after a General Meeting in the Playhouse one year, in which an entire Box Office queue outside the Portakabin expired in the snow! When a Box Office was later provided in Mattock Lodge, the Portakabin was seized upon gratefully as additional storage space and, tucked away to the side of Mattock Lodge, it eventually became a notoriously impenetrable den of properties.

In the fortieth birthday year of the founding of The Questors, 1969, the Playhouse lighting systems were expanded from 48 to 72 circuits, a process which almost resulted in two fatalities although not from the most likely cause. Roger Kelly and Peter Kendrick, heavily involved in the intricate rewiring process in the old dimmer room under the seating of the Playhouse one hot summer Saturday afternoon, found themselves getting extremely giddy and light headed, which they attributed to the heat and the stuffiness of the room. It was some time later they realised that they were actually slowly being poisoned by their blissfully unaware lighting department colleague, who was repairing his car with the engine running just outside, with the exhaust pipe pointing directly into the room!

In the same year an appeal was launched to pay for a new Foyer and scenestore. It took two years to design and complete the first-floor Foyer extension right across to the Shaw Room block, providing a much larger space, an additional staircase at the Shaw Room end and independent catering facilities. One consequence of the latter, quickly seized upon, was the opportunity to provide a more elaborate refreshment service for the audiences, first with the Bistro which opened in 1972, serving an after-show meal on the first night of each Playhouse performance, and leading eventually to the setting up of the Hotplate in 1981. Under the dedicated management of Dorothy Dent, this has developed into a full meals and snacks service running on every performance evening and contributing upwards of £8,000 profit to the Theatre's funds annually. The scene store underneath the Foyer provided a space the length of the Stanislavsky Room. On February 13th 1971, George Benn stage-managed one of The Questors' more outrageous photo-opportunities, to provide publicity for the Foyer Appeal, when Sir Michael Redgrave blew up the infamous covered way, with the comment "The Questors is in the forefront again".

Improvements to both the front-of-house and backstage areas continued through the late 1970s and into the 1980s. For example—and this is not a comprehensive list: in 1975 a flexible matrix was added to the Playhouse lighting console; installation of lighting facilities and a sound desk for the Stanislavsky Room was undertaken in 1976; in 1976/77, The Grapevine was extended and a new lower Foyer with Box Office area was built; a wardrobe extension was provided in that same year, although this meant the loss of the actors' Green Room, a loss which has never been made up; shortly afterwards, a music and paging system was installed in the Foyer; in 1979, parking spaces for about 20 cars were provided at the front of the theatre; in 1980, new lavatories above the Stanislavsky Room corridor were built and the old lavatories below later converted into a print room and dubbing suite; new office accommodation was built below the main Foyer for the employed administrative staff (by then numbering three) in 1984; and in 1983/84, a new heating system and a computerised lighting control system were installed in the Playhouse.

Throughout this period of course, the fund-raising continued relentlessly, each stage of development being funded by a combination of borrowing, some grants and donations, and cash raised by the membership from additional activities. The fund-raising mixture remained much as before, although there could regrettably be no more Garden Parties (not a lot of fun in a car park!). There was plenty of initiative around, however, including the 'official' birth of Coarse Acting, which sprang up out of a special performance put on in 1970, as Michael Green explains in Chapter 14.

Most recently, a major redevelopment of the only part of the site which had remained virtually untouched, the old workshop in the North-East corner, resulted in the erection of a new high-quality fully equipped Workshop and the provision of a separate Dressing Room and backstage area for the Stanislavsky Room. This development was commissioned in 1986 and completed in 1987 within the budgeted cost of £220,000; comparison with the £85,000 needed 25 years previously to build the entire Playhouse, including the Shaw and Stanislavsky Rooms, gives an eloquent illustration of the extent to which costs of building have changed. It was again financed by overdraft and the establishment of a Redevelopment Fund and once more, members threw themselves into fund-raising with gusto, devising ever more ingenious ways of persuading people to part with their money. A 50-hour sponsored Shakespeare marathon organised by Tony Barber and Roger Kelly, during which teams of members from all departments read non-stop from the works of Shakespeare, proved an enormous financial success (raising over £3,000) as well as a great deal of fun for all participants—even the unlucky group from the Committee of Management who had to embark on *Antony and Cleopatra* at 3am. Members of the Young People's Groups and, on a separate occasion, the active members and the Student Group improvised non-stop for 24 hours, again for sponsorship. And a highly enjoyable and successful Promise Auction was held in 1988, when the Artistic Director, Geoff Webb, demonstrated hitherto unsuspected talent as an auctioneer and managed to realise more than satisfactory bids for a wide variety of intriguing Promises, ranging from a Singing Telegram, through a Champagne Breakfast and various sailing trips, to a Visit to a Fringe Theatre on the Back of a Motorcycle!

Planned for the future is the construction of yet another rehearsal room, above the Stanislavsky Room, to alleviate the space problems created by regularly having as many as four shows (sometimes more) in rehearsal simultaneously, plus Student Group and Young People's Group classes, actors' training classes and meetings. Better facilities for the disabled, in terms of access to the Playhouse and Foyer, are also scheduled for provision in the next few years, as and when finances permit.

During all the building and redevelopment work chronicled above, The Questors has maintained and indeed increased its output in terms of performances—150 or more are now staged each year; the following tabulated summary indicates how the scale of operations has changed since 1945:

Year	No. of productions	No. of performances
1945	6	47
1955	8	70
1965	14	94
1975	22	129
1985	23	148
1988	23	184

Around one-third of all productions have since the mid-1970s been mounted in the Stanislavsky Room. This room is often referred to as 'The Studio', although, strictly speaking, Studio is what goes on there rather than the name of the space itself. The development of the Studio programme, presenting a full season of productions to complement the Playhouse programme since 1973, has been of great value to the artistic development of The Questors. Not only has it allowed the company to stage plays not suitable for the larger Playhouse space, and provided the audiences with a wider choice of programmes, but it has also provided actors, directors and technicians with a space in which to experiment with new plays, styles of performance, playing spaces, and so on. Above all else, the Stanislavsky Room at The Questors has become one of the most attractive intimate theatre spaces in London. Chapter II traces the development of Studio Theatre at The Questors in more detail.

Audience numbers, too, have naturally increased over the years. A campaign to double the membership from 1,500 to 3,000, the level believed to be necessary to sustain the new theatre, was launched in 1960. This had been achieved within a year of opening the Playhouse. Membership in the ensuing quarter century has fluctuated between 3,000 and the 1980 peak of over 4,500; a steady slow decline through the late 1980s, to bottom out at around 3,600, has been caused by a number of factors. Several of these—the proliferation of fringe theatre competing for non-West End audiences, the advent of home video and sophisticated leisure activities—are obviously not unique to The Questors, but they have meant that rather more professional marketing techniques than were used in the past have become necessary to maintain the inflow of new members, both active and audience, on which the company's progress depends. And it must be admitted that in this respect, The Questors has been slow to find an effective response to the problem.

For many years, new members were principally attracted (other than by word of mouth, which is still considered to be the most effective method of all in percentage 'hit' terms) by the so-called 'Door Drops', huge undertakings in which literally thousands of literature packs were delivered by hand of members to homes in various catchment areas. These were extremely successful for a considerable period—typically, in their heyday in the mid-1970s, as many as 20,000 envelopes would be delivered in the annual Door Drop in September, from which around 600 new members would result. The sheer logistics, and members' goodwill, involved in such an exercise were extraordinary, but The Questors has certainly never been short of the latter. A good illustration of this, which also gives an indication of the work involved in organising the Door Drops, follows in the form of Barbara Emmet's account of the handling of the crisis caused by the national postal strike of 1971, which she calls 'How We Beat the Postal Strike and Brought the News to the Four Thousand'.

"It was in 1971, when the latest edition of *Questopics* had just rolled off the presses and been stuffed into the waiting envelopes that all collections of mail came to an abrupt halt: the postal services were on strike. Appalled, we faced the probability of playing to small or even non-existent audiences, a flagging membership drive and the almost total loss of communication with the lifeblood of the theatre—its members.

"With the foolhardiness of despair, I remember proposing to the Administrator that we should endeavour to deliver as many copies of *Questopics* by hand as we possibly could; I also remember the blank look that he turned on me, behind which he was obviously trying to work out whether I was as mad as I sounded or just joking. Having convinced him that I was indeed serious about making the attempt, he installed me in the Portakabin (which at that time was standing, unused, in the front garden of

Mattock Lodge) and rigged up cables from the house to provide me with light and warmth.

"I set to work, aided by a large street map of the London Borough of Ealing and numerous cardboard boxes, sorting the envelopes into areas. I wasn't alone in my task for long. Enquiring souls would appear in the doorway and stay to help. We concentrated first on Ealing and its environs, anything outside the Borough being thrown into a special box for future consideration. Smaller areas we kept all in one box, but Ealing itself was divided into many sections. In a couple of days all the envelopes were sorted and grouped in blocks of streets and we could turn our attention to the task of getting them out to the membership.

"First we duplicated a small slip which we inserted into the envelopes. To the best of my recollection, it said something like this:

'This copy of *Questopics* has come to you through the kindness of a fellow member who has put it through your letterbox. If you should happen to be passing the theatre and felt able to call and collect a few to deliver in the same way, this would be very much appreciated'.

"This brought a splendid response: members would drop by and take a bundle of envelopes for roads near where they lived to 'post' on their way home. Enterprising souls organised car trips and would work out routes criss-crossing Ealing. Before many days were up we had disposed of a very high proportion of envelopes to local residents and were able to turn our attention to people living elsewhere.

"This was obviously not going to be so successful, since we had to rely on learning who could help, for instance by taking a couple or so to work to give to colleagues who did not live in Ealing. But we did make a small dent in the 'ELSEWHERE' box and perhaps our greatest triumph was getting one to Paris, two to Dublin and even one to the USA, carried, and posted in those countries, by members going there on visits!

"One of our great strengths at The Questors is the way in which we can rise to a challenge, and this was no exception. It was an episode I always remember with much pleasure and satisfaction. And above all—it was such fun!"

The *Questopics* referred to above is the newsletter which has been sent in advance of each show to all categories of members since 1965; and although the format and the editor have changed many times since then, it has appeared consistently and well over 300 issues have been published. Its prime function is to advertise the forthcoming production (and to give advance publicity for the next few), to encourage the membership to attend. Since The Questors is a theatre club, only members may buy tickets although each member may of course bring as many guests as he or she likes. With a membership of approximately 3,500 receiving the publication and an average capacity per Playhouse production of 2,100, an attractive selling piece in *Questopics* can be a considerable advantage in ensuring good houses, particularly as postal booking forms are included in each mailing.

The changes in total membership and audience figures over the years since 1945 are summarised below:

Year	Membership	Total audience
1945	744	6,780
1955	1,303	9,344
1965	3,125	25,349
1975	4,030	32,286
1985	3,841	27,803
1988	3,632	25,158

The Acting Membership of The Questors over the same period has increased from around 50 in 1945 to 293 in 1988. Around 500 others are on the Active Membership list, involved in some way or other in the running of the Theatre, be it directly on productions in technical, backstage or front-of-house capacities, or more generally in the administrative, technical, catering or box office functions, not forgetting the Grapevine Club of course. Communication with the Active Membership is maintained through the intriguingly named TOAD (Theatre Organ for Active Departments), founded by David Emmet in 1976 and mailed with each *Questopics*.

It is worth noting that the Active Membership by the mid-1980s numbered more than the total membership of The Questors in 1945, an expansion necessary to cope with the increased workload. Inevitably, as the organisation has grown, the family atmosphere which people remember so vividly from the early years has to a large extent disappeared, although it is recreated on one level around 23 times a year—the company spirit engendered through working on a show four nights a week and every Sunday for eight weeks remains as strong as ever. Many members do however regret the passing of the 'personal touch era', when it was possible for one person to know every other active member by name—and most of the audience members as well. This is doubtless one of the main reasons why the discomforts and deprivations of the Tin Hut are still remembered with such affection by so many, along with the tea-breaks midway through each evening's rehearsal when literally everyone on the premises would congregate at the back of the auditorium for 15 minutes. The attitude of members to The Questors, even many years after leaving 'active service' is well-summarised by this note from former acting member Gerald Rawling, published in *Questopics* in 1967:

> "The truth about The Questors as I understand it after six years of working within the organisation and nine more spent on the outside looking in is that 'our' theatre gains its strength from being a community, a group—almost a family ... I have always been aware that everybody involved had the same attitude to the job in hand ... active members are respected only for what they achieve in the theatre, whether it be on the stage or in committee or in some other department of the organisation ... There were a number of people working at The Questors in my time whose jobs in private life I never did find out despite the fact that I knew them tolerably well."

And possibly the best example of all is that of Pat Bowley, who returned to Australia in the 1950s but has maintained close contact with several of his Questors friends; indeed, the *Questopics* report of the Members' Reunion organised by Wilf Sharp as part of the Golden Jubilee celebrations in 1979 notes the following:

> "a small ceremony took place in the Office which perhaps most aptly symbolised the spirit which had informed the whole evening. About ten of us clustered round the telephone to hear Pat Bowley speaking ... from Tumutu, NSW, Australia, where he had received notice of the event he would so dearly have liked to attend."

The steady growth of the Club through the years is also reflected in its financial history, from that first balance of a mere 7s. 11 ½d in 1929 to the record surplus of £26,492 in 1987, the latter achieved, it must be said, with the aid of a certain amount of creative accounting. Through the 1930s and 1940s, although the theatre lurched from financial crisis to financial crisis, modest surpluses were achieved. Then in the 1950/51 season came the first published Annual Report of The Questors Limited, in accordance with the requirements of the Companies Act. The balance of income over expenditure as recorded in the Annual Reports has grown steadily since, with a few hiccups from time to time. Turnover by the late-1980s was typically in the region of £150,000, compared with £2,000 in the early 1950s; the following table summarises the rate of progress:

Financial year	Turnover £
1950/51	2,187
1960/61	4,464
1970/71	18,079
1980/81	68,345
1987/88	128,211

Of the most recently-quoted figure, over £40,000 represented membership subscriptions and over £35,000 ticket sales; comparable 1950s figures were £700 and £750 respectively. Other major sources of income now include Front-of-House sales and the Hotplate refreshment service (£10,000 or more), letting of the premises to other organisations (£15,000 plus), Grapevine Club donations (approaching £30,000 a year), sponsorship (which, thanks to the efforts of Geoffrey Sellman, the Sponsorship Co-ordinator, has grown from a mere £30 in 1983/84 to over £6,000 a year) and other donations. Of total annual expenditure in the late 1980s, the largest single element is staff salaries. The production expenses bill for the Playhouse is around £13,000 a year and nearly £7,000 for the Studio; that the latter is somewhat difficult to reconcile with the 'official' budget for a Studio production which remains £50 shows a certain indulgence—or perhaps inefficient budget control—on the part of the financial management! Production expenditure in 1955/56, for comparison, was £760 (for only nine productions, of course, and no Studio), representing the largest single item of expenditure quoted in that year's total of £3,319. Average expenditure per production has thus grown from £84 in 1955/56 to £999 (for the Playhouse) in 1987/88. In addition to the individual show expenditure, around £10,000 a year are spent on equipment by the technical departments and £10,000 or more on publicity and administration.

Membership subscriptions and ticket prices have gradually increased, as illustrated in the tabulated summary below. These figures are of necessity a gross over-simplification—several different classes of membership, each paying a different rate, have been defined over the years, including joint membership for married couples, student membership, associate membership and concessionary membership for the long-term unemployed and other low-income categories. Likewise, there has always been a multi-tier ticket price, depending on the position of seat or on the night of the run. The table gives, for the years indicated, the price of the basic membership subscription for an individual and the top price of a ticket.

Year	Membership fee	Ticket price
1951	£1/ = / =	5/ =
1961	1/10/ =	5/6
1966	2/10/ =	5/6
1971	3.50	£0.50
1976	6.00	1.00
1981	10.00	1.70
1986	17.00	3.00

A survey of the audience membership in 1970 was completed by 20% of members. It revealed that 60% lived in the Borough of Ealing, and that over 75% had joined the theatre in the six years since the Playhouse was built. Nearly 50% had been introduced to The Questors by existing members, but a further 37% had joined on the strength of the company's reputation. Over two-thirds of members booked their tickets by post. Although this survey was conducted nearly 20 years ago, it is probable that the percentages will have remained fairly constant. The percentage of members who take up their free seats for each production has declined over the years, but has averaged around 25% since the late 1960s. It obviously depends to a certain extent on the popularity of an individual show.

Over the years the administrative structure of The Questors has, of necessity, changed and developed markedly, although it has always been governed by a Committee of Management (originally called the General Committee) elected by the membership, with overall control of artistic and financial policy. Artistically and administratively, for the 40 years until his retirement as Honorary Director in 1969, the reins were very firmly held by Alfred Emmet. Although he was of course assisted and supported by a number of committees and colleagues, notably a Plays and Productions Committee which was responsible, from 1947 onwards, for play selection and the General Purposes Committee, with executive responsibility for administrative matters, Alfred was the artistic pulse of The Questors, with a say in virtually all decisions, from auditioning candidates for acting membership, to selecting directors for particular shows, to setting the syllabus for the Student Acting Course. It was because of his single-minded determination to stick to the original principles that The Questors achieved the reputation and international recognition it undoubtedly has for innovative and exciting dramatic work. As *Questopics* commented in 1971, when Alfred's enormous contribution to the development of the amateur theatre at large was finally recognised with the award of an OBE, "There can be few active members of the Theatre who have not been infuriated by his persistence in getting them to do something they would rather not do, or at least not do now. No-one who has ever served on a committee with him will forget his dogged way of refusing to admit that the impossible cannot be achieved, only that it takes a little longer to do."

In 1969, an entirely new administrative organisation was implemented. The General Purposes Committee was replaced by an Executive Committee with full executive powers to plan the Theatre's programme in detail; the Committee of Management remained the governing body and the only body with authority to vary in any way the artistic and financial policies of the Theatre. The Executive Committee consisted of the Chairman, the Secretary, the Chairman of the Plays and Productions Committee, the Stage Director, the House Manager, the Chairman of the Publicity Committee and the Administrator (as the theatre manager was then known). In addition, there were three main advisory committees, reporting directly to the Committee of Management—the Plays and Productions Committee, the Development Committee and the Theatre and Youth Committee.

'The Quest and What it Means', the policy document originally issued in 1947, was reassessed by a Working Party under the chairmanship of Nevile Cruttenden and updated in 1972 with the publication of the 'Statement of Aims'. Both these documents, together known as 'Our Quest', were reaffirmed in 1985 as the guiding policy of The Questors and are reproduced in full in Appendix 3. Implementation of the policy was facilitated in 1974 by the establishment of an Artistic Directorate, to replace the old Plays and Productions Committee and "to promote a vigorous and unified artistic policy for The Questors Theatre", headed by a Director of Productions and having five other members—the Productions Manager, the Stage Director, the Head of Design, the Plays Adviser and the Studio Theatre Director. A separate Stage Directorate, bringing together the heads of the technical departments, was also established.

This structure was again reviewed in the 1978/79 season, when the Committee of Management set up a Working Party under the chairmanship of Tony Barber "to examine the artistic development of the Theatre in the 1980s and any consequent financial and administrative changes." As a result of this Working Party's recommendations, the Executive Committee was abolished in 1980 and replaced with four Directorates, responsible for Administrative, Artistic, Financial and Stage (ie. technical) matters. Each Directorate was headed by an individual Director who was to be responsible for all day-to-day executive decisions. The Working Party also recommended a more interventionist role for the Artistic Directorate and a more positive Studio policy, hoping that this "will allow a more coherent artistic philosophy." Ten years later, the Committee of Management again felt it was time to review the role of The Questors, for the 1990s and beyond. Another Working Party, this time chaired by Martin Bowley, was set up: "to review the artistic practice and policy of the Theatre; to seek to define the role of the Theatre for the next ten years; and to consider ways and means of improving the artistic standards of the Theatre and its members".

Martin Bowley, who was Chairman of The Questors at the time, commented in the 1980/81 Annual Report: " … We are at one and the same time a club, a theatre and a business." This, indeed, sums up the continuing dilemma for a company such as The Questors—it is by now such a large organisation that sophisticated business management techniques must be employed. However, it also remains a club, whose members participate actively on a voluntary basis, principally for their leisure and enjoyment. The difficulty is always in maintaining the delicate balance between involving the membership in the decision-making process and running the business efficiently—a balance which is maintained more happily at some times than at others. What has held it together for 60 years, and continues to hold it all together, is a shared belief in 'worthwhile' theatre and in the importance of continuing The Quest.

Chapter 16

Under the Grapevine

by Alan Chambers*

The progress from the first apocryphal debate in July 1959 over whether to order six or twelve bottles of brown ale to the 1989 average turnover of £1,800 a week is a good indication of the growth of the Grapevine Club's popularity and its importance to the Theatre's finances during the 30 years of the club's existence.

Originally, it only opened at weekends and while a show was running, but during the rehearsals of **Henry IV part** I in 1961 a number of members of the Committee who were in the play felt that valuable drinking time was being lost getting to The Three Pigeons or to The Black Lion in Hammersmith which stayed open until 11.00pm. The bar began to open more regularly as a result, although it was not until November 8th 1963 that the Committee agreed to the system of opening each night and Sunday lunchtime.

The first Bar took up only about a third of the space now used and the entrance was through the present bar helpers' door. The counter occupied the opposite wall and washing up was done in what subsequently became known as The Snug. The glasses were carried over in small wooden boxes made by Ruth Howard and taking them to the kitchen on a busy night was equivalent to being in a grape press at the height of the grape harvest! The then Treasurer put up a solemn notice totalling the glass breakages during the financial year only for another member to add the comment, "With a little more effort we'll do better next year!"

One of the first extensions was the removal of a small committee room at the North end, followed by the moving of the bar counter more or less to its present position. John Howard proved this could be done with two inches to spare by swivelling bits of paper on an alleged scale drawing. To everyone's surprise,

---

* Alan Chambers has been an actor and director at The Questors since he joined in 1961. He was Director of Productions from 1977 to 1981 and served on the Committee of Management from 1968 to 1986. Alan has been Chairman of the Grapevine Committee since 1981.

it worked. A new entrance was made in the North wall and a sink was put under the bar. With the kitchen becoming redundant, a hole was knocked through the dividing wall and the old front door was blocked up, to make The Snug. Alarm was being expressed at the state of the floor, which was creaking ominously, and there was a danger of many eminent Questors being thrust into the role of Demon King and disappearing through the floor in a puff of beer and brickdust. This was temporarily alleviated by the use of Acroprops until, in 1977, there was a major alteration which provided an extension, by knocking through the West wall, and a new concrete floor. During these changes The Grapevine moved for two months into the Shaw Room. The process of removing the bar counter needed 20 strong men, seven of whom it was rumoured were never seen again, though it is thought that the remains of one can still be seen faintly on the plate glass window of the lower foyer. Perhaps the most traumatic change was the straightening of the entrance steps, which used to bend to the right. For months, dazed and winded regulars would be found hanging over the new rail, their legs feebly seeking the non-existent steps.

The original decorations in black and white, designed by Graham Heywood, were in a contemporary style, but these were replaced by more traditional theatre pub designs by Nigel Woolner in the early Sixties. Since then the decorations have stayed within this convention. The bust of Queen Victoria, painted gold over its original terracotta, has been with us all this time, though Jill Champion-Torrance's Can Can Lady was reluctantly painted out, due to age and decay, in 1986. A new, more comfortable and convenient scheme was designed in 1989, to celebrate the Theatre's Diamond Jubilee and the Grapevine Club's thirtieth birthday.

Whenever it has been a case of simple redecoration, the Committee members and helpers have carried out the job themselves and without closing the bar. Only a few drinkers have complained of emulsion in the beer and it is not true that most of them could not tell the difference. The major problem for redecorating has been the ceiling, through which a succession of Administrators and Theatre Managers have poured the contents of their sinks, baths and washing machines from the flat immediately above. Again, few drinkers have complained, though some may have been incapable of noticing. In the contest between Grapevine din and Administrator noise, the Grapevine has won handsomely, though one or two incumbents have run us pretty close!

With the development of the new Foyer by the Theatre in 1971, the Grapevine opened the Foyer Bar with a separate licence for performance nights and open to all attending the show. Since the inception in 1981 of The Hotplate catering service in the Foyer on show nights, The Grapevine has been happy to supply the wines.

Of the original Grapevine Committee, none is still serving, but three, Kath Harrington, Alan Drake and Neville Bradbury, remain members of the Theatre. Roy Montgomery and Frank Smith, who became the first Life Member in 1961, were also founder members, with Bill Wall as Secretary and Arthur Boyd Taylor in the Chair. Bill's antipathy to pub games led to his hiding the shove halfpenny board, which was fortunately made of slate, in a number of insalubrious places where a variety of unmentionable things were done to it by overtaxed and emotional male Committee members. He also instituted sausages on Sunday evenings, which quickly became de-instituted due to the elderly cardboard nature of the sausages and the clouds of smoke. The electric frying pan was never seen again.

Arthur did more than anyone to establish the informal yet efficient teamwork that has characterised The Grapevine's approach to its affairs. His relaxed, familial style at Committee meetings ensured that an unruly bunch of individuals had an enjoyable evening in Committee, yet by the end of the meeting the necessary decisions had been taken. Despite the increased pressure that serving behind the bar involves, it is good to see that the Committee members still feel it a privilege, and the responsibility and mutual trust that they share arise from the atmosphere that Arthur created. His attention to detail in ordering and accounting was carried on right until his death in 1981. The Theatre and The Grapevine owe a considerable debt to him and it was with great pleasure that we were able to see Norman Barwick's portrait of him in characteristic pose placed in The Snug, where we intend to see it remain.

There have been well over 150 members of the Committee since 1959. It has been noticeable how many of them have been busy in other areas of the Theatre, yet how they have been ready to give their voluntary efforts even when pressed in other ways. Bar helpers have been legion. From the beginning, it has been the aim to keep the operation as simple as possible.

Volunteer labour that changes every night means that there must not be too much to learn and that the work is kept to a minimum. As a result, from the start there has been a restricted number of lines for sale. Whitbread was our sole supplier at first, and we sold Flowers and Tankard at 1/10d a pint. Flowers was replaced and, for a time, draught Bass was stocked. This had to be withdrawn because of the effect it was having on its regular but over-indulgent drinkers, although this theory has never been fully proved! For some years Tankard and Trophy were our only beers, but by popular demand Fuller's London Pride was introduced and we embarked on a two brewery system. Pride was so popular that Tankard was withdrawn and then, in 1985, we decided to change from Whitbread to Greene King. With new cellar cooling and organisation, two draught lagers, draught Guinness and cider could be introduced. Coca Cola, lemonade and soda are also on draught.

The biggest expansion has been in the sales of wine. In the early days of The Grapevine, the problem lay in getting a wine that was consistent in taste at a reasonable price. Many were the experiments and the only time Committee meetings got acrimonious was at a wine tasting. This may have been due to arguments over quality, but was more probably due to the quantity tasted. A more than immodest Spanish white called Spadela stands out on the writer's scarred palate. Red wine was never as popular and was consequently difficult to keep. However, these problems have been largely overcome and at any one time, The Grapevine can usually offer a choice of around ten to a dozen wines.

Soft drinks have always been part of The Grapevine, though changing patterns of drinking, especially with the increased awareness of the problems of drinking and driving, meant a sharp upturn in sales in the late 1980s. We have developed the range and added a number of low-alcohol bottled beers and wines, as well as selling coffee on non-show nights. The range of snacks and sweets has been extended and we have investigated ways of improving this service without going into competition with The Hotplate.

Keeping the bar easy to work has meant that simple wooden drawer tills have been used throughout, though an innovation has been the introduction of hand calculators for those who find adding up an embarrassment. An attempt to use an electronic adding machine failed when sherry somehow got into the works!

All this calls for a high degree of trust in our bar staff, but our consistent profit margins show that this trust is rarely abused.

Undoubtedly, the greatest labour-saving device has been the glass washing machine. Introduced first in 1979, with a second, larger, machine substituted a few years later, no-one can think how we ever managed without one. Modern technology has also given The Grapevine the 'smoke eaters'—devastating pieces of equipment which, despite the mockery, have produced an improvement in the atmosphere.

Although keeping in mind its prime function of keeping the Bar open and properly staffed, The Grapevine has hosted a number of social events both on and off its premises. Perhaps the most notable of these have been the dances. The present Chairman at an early dance, having sampled the lavish hospitality given at the beginning of the evening, thought he would go and have a dance and arrived as they finished The Last Waltz. On a later occasion Beth Crowley (now Josh) was alleged to have said "What dance?"

In the first year of The Grapevine's operation the turnover was £1,162/14/11d and £300 was handed over to the Theatre. In 1988, the turnover was £82,745 and the sum of £29,500 was given to the Theatre. In total The Questors has received a quarter of a million pounds from The Grapevine and it is perhaps significant that the last £50,000 has come in under two years.

This is an achievement of which The Grapevine is proud, but it is prouder of the amateur tradition which has' provided the service enabling this to take place. We have attempted to provide a focal point where Questors members can meet, whether for an after-show drink, to discuss the next production or just to be sociable with like-minded people. We also hope that we make drinking a little cheaper than elsewhere! We shall strive to continue to do this as successfully for another thirty years.

The Questors' first production, The Best People, Park Theatre, Hanwell, 1929

The Old Theatre (the 'Tin Hut')

The first production in the Tin Hut, Dragon's Teeth, 1933

The Witch, 1934. Produced by Alfred Emmet

One of Dudley Clark's designs for
Wonderful Zoo, 1935

The first Questors symbol, designed by
Ernest Ives

Icarus Preserved, 1941. Produced by Alfred Emmet

The Cherry Orchard, 1943. Produced by Alfred Emmet, designed by Graham Heywood

The first Student Group production, Cradle Song, 1947

The Thracian Horses, 1949

Set design by Graham Heywood for Othello, 1949

Making up in the dressing room in the Old Theatre (for Poor Man's Miracle, 1951)

Alfred Emmet and Student Group in the Old Theatre (ca. 1961)

Tea break during a dress rehearsal in the Old Theatre (1950s)

Marius Goring cuts the first turf, 1955

Tom Boyd pointing the Shaw Room, 1956

Building the Bernard Shaw Room, 1956

At the switchboard in the Old Theatre, Gerry Isenthal on left

The prompt corner in the Old Theatre

The Wardrobe at work (1950s), Hilda Collins second from right

George Benn, set painting in the Old Theatre, 1950s

Alfred Emmet with IVS students during building of the Stanislavsky Room, 1959

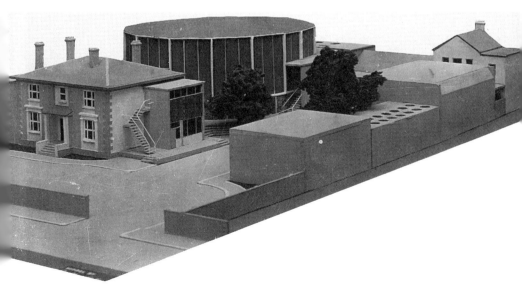

The original model of the new Questors complex

Dame Sybil Thorndike presents the wreath for Norman Branson to place on the Shaw Room roof, 1956

Detail from the set for The Master Builder, 1956. Designed by Billee Lawrence

Alfred Emmet and Norman Branson show Dame Edith Evans around the site, 1957

Victor Stanitsyn of the Moscow Art Theatre laying the foundation stone of the Constantin Stanislavsky Room, 1958

Schools Tour of Double Double, 1965

Alfred Emmet and the cast of Brand discussing the script, 1964

*Alfred Emmet welcomes Her Majesty Queen
Elizabeth, the Queen Mother to the Gala
Opening of the Playhouse, April 1964*

Brand, Playhouse, 1964

Example of thrust stage arrangement, Playhouse

Example of proscenium stage arrangement, Playhouse

Example of in-the-round stage arrangement, Playhouse

The Questors Theatre exterior (taken in the early-1980s)

Bill Wall in the Grapevine bar, 1960s

Sir Michael Redgrave at the opening of the Redgrave Room, 1968, flanked by George Benn (L) and Alfred Emmet

Peer Gynt (40th birthday production), Playhouse 1969.
Directed by David Gower, designed by Mary Anderson

Hans Kohlhaas, Stanislavsky Room 1972. Directed by Bill McLoughlin

The Lark at the Minack Cliffside Theatre, The Questors tour, 1976.
Directed by Ron Bloomfield

The Questors at Edinburgh
(Michael Green second from right), 1988

The Ghost Sonata, Playhouse 1979. Directed by Tony Rushforth

Mother Courage and her Children,
Playhouse 1967. Directed by David Gower

Sisters, Playhouse 1982.
Directed by Spencer Butler

Set for Prometheus Bound, Playhouse 1977. Designed by John Stacey

Set for Lear, Playhouse 1976. Designed by Norman Barwick

Set for The Seagull, Playhouse 1989. Designed by Ray Dunning

Bartholomew Fair, Playhouse 1986. Directed by John Davey

Junior Drama Workshop improvisation evening, ca. 1979

Alfred Emmet and the Student Group, 1979

Electra, Student Group production, Stanislavsky Room 1975

The Brick, Studio production 1987. Directed by Peter Whelan

Hamlet—What Dreams May Come, Studio production 1989. Directed by John Wilson

Alfred Emmet and Sir Michael Redgrave at their joint 75th birthday celebration at The Questors Theatre. (Inset) Bronze bust of Alfred Emmet, by Colin Walters

Chapter 17

Playing Away

by Ken Ratcliffe*

Taking shows out to other venues—known in Questors parlance as 'touring' although it usually refers to the visit of a single production to a single venue—has long been a popular feature of our activities. In the early years and, of course, during the second world war, touring was not as we know it today. The first tours, apart from an entry in the Welwyn Garden City Drama Festival in 1937, were confined to seven appearances, from 1931 to 1937, in One-Act Play Festivals organised by the British Drama League. Then in the early years of the war—1940/41—there are records of plays, including *She Stoops to Conquer*, *The Romance of the Western Chamber*, *The Fantasticks* and *Arms and the Man*, taken out to ARP depots, factories, hospitals, gun-sites and community centres. Later in the war a 'Travelling Theatre' was established, performing mixed bills of short plays with props, costumes and even scenery that could easily be transported by tram and Underground. In the last year of the war, it became a little easier to acquire petrol coupons and motorised transport was used.

In the eight years immediately following the war, the only official tour under the Questors banner was the visit of *The Gentle People* by Irwin Shaw to the Palace Court Theatre in Bournemouth as part of the BDL's Amateur Theatre Week. Then, in 1953, a production of *Tartuffe* was taken to the Crescent Theatre in Birmingham—another amateur theatre company similar in status to The Questors. And between 1956 and 1958, we had our first taste of open-air theatre, when three productions—*She Stoops to Conquer*, *Pygmalion* and *The Miser*—played in Torquay.

The first foreign tour took place in 1965, when we were invited to West Berlin by the Literarisches Colloquium to perform two recently produced new plays, James Saunders's *Neighbours* and

---

* Ken Ratcliffe has been an acting member since 1962 and has played almost 100 roles on The Questors' stage during the ensuing 27 years. He also edited *Questopics* for a brief period and is currently Editor of the Playhouse programmes.

Barry Bermange's *No Quarter*, at the Akademie der Künste, as part of a Festival of New Drama. The production of *Neighbours* also played in Paris on the way back. Both plays were directed by Alan Clarke, who shortly afterwards turned professional and has since gone on to direct numerous highly controversial plays for TV. We had the accolade while there of performing both plays 'live' on late-night German TV. The company, of which I was a member, was also able to make a pilgrimage to the Eastern sector to see the famous Berliner Ensemble in a production of the Brecht play *The Good Soldier Schweyk in the Second World War*. Both the production and the theatre remain vividly in my memory.

Following a visit to Felixstowe in 1966 with *A Scent of Flowers* by James Saunders, a second tour was planned there the following year, of Fred Watson's *Private Fires*. The hosts however decided that this play, with its six coffins on stage, would be too much for their audiences, whose sensibilities had apparently been upset by *A Scent of Flowers* (with only one coffin!). We at The Questors were vastly entertained that they substituted another company presenting *The Killing of Sister George*—surely a play which, with its fairly obvious lesbian theme, was likely to upset several sensibilities back in 1966!

Also in 1967 came the first of what became biennial visits to the delightful open-air Minack Cliffside Theatre in Porthcurno, Cornwall. The production in 1967 was *Phaedra*, directed by Alan Chambers. The company very soon discovered that performing in the open air has the disadvantage of being totally at the mercy of the elements, as the following account by Tony Shipley, published in *Questopics* some years later, shows:

> "One memory of Cornwall that will haunt me evermore is of a dress rehearsal at the Minack on a cold Sunday evening, with the rain coming down in torrents, a 'strong to gale' wind blowing right through the lighting box, enormous waves crashing on the rock below and the stage crew stomping about in oilskins and sou-westers. Suddenly there appeared on one of the highest rocks an apparition in the form of Mike Green, dressed like an advertisement for a famous brand of pilchards. He raised his right arm, pointed sea-wards and announced in a penetrating voice 'Sail on the port bow'. It was shortly after this that we gave up and went back to the hotel."

The experience did not, however, put us off and that first tour was followed two years later by *The Comedy of Errors*, again directed by Alan Chambers. Then came *The Italian Girl* (1971) and *Relatively Speaking* (1973). Nearly all of the productions which toured to The Minack were also presented in the Playhouse, either before or after the tour. But in 1976 one of The Questors' most successful productions, both artistically and financially, was one produced for the Minack tour only. This was Ron Bloomfield's production of Anouilh's *The Lark*. It was my first visit to The Minack and it coincided with one of the hottest and longest summers of the century. The sun shone every day and the supplementary lighting afforded by the moon on cloudless nights enhanced all the evening performances—and proved very necessary on the first night, when a fire in the electricity substation in nearby Porthcurno caused all the lights to go out before the end of the performance! We drew large and appreciative audiences. The company comprised upwards of 60 people, most of them, like me, new to The Minack and Questors tours. Some say you need a holiday after working a week at The Minack; this was one of those occasions when the week was a holiday in itself.

I have equally vivid recollections of other Minack tours, where the dramatic natural backdrop of Cornish cliffs and wild sea adds another dimension to any production. For instance in 1978, with *Penny for a Song*, in which Ted Srivener risked life and limb by taking off in an air-balloon! And in 1980, when we took *Macbeth*, a play ideally suited to the open-air setting. John Davey's production put some of the battle scenes on the tops of the cliffs surrounding the stage to breathtaking effect. After the battle, Macbeth's body was rolled off the back of the stage down a sheer drop and caught on a specially-rigged platform which was removed before the performance finished. At the end, audience members invariably rushed to see where the body had gone and were astonished to find a yawning space.

The Questors was pleased to be invited to help celebrate the Golden Jubilee of The Minack in 1982, with a production of *Twelfth Night*, again directed by John Davey, and we were back again the following year with Alan Chambers' production of *Sir Gawain and the Green Knight*. Both productions played to record and appreciative audiences.

Then in September 1985 we paid the price of inclement weather with a late appearance at The Minack. The play was *Tom Jones* and with a storm brewing up on the opening night the local newspaper critic compared the four-poster bed in the opening scene to a ship in full sail as the curtains billowed in the wind, while the doll representing baby Tom was brought most unexpectedly to life, bobbing about on the bed! Very heavy rain during one matinée obliged us to omit one act which required much chasing about, both on stage and backstage—an extremely perilous occupation on a muddy clifftop with a sheer drop behind. A saturated cast and crew applauded Jack Wood, the director, as we heard him apologise to the small and equally saturated audience and give them a resumé of the plot of the act! Very few performances are ever completely cancelled at The Minack and this week was no exception—although we sailed pretty close to the wind.

The next Minack tour was another triumph—Jeffrey Smith's production of *Animal Farm* in 1987, which played to record houses and made a handsome profit. It was hard work on the actors, gambolling about the rocks playing the animals in masks and on crutches, but the audience reaction was more than worth it. In total contrast was the play chosen for the 1989 tour— Thomas Kilroy's 'Irish' adaptation of the Chekhov classic, *The Seagull*, which was perfectly in tune with the Celtic atmosphere of the Minack setting. John Davey directed.

Apart from the regular visits to The Minack and the Edinburgh Festival Fringe—the latter of which form the subject of a separate chapter by Michael Green—tours to many other venues have continued throughout the past 20 years or so. In the UK these include visits to the Barn Theatre at Dartington Hall in Devon (Harold Pinter's *The Homecoming* in 1968 and David Storey's *The Restoration of Arnold Middleton* in 1969), the Piran Round near Perranporth (*The Fall and Redemption of Man* by John Bowen, 1970), Bolton Little Theatre (*Agitator* by John Norman in 1976, Ibsen's *Little Eyolf* in 1984), Bradford Playhouse (*Ashes*, 1977), Woburn (*The Killing of Sister George*, 1978), Guernsey (*Educating Rita*, 1987) and the Niccol Centre in Cirencester (Jane Dewey's adaptation of Jane Austen's *Lady Susan*, 1988).

One particular occasion that sticks in my mind was a somewhat bizarre production in 1975 of Edward Albee's *All Over* which was the focus of an equally bizarre tour, a one-night stand at Bath University. We were there simply to provide entertainment to the resident undergraduates on the first day of the academic year. Although the play as written was contemporary American both in style and setting, the director had decided to costume the entire cast in Elizabethan dress to denote the timeless quality of the play. A production which had puzzled audiences in Ealing totally confused the undergraduates at Bath who, due to an administrative error, were without programmes! Confronted, explanation-less, by actors dressed in elaborate Elizabethan costume answering telephones, talking of automobiles and smoking cigarettes, many were utterly defeated and noisily opted out. One wide-eyed student came round afterwards and asked: "What on earth happened—didn't your costumes arrive?" As we drove away into the night I reflected that it was perhaps just as well that on this occasion we had had no publicity!

In neighbouring theatres in the Greater London area, a total of seven Questors productions have played since 1976, when one of the new plays from that year's New Plays Festival, John Norman's *Agitator*, visited the Cockpit Theatre. That was a busy year—the productions of *Staircase* by Charles Dyer and the late-night revue *The Gentle Art of Seduction* also toured, to probably our nearest neighbours, the Teddington Theatre Club. The Tower Theatre in Islington, home of the Tavistock Theatre Company our London-based LTG fellow-member, has hosted The Questors twice—with Tennessee Williams's *Small Craft Warnings* in 1977 and Pinter's *Betrayal* in 1981. And across the river Thames, to the South Bank Polytechnic, went Brecht's *Man is Man* in 1977 and, to the South London Theatre Centre, went David Fletcher's 1984 Studio production of *Julius Caesar*. Particularly effective was the visit of TS Eliot's *Murder in the Cathedral*, another Studio production, to St Matthew's Parish Church in Richmond, Surrey, in 1981, where the play gained a dimension from the ecclesiastical setting.

International touring, as might be expected, has been less frequent but has been spectacular. European visits, apart from the West Berlin/Paris trip already mentioned, have been limited to two—the 1976 Studio production of Michel de Ghelderode's *Escurial*, directed by Georg Malvius, went to the International Drama Festival at Villach in Austria, while David Emmet's 1983 production of *Bonjour Là, Bonjour* by the Canadian author Michel Tremblay, was invited to take part in a theatre festival in Sweden. This was played in a theatre-in-the-round, specially built for the occasion on the stage of the large professional theatre which was acting as host, to a prolonged standing ovation and flowers flung on the stage.

Further afield, there have been two tours. In 1977, a small Questors company of ten embarked on a tour of the USA.

The Florida Theatre Conference, an organisation representing amateur theatre throughout the State, invited The Questors to give the only international contribution to its annual festival. The play chosen was Joe Orton's *What the Butler Saw*, accompanied by *The Man Shakespeare*, a selection of extracts from Shakespeare devised and directed by David Gower. The set was specially built to Questors specifications and most of the properties (apart from a British policeman's uniform and three straitjackets, the last-mentioned being taken through US customs in a rather worried Tour Manager's briefcase!) were provided by the hosts. The tour lasted three weeks, covered 1,000 miles, gave nine performances of the two shows in six different venues and played to 90% capacity. Roger Kelly, who was Tour Manager, recalls that *What the Butler Saw*, which was the sort of play that a US company could not have got away with putting on at that time, proved too much for some of the American audiences; large numbers regularly got up and walked out at the point at which Mrs Prentice begins to discuss her gynaecologial details! Local publicity for the visitors was extremely high-profile, with interviews on local radio and television stations being arranged in nearly all venues. Hospitality was also extremely lavish and one member of the company, during an early-morning radio show after a particularly generous party, could not remember her own name.

Then, in November 1985, came the longest journey to date— halfway round the world to Japan. Barbara Emmet's production of Peter Shaffer's *Black Comedy* took part in the First Kanagawa International Theatre Festival, along with representatives from nine other countries, France, West Germany, Belgium, Yugoslavia, Canada, the USA, Northern Ireland, Finland and Japan. All the companies were billeted in one hotel and although the Festival was non-competitive, there was an opportunity to see all the performances and compare standards. The Questors gave the last performance on the last day and the production received much acclaim. Simon Higginson, one of the actors in the company, wrote the following account for *Questopics* on his return:

> "We entered the magnificent 1,000-seat auditorium in Yokohama to find an army of stage hands busily erecting a carbon copy of our Mattock Lane set—all based on photos of the MODEL we had sent! ... All went very well—despite the language barrier, we were well received. Although the Festival was over, to ensure

our total relaxation our hosts then bussed us to a Japanese-style hotel in the Hakone National Park, passing the magnificent Mount Fuji on the way. Hot springs, kimonos (*de rigueur!*) and a truly breathtaking last-night Japanese feast overwhelmed the senses and typified the depth and charm of the welcome extended to us all.''

Touring, whether it's to Teddington or Tokyo, is an unforgettable experience and one which often seems to bring out the best in The Questors. Companies become like families, there are no petty rivalries and everyone works for the common good, of promoting The Questors and what it stands for to the outside world. I hope this brief history of our tours revives pleasant memories for the hundreds of members who have Played Away with The Questors over the years and gives those who have not an idea of what it's like.

Chapter 18

The Questors on the Fringe

by Michael Green

The Edinburgh Festival Fringe is unique. No other occasion offers anything like the same concentration of drama, with nearly a thousand separate shows jostling each other in the space of three weeks (and most of them performing within an area little more than a mile square). Not to mention the official festival, which runs at the same time, with its international stars and famous companies. No wonder that success at Edinburgh can bring rewards not available anywhere else. For one thing, there is a splendid chance to be noticed by the world's press and other media, who are concentrated in Edinburgh for the Festival. Shows which would not stand a hope of being reviewed in London may be written up by a dozen papers and the cast interviewed on radio and television. A great part of the theatre world visits Edinburgh during the Festival and companies have a good chance of getting their name known where it counts, among people who like going to the theatre and people who matter in the theatre.

To be weighed against these tempting possibilities is the enormous expense involved and the fierceness of the competition. Every year something like a dozen companies go home because not one person ever comes to see them, which isn't surprising considering the public have hundreds of shows to choose from. One aspiring author travelled 400 miles to see the première of his play, only to find he was the only person in the audience, so he solemnly sat there and applauded loudly by himself at the end (he denies he called "Author! Author!").

However, this jungle atmosphere does make Edinburgh a wonderful training exercise. Companies learn to create their own theatre under the most unpromising conditions. In a world far removed from the cosy atmosphere of a Little Theatre, with its regular permanent playhouse audience, companies rapidly learn skills in publicity, promotion, public relations, front of house and administration. Most of all, perhaps, they learn to keep fighting, to bite back the bitter disappointment of getting audiences of six or seven every night. And if they overcome all the obstacles and triumph, there is no success like an Edinburgh success. Suddenly the company is the toast of the city and total strangers see the sweatshirt and stop members of the company in the Royal Mile with "Hey, I did enjoy your show last night".

The Questors has tasted both triumph and (partial) failure at Edinburgh. However, success on the Fringe is not entirely to be measured in box-office returns or favourable notices and some shows, unsuccessful on paper, paid dividends in lessons learned. Much of the value of Edinburgh is as a tough school which sharpens up those who attend.

The first venture to Edinburgh was with *The Coarse Acting Show* in 1977. It went almost by accident, largely because I thought another company might be pinching our ideas at Edinburgh. However the show was an immediate success and the rapturous reception is described more fully in the chapter on Coarse Acting and The Questors.

Two years later, in 1979, the company returned with *Coarse Acting Two* (and the publicity slogan, "Just when you thought it was safe to go back into the theatre..."). This was even more successful than its predecessor, transferring to the Shaftesbury Theatre in London's West End. Neither of these two productions was an official Questors venture and they had to finance themselves by borrowing, although both made big profits.

In 1980 came what is still regarded as The Questors' greatest artistic success in Edinburgh. This was Tony Rushforth's promenade production of Strindberg's *The Ghost Sonata*, in a tour organised by Barbara Emmet. Once again, official backing was refused (although the show had run very successfully in our own Playhouse) and the company had to finance itself. However, critics in Edinburgh raved about the production and within a few days it had become one of the Edinburgh 'cult' shows and was playing to full houses. The venue was a converted church in Morningside, which provided a perfect atmosphere for this macabre play, the dying sun shining through the stained glass windows as the show began. Afterwards, the audience was invited to have coffee and discuss the production with the cast.

"One feels that one has experienced the definitive performance", wrote *The Scotsman*.

The Ghost Sonata was accompanied by another Questors show, *The Gentle Art of Seduction*, by David Pearson. This was a late-night revue which had already been seen at Mattock Lane, and it was enthusiastically received by good audiences. Thanks to the success of both shows a profit of £800 was made, and placed in a special fund to help future touring companies from The Questors.

So far, so good, with four hits out of four shows in three tours. Perhaps it was too good to last and in 1982 came The Questors' first tough trip. Ironically, it was the first tour sent up with official financial support. The play chosen was James Saunders's *Hans Kohlhaas*, which originally had a very successful Studio première in the Stanislavsky Room some years previously, but which had not had the success it deserved when performed professionally. It was based on the legend of the 17th Century German horse-dealer Kohlhaas, whose obsessional efforts to secure justice over the sale of two horses threw the whole country into war and rebellion. The venue was excellent, Carlton Studios, a small cinema and restaurant near the Royal Mile, but The Questors fell victim to an experiment by the Festival Fringe organisers, who persuaded us and other companies to play in the week preceding the official opening of the Festival. Thus The Questors, in common with many other companies, had poor houses during that first week and the tour lost money, although the production was highly praised by *The Scotsman* and other papers. One performance was actually cancelled because there were fewer than six in the audience, an example of how tough the Fringe can be.

In addition to *Hans Kohlhaas*, Questabout, our schools touring company, played a very successful morning show for children, Don Kincaid proved popular with his late-night guitar performances and I performed my own illustrated lecture on Coarse Acting.

Our next venture to Edinburgh was in 1985, with Geoff Webb's original comedy, *Foul Play* (earlier performed at The Questors in the Studio under the title *Fair Play*). A small-scale intimate piece, based on improvisation by the cast, it was perhaps better suited to a studio theatre than the venue at Edinburgh. This was the Pleasance Theatre, quite a large conventional playhouse, complete with proscenium arch. In fact, audiences were good by Fringe standards (the average audience over all Fringe shows in 1988, for instance, was only 14 per performance), but because it was an expensive venue The Questors lost money, although some valuable lessons were learned.

Foul Play was officially backed by The Questors but another unofficial tour followed the next year (1986). Helen Walker and a small company took up Geoff Webb's adaptation of Ödön von Horváth's novel *The Age of the Fish*, under the stage title **Cold Times**. This was probably The Questors' most difficult tour. An original offer of a good venue having fallen through, the company was forced to hire an evil-smelling building on the edge of a slum clearance area. It was promptly nicknamed The Armpit and was so dirty that most of the first weekend was spent wiping unpleasant stains off the stairs. Undismayed, the cast and crew fought their way through with praiseworthy determination. The place was so unfashionable and so far out it was obvious that audiences would not come easily (in fact, a one-man show playing at the same venue consistently played to an audience of two, one of whom was the performer's wife). But everybody struggled to raise an audience with intensive leafletting at other venues and propaganda in the Royal Mile, the traditional Edinburgh methods of getting them in when times are bad.

So in the end, attendances, though small, were respectable by Fringe standards, and only a small loss was recorded. Artistically, the show was a great success, being well received by critics from several papers, and audiences were enthusiastic, often staying behind to discuss the play.

After this there was a gap of two years until 1988, for which I, as the oldest Edinburgh campaigner, was asked to organise a special effort. No fewer than four plays were taken: **The Brick**, by Nigel Swain (runner-up in our 1987 Student Playwriting Competition), directed by Peter Whelan; Steve Fitzpatrick's adaptation of Aristophanes' **Wealth**, which had played previously in the Studio; **Coarse Acting Strikes Back** (a mini-version of the previous successes, directed by myself); and **State of the Art**, by B F Herst, winner of the 1988 Student Playwriting Competition, directed by John Davey.

It was easily the biggest touring venture ever launched by The Questors, with well over 100 people involved. A good venue was secured at Old St Paul's Church Hall, just off the Royal Mile, and within this rather dour, typical church hall a new mini-theatre was created, wiping out all traces of what the building had been. Cast, crew and front-of-house all pulled together magnificently, and most of the company found themselves doing two or even three jobs. Everybody agreed the spirit was superb. A dedicated team ran a refreshment buffet thirteen hours a day and a huge publicity blitz was launched, including a vast yellow and blue Questors banner which dominated the

Royal Mile and was featured on television.

Fortunately, the hard work was rewarded. No other Questors project had ever attracted so much concentrated national attention. *The Brick* was the subject of a half-page in *The Guardian*, who called it "the most politically significant play of the Festival", and a third of a page in *The Independent*. The success of *The Brick* was due in no small measure to its topicality. Author Nigel Swain drew upon his experiences as an Army officer in Belfast to paint a picture of urban guerilla warfare in mainland Britain in future years with terrifying authenticity. He himself played the leading role of the tormented undercover man, under pressure from all sides. As a result, Nigel became the most-interviewed actor on the Fringe.

The Times said of Coarse Acting: "if only all bad acting was as funny as this". Altogether something like 25 mentions in the national press were recorded, as well as those in Scottish papers and on national and local radio and TV. Both *The Brick* and *Coarse Acting* had full houses on some evenings, while *Wealth* registered persistently large audiences and became one of Edinburgh's most popular late-evening shows. *State of the Art* drew the short straw, opening in Week Three when interest flags and despite a good review in *The Scotsman*, audiences remained small. However, company morale stayed high and in the best Fringe tradition they 'fought it'. So The Questors was generally reckoned to be among the most successful companies of the 1988 Festival. And the venture actually made money—a profit of nearly £2,500. As tenants of the hall, we sub-let to several other companies and a spin-off from the venture was the contacts we made this way. In particular, we welcomed another Little Theatre, the Garrick, of Altrincham, and a close friendship ripened as we both struggled under the uncertainties of the Fringe.

The Questors is now firmly committed to Edinburgh and we have built up a great deal of experience and expertise. It is hoped to take more tours there in future. As token of our commitment, since 1985 The Questors has been a corporate member of the Festival Fringe Society, the body which organises the Fringe, and, when possible, representatives attend the annual meeting of the Society, held during the Festival. As a member of the Society, we have a say in how the Fringe is run and in the election of officials and we have established good relations with those who run it (the secretary of the Fringe Society was responsible for letting us have our splendid venue at Old St Paul's, where he is church secretary). So besides attending the Fringe, we are part of the organisation and hope to continue to play an active role.

Chapter 19

IATWs: Some Personal Reminiscences

by Alfred Emmet

Internationally, The Questors has always played a key role in the development of the amateur theatre movement, and participated in the formation of the International Amateur Theatre Association, back in 1952. The Questors later co-operated with IATA in organising an International Technical Symposium and in 1987 hosted an IATA seminar on Directing Theatre in the Round. The Theatre first played host to a visiting foreign company in 1947, when a Dutch company from Buscum gave a single performance. Several other foreign companies have played at The Questors since then, two of the more memorable of which are discussed in Chapter 22. In the 40th Anniversary year (1969), the first of six International Amateur Theatre Weeks was held at The Questors Theatre. This aspect, like so much of the history of The Questors, is really Alfred Emmet's story and he tells it in his own inimitable way in this chapter.

The Start

I ASKED FOR IT! The idea came to me in a flash at an IATA (International Amateur Theatre Association) Congress in Hamburg in 1967, where there was much talk of International Drama Festivals, the usual concept being of theatre groups coming to some festival venue, usually with a one-act play, performing it once and then going home again. It struck me that at The Questors, with our own theatre, we were in a unique position to host something more interesting: three carefully selected top quality groups from foreign countries would be invited to Ealing for a week, each giving two performances of a full-length play. The members of the groups would stay for the week in the homes of members of The Questors. This would be a real sharing of a week of theatre.

So I returned to The Questors and reported with enthusiasm on this idea: an International Amateur Theatre Week (avoiding the use of the rather debased word 'Festival'). "OK", said The Questors, in their usual way, "Get on with it". As I said, I asked for it!

I soon found that the idea was appealing and countries were eager to participate, France was the first shot. I was invited to be a guest at the final of the competitive French amateur theatre festival at Aix in the French Alps. The hospitality was generous, the scenery delightful, the fondue memorable, the formal speeches endless, the dramatic fare disappointing and traditional. This was supposed to be the best that France could offer; it was much the same as in any reasonably proficient British amateur group except that it was in a foreign language. That was hardly the idea. We were looking for something more exciting or it would not really be worth while. Doubts began to arise. Had the idea been no more than a dream?

I explained as tactfully as I could to my host that I was really looking for something a bit more adventurous, more special. He put me in touch with a group in Lyon and I arranged to visit them.

I should explain here that my job entailed occasional visits to Sri Lanka, and I discovered that with a scheduled flight air ticket it was possible to stop over *en route* as often as one wished and also to make diversions of such and such a percentage of the direct flight mileage without any additional cost. I was to take full advantage of this on journeys to and from Colombo. British Airways unwittingly made many material contributions towards the costs of our IATWs!

January 1969 saw me flying via Lyon and Venice (for Chioggia) to see the work of possible groups. I had been told that the Lyon group (Théâtre du Béguin) was somewhat *avant garde*, and *avant garde* it certainly was. I didn't understand a word of it. But there was something about the almost frenetic dedication with which the group's leaders approached their work and their undoubted imaginative and inventive quality that impressed me. We talked long into the night and when the next morning I was sent off to look round the town and returned to my hotel to find that in my absence my bill had been paid, it was a first example of the generous hospitality I was to receive everywhere in the course of my quests.

At the airport, a 'one-little-plane-a-day' set-up, we talked again over coffee until we realised that the flight had been called some minutes before and all the other passengers were already aboard. It was to cries of "Vite! Vite!" by all the airport staff that I rushed through the barrier and across the tarmac, escorted by an official. Halfway to the plane I suddenly realised that I had left my briefcase in the coffee lounge, so I turned and ran back. By now the entire airport was alerted to this mad English-man and I had no difficulty in re-crossing the barrier to retrieve the briefcase. I set off again at a sprint to the plane to redoubled, but by now rather amused, cries of "Vite! Vite! Vite!" (for God's sake, I was running, wasn't I?). This was the first of many near-misadventures that were to dog my travels.

I arrived in Venice in thick fog. My host had driven from Chioggia to meet me with his young son, who had a few words of English, but the fog thickened and the only way to proceed was for the son to walk in front of the car with a white handkerchief. This rather hindered conversation on the hour-long journey, as my host knew no English and I no Italian. I found that arrangements had been made for a performance of their current Goldoni play to be given in a local hall to an audience of one—myself. This was played with such infectious verve and spirit that the language problem really seemed no barrier to enjoyment, and I invited them on the spot, to the great delight and excitement of the company.

Having fixed one more or less traditional production, it was easier to accept the *avant garde* of Lyon. The IATW had been scheduled for September; two up and one to play!

In March I returned home via Czechoslovakia. It was only a day or two before leaving Colombo that I cabled to Kit : MEET ME PRAGUE MONDAY STOP BRING MONEY. Kit dutifully organised foreign exchange and booked her flight to Prague where she arrived on that Monday without the slightest idea what time I was likely to arrive or, indeed, where I was coming from. Nobody could have been more surprised, or relieved, when after some hours of waiting, I walked off a flight from Rome! In Czechoslovakia, after discussions with very friendly officials, tours of Prague and a theatre visit, we were put on a local flight to Brno to meet the Studio Josefa Skrivana, the theatre group put forward by the Ministry. Here we did have a little language difficulty until Kit remembered a little schoolgirl German with which we managed some communi-cation, with the help of much excellent Moravian wine. We were not able to see a performance by the group but we learned and saw enough to convince us that it would be well deserving of an invitation, and their official permission to travel was already assured. So the programme was complete.

The result was a fascinatingly varied and very high standard week of theatre: The Little Theatre of Chioggia in Goldoni's locally written comedy, *The Squabbles of Chioggia*, charming, vivacious and skilful (it had been in their repertoire for 15 years); Théâtre du Béguin in three short pieces created with the group, experimental, puzzling, but eye-opening; and Studio Josefa Skrivana in *The Near and Dear*, the English title adopted for a satirical farce about relatives gathered for a funeral, a quite brilliantly stylish and amusing production with a witty set. Each night after the performance the groups all had supper together in the Shaw Room and when the tables were cleared there were no signs of international barriers during the singing and dancing that followed.

The Search is on Again

It was immediately decided that we must have another IATW in 1971, and so, on the way to Colombo again in March 1970, I visited a group in Rapallo, which seemed to have an interesting programme. I watched a rehearsal of Arrabal's *The Cemetery of Cars*. It was too unfinished for me to be able to assess it and anyway if we had an Italian group, we would prefer to see it in an Italian play. It was clearly an adventurous group, however, and we agreed to keep in touch.

Two months later, on my way back from Sri Lanka, I visited Basle and Karlsruhe. The charming little group in Basle was clearly not IATW material. In Karlsruhe, I went to see the Sandkorn Kellertheater. This was a very publicity-minded group. I was immediately rushed off for a radio interview and a meeting with the local press, finding myself built up as some kind of VIP in order to boost the group's local image. The play, a Soviet comedy by Valentin Kataev, *Squaring the Circle* (which we had done at The Questors in 1942), was presented in their tiny cellar theatre, quite well done but not itself a suitable choice. Later that year, having heard that the group was presenting *Herr Mockinpot* by the prestigious Peter Weiss, a play then unknown in England, I decided to see them again and a visit to Munich for a television programme about The Questors provided the opportunity. *Herr Mockinpot* proved a sad disappointment, both the play itself and the production, in a rather forced 'experimental' style.

A member of the group had promised to call for me the next morning and drive me to the station to catch my train to Frankfurt. Remarkably, I had breakfasted and packed and was ready waiting in the hotel lobby at the appointed hour, but there was no sign of my friend. The minutes ticked relentlessly away, but still no sign and my apprehension was rapidly increasing. At last, half thinking I had already left it too late, I summoned a taxi, left a message with the hall porter, and leapt into it. Had I known the German for "Vite! Vite!" I would have hissed it all the way to the station. A frantic rush got me onto the platform just as the train was drawing in. (Later, a letter of apology from my intended chauffeur confessed that he had forgotten all about it.) Phew!

The second IATW was now only ten months away and I was drawing blanks. It was decided that it would be a good idea to invite again one of the three groups that had appeared before, partly because it might mean that the initial ice would be broken more quickly, so an invitation was sent to Czechoslovakia for the Brno company and this was accepted.

Having heard of a group in Paris that sounded more interesting than any I had seen in Aix and less outré than the group from Lyon, I flew over to Paris in January to see Le Cercle d'Art Populaire in Sartre's *Les Troyennes*, performed in appallingly difficult conditions. This was well directed, had a quality and style which seemed to me particularly French and was a good choice of play; most of the audience, even if not understanding French, would at least have some general idea of the gist of Euripides' original.

The following month I set off on another European tour to find a third group. I have not the space here to recount all the hair-raising experiences of that tour. First of all to Rapallo, where I saw a performance of Ugo Betti's *The Queen and the Rebels*, which might seem a good choice of play. Unfortunately the standard of performance, in a miserably makeshift hall, was indifferent. From Rapallo I was headed for Lugoj in Romania where I was to see a group that had been highly recommended to me by a friend in England. This involved a train journey to Milan, a flight to Belgrade and a train journey from there to Timisoara. The distance from Belgrade to Timisoara is only about 80 miles and I had reckoned on arriving in good time for dinner. But that, it seems, is not the way with international train travel and after sitting about in various places for literally hours for no apparent reason, it was well after midnight when we pulled into Timisoara. "Would I be met at this hour?", I wondered, "and if not what the hell will I do?" I need not have worried; a charming lady interpreter had been laid on to look after me throughout my stay, and there she was to take me to my hotel.

During the next two days I sat in the theatre of the Lugoj House of Culture while the theatre group performed for me its entire repertoire of three full-length plays, the idea being that I could then choose any one of them. One was a modernist political piece which was quite incomprehensible (the fact that the author was sitting beside me explaining in whispered French what was going on made it more rather than less difficult); one was a farcical comedy in which great play was made of a bowler hat (''le melon'', as my companion kept referring to it, which had me confused as I had not realised that 'melon' is French for bowler hat); the third was a brilliant company piece about Christopher Columbus, full of witty humour and exciting theatre. I was able to invite them on the spot and so (I supposed) we had the programme complete for the following September.

The groups were due to arrive on Saturday 18th September. Late on Friday 3rd, we received a telegram from Bucharest: TWO PRINCIPAL ACTORS UNAVAILABLE WOUNDED STOP IMPOSSIBLE PARTICIPATION THE POPULAR THEATRE OF LUGOJ REGRET PRESENT OUR APOLOGIES.

The events of the next five days were reported in a News Sheet sent to all the IATW helpers:

"A telegram was sent off on Sunday 5th September urging reconsideration even with another play (such as the one about the 'melon') particularly in view of the worldwide publicity for Romanian participation through the IATA.

"Meanwhile a German group from Hamburg was invited by telephone to consider whether they could come in place of the Romanians. They asked for 48 hours for consideration.

"On Monday morning (6th) we contacted the Romanian Embassy, who promised to telegraph through their own channels. On Monday evening, at the expiry of the 48 hours, another phone call to Hamburg elicited the reply that the company could come, but their play lasted only 55 minutes. We obtained 24 hours' grace to give the Romanians the opportunity to reply. On Tuesday evening there was still no reply from Romania and in a telephone conversation with Hamburg it was agreed to make 1 pm the following day the absolute deadline. Meanwhile we had an indication that an English company could play to make up a double bill with the Germans.

"On Wednesday morning it was agreed with the Romanian Embassy that if there was no reply from Romania by 1 pm we were justified in settling with the Germans. A telephone call to Bucharest was booked. The English company dropped out. At 1pm the call to Bucharest was cancelled and an attempt was made to telephone Hamburg to arrange for them to come. As it happens there was difficulty in getting Hamburg on the phone and before we could get through Bucharest was on the line.

"The outcome, ten minutes after the deadline, was that the Romanians are coming, but with another play."

This was confirmed by telegram from Bucharest on the 10th. We heaved a great sigh of relief, while wondering what the other unknown play would be like. But relief was short-lived, for on the 14th a further telegram from Bucharest said that the difficulties in remaking a production which had been off the stage for a long time were insurmountable and participation was impossible.

Four days later the other two groups arrived. Although truncated, we had a very successful week; both shows were notable for their distinctive styles (the Czechs' hilarious production of Chekhov's **The Bank Anniversary** being particularly popular); the Czechs and the French got on extremely well with each other and with us, and the international camaraderie was outstanding. We had however been saddened to learn that one of the Czech actresses, Alena Hradilova, had been refused permission to leave the country at the last minute and had had to be left behind in tears on the station platform at Brno.

Third Time Lucky

So now the search began for IATW No 3. It was to be in April 1974. I was due to visit Sri Lanka again in March (1972). *En route*, I visited Poland, Czechoslovakia, Hungary and Yugoslavia. This time there were no mishaps (or hardly any) but it was a tour of very great interest. In Poland I was the guest of the Polish Socialist Students Association (Student Theatre was leading the way in Poland), and my purpose was to meet Theatr STU in Cracow, recommended as perhaps the leading student theatre group in the country. Their performance of **Sennik Polski** was put on specially for me in the Cracow Students Club. The play itself, a collage based on Polish myth and legend, might have a limited appeal, but the performance was stunning, theatrically exciting and very visual. Clearly Theatr STU would be a strong candidate for IATW3.

The visit to Czechoslovakia was chiefly to cement relations and explore possibilities of The Questors taking a show to Czechoslovakia sometime. Even so I was given the usual VIP treatment. These Eastern bloc countries spare no money to look after their guests on a scale that can seldom be returned, as greatly embarrassed the late Sir Peter Daubeny during his historic World Theatre Seasons at the Aldwych Theatre from 1964 to 1976.

In Hungary I was taken to visit four very different groups: a brilliant school drama group (I tried hard but unsuccessfully to persuade ILEA to bring them over for a tour of English schools: it would have been an eye-opener); a curious presentation of Hungarian ballads, the first fifteen minutes of which consisted of a silent, ritual painting by one actor of the faces of three others, followed by a recital of text directly to the audience without movements of any kind whatsoever (I was told that the amateur theatre, rejecting traditional modes, was going back to basic origins to find a new way); a university group in what amounted to a workshop type exercise in choral speaking based on a well-known poem; and finally a 'Miners Theatre' group which I saw in rehearsal under the direction of their Olympic-standard athlete leader, who imposed a strong discipline but with emphasis mainly on externals. (The group's recent repertoire was astonishing, including Aristophanes' *The Birds*, Jarry's *Ubu Roi* and a studio in-the-round production of an adaptation of Agatha Christie). I felt that if these were the best they could show me, I was not likely to find a Hungarian group for 1974, although there had been signs of an interesting potential (fully realised some years later in visits by Studio K).

In Belgrade a number of visits had been arranged for me, in one or two cases special performances being put on. Here also the amateur theatre was mostly young and student based. This results in a continuous turnover of membership of any group and consequent fluctuation in standards. The aim of most amateurs, I was told, was to gain a foothold in the professional theatre. In these circumstances very few groups would be able to take any long term view of their work. A straining after the 'experimental' and *'avant garde'* for its own sake was an impression then, reinforced on a later visit. While I gained considerable insight into Yugoslav theatre, I found no likely candidate for IATW; earnest, adventurous work, but little talent.

Leaving Belgrade was not without its moment, if hardly of serious crisis, at least of humour. Passing through security at the airport, the security officer opened and rummaged through my briefcase.

"Ah! Pilce", he said, with what seemed to me a note of triumph in his voice, holding up a small bottle of sleeping pills which he had discovered. A trifle nervously I tried to explain what they were and he seemed to be satisfied. He continued to rummage.

"Enny gunce?" he asked a little sharply.

"I beg your pardon?" I said, not understanding.

"Enny gunce? Bang-bang-bang-bang", with mimed accompaniment.

"No" I replied aloofly, "I don't have any guns." And with that he let me through.

That was the end of that reconnoître, although I was later to visit again Le Cercle d'Art Populaire in Paris, the group from IATW 2 to be invited back for a second visit.

It was also thought that it would be a good idea to include one English-speaking group in IATW 3. The Festival of American Community Theatre was to be held in June 1973, so I decided to fly to Lincoln, Nebraska, for the weekend to see what was on offer, my fee for speaking at their gala dinner paying for most of my flight cost.

The work was mostly what one would see in any English Little Theatre, but there was one piece, Arthur Kopit's *Indians*, played by the Tulsa Little Theatre, that had a particularly distinctive flavour. Not only did this seem a very typical American play, but the performance had a unique 'plus' in that the parts of the Indians were performed by Red Indian members of the company.

This virtually settled the programme, and we were all set for another highly successful IATW, though not without a last minute panic because the Poles had not got their visas through two days before they were due to leave and we had to engage the urgent assistance of the Foreign Office in London (spelling out the full names of 20 Poles over the phone was no joke). Even then, we learned, there had been problems because on the actual day of departure the airline had only written out half their tickets when the lunch break intervened. The Americans, who had had to slave away for months to raise the funds to pay their fares (unlike Eastern European countries where travel costs were paid by the State), coupled van Italie's *Interview* with *Indians* which is a shortish play. The theatrical excitement of the Week was Theatr STU's quite stunning production of *Sennik Polski* (The Polish Dream Book). It was a pity that the Americans were, understandably, so keen on sightseeing and shopping that they made but little of the opportunity to share the overall experience with the European groups.

On to Number Four

Theatr STU would have been the obvious group to be invited back for a second visit in 1976, but it had in the meantime become fully professional. In fact, their performance at The Questors was their last as amateurs. So I had to start from scratch.

Sweden was the first port of call, in November 1974. The occasion was the 10th Anniversary Congress of the Amateur Theatre Federation of Sweden, to which I had been invited. There were included performances by what I understood to be leading amateur groups. A most interesting weekend during which fruitful contacts were made, but no obvious candidate for IATW emerged.

In March I was invited to a conference at the Catholic University of Lublin (KUL) in Poland, to celebrate the 5th anniversary of the student group's 'Visual Stage'. There is of course some political division between the independent Catholic University and the Socialist Students Association. Nevertheless the latter hosted me generously in Warsaw and put me on a coach for Lublin. It struck me as ironic that the Catholic university, the Communist Party Headquarters and a modern luxury hotel stood adjacent to each other in the same street (a further irony was that if the Catholic University had been Socialist instead of Catholic, I would probably have been accommodated in the luxury hotel instead of the rather spartan students' hostel!). The talks and discussions were outstandingly stimulating, and the three (wordless) productions I saw were truly unique and visually stunning. The snags were that each show was only 45 minutes long, there were no actors in the ordinary sense, the members of the company appearing only in giant-sized masks, and the shows having to be performed in a long, narrow restricted space of great depth which could only accommodate a very small audience. I decided to leave open an invitation until after seeing other Polish groups at the Wroclaw Festival later in the year.

On my return to Warsaw the Students Association had laid on for me a performance by another mime theatre group. This was played in a large professional theatre with full stage and FOH staff, arranged specially for me with a small handful of friends of the company. There are lavish aspects of a communist economy! After the show, over dinner in a delightful restaurant, I had the embarrassing task of explaining to my hosts that I did not think the group's work, which was not very audience-oriented, was quite what I was looking for.

The search continued. 1975 was a busy year. An invitation to a week's international festival of one-act plays in Belgrade in May, again very *avant garde*, led nowhere. In June was the IATA Congress in Oklahoma, followed by the International Theatre Olympiad in Detroit and a visit to Canada Day. This last was at the University of Windsor, where I saw three productions; one of these was a find, a French-speaking secondary school production based upon some of La Fontaine's fables, brilliantly directed with the young cast by a talented teacher at the school. This was short-listed for IATW 4.

In August to a festival in Hronov in Czechoslovakia. This turned up nothing to measure against other candidates I had in mind. Wroclaw in October. The Wroclaw International Festivals were stupendous affairs. I saw 17 shows (out of a possible 35) in seven days, from twelve different countries, and all packed out with ticketless crowds at the door scrambling to get in. One other Polish student group seen at Wroclaw seemed a possible alternative to KUL, but in the course of discussion it was found that the group was going to a festival in Venezuela at about the same time as the IATW. So KUL was invited.

Before leaving Poland I had arranged to visit Olsztyn to see the Olsztyn Pantomime group of which I had heard. This is a remarkable deaf and dumb group which performs spectacular musical mimes. Regardless of their disabilities, the standard of the show was superb. I spoke to them warmly at an after-show supper to which I was invited, when I had the unusual experience of speaking to an audience who could not hear a word and were not even looking at me but at the simultaneous translation in sign language. Clearly it was not possible to invite the group to the IATW because of the impossibility of communication between host and guest and between group and group, but I strongly felt that it should somehow be brought to The Questors. Later, with the help and backing of the Polish community in Ealing, we hosted them at The Questors for a week in December 1976 (*Apocalipsis and Caprichos*).

We needed an English-speaking group for the IATW. A leading group in Dublin, The Sundrive Players, had been recommended to me. While I had not been all that impressed on a quick trip to Dublin by their *The Importance of Being Earnest*, valiantly put on in the most appallingly difficult conditions in a YMCA hall, the show they were offering us, Mary Manning's *The Voice of Shem*, a stage version of passages from *Finnegan's Wake*, was of exceptional interest. We had ourselves presented the European première of the play in 1958, when following a review by Kenneth Tynan we had never had so many people ringing up from all over London wanting to come and see it...and never had so many people walking out, bemused, before the end. It would be interesting to see how it would work nearly twenty years on, particularly with a Dublin company.

So that was IATW 4 in May 1976—Ireland, Canada and Poland. There were stories to tell. The James Joyce play required a large coffin. The group would not trust us to build it for them and as they were travelling in cars, the coffin was strapped to the roof of one of them. This was the source of the utmost suspicion on the part of the British Customs and not at all easy for the driver to explain convincingly. Theatre KUL in accordance with regulations were required to bring with them an official observer from the Ministry. They travelled by coach and at the frontier it was found that it was the official whose papers were not in order and who had to be left behind.

On the whole, IATW 4 was not the most successful of the series. There were complaints from the audience because Theatre KUL's show was so short that they felt they had not got their money's worth; the Canadian youngsters were full of complaints about where they were staying and were not the most courteous of guests, nor did they mix well with the other groups (their show was excellent and drew a nightly ovation from the audience); while The Sundrive Players' performance was a joy for the connoisseurs, Joyce proved as baffling to most of the audience as we had found before. Though the bar profits soared dramatically when the Irish were around, that is not what IATW was really about.

That was the last IATW for which I was responsible. The Polish group had to stay on a further day to catch their ferry and on their last night there was a merry party at a local, Polish-owned restaurant. My last memory of the week was of the lady Professor of Drama at Lublin University dancing a jig on the pavement outside the restaurant, to the mild astonishment of passing Ealing residents. It was a good evening.

Finale

Tony Rushforth then took over as IATW director. The group invited to return in 1979 was The Sundrive Players, whose musical version of *The Playboy of the Western World* (*The Heart's a Wonder*) I had seen at the Dundalk Festival and recommended. Tony decided to invite again the group from Chioggia which had participated in the first IATW and they brought another lively Goldoni comedy. The third place was filled by a talented group from Antwerp (Flemish-speaking) which Tony had seen in Monaco, in a richly theatrical and imaginative satyr-comedy, *The Goats*. It was a week of high standards and much enjoyment, the Irish show being so popular that an extra performance had to be put on on the Saturday afternoon. We felt only that the social side was beginning to wear a bit thin, with rather minimal involvement by The Questors' own actors. Perhaps we were losing something of the sense of occasion of the earliest Weeks.

The sixth and last IATW in 1982 finished the series on a splendid artistic high. Tony had discovered in the course of his travels a remarkable Hungarian group, Studio K, which he arranged to bring over to do a promenade production of *Woyzeck* in the Stanislavsky Room, the impact of which will be long remembered by those who saw it. This production was probably the inspiration behind Tony's own promenade production of *The Ghost Sonata*, which was such an outstanding success at the Edinburgh Festival in 1980. Studio K was invited back to the IATW with another play by Büchner, *Leonce and Lena*. Though a bit difficult to follow for those who knew neither Hungarian nor the play, it had many superb theatrical inventions.

Tony had also discovered an exciting group from Stockholm, Teater Schahrazad, who came with their stimulating and breath-taking production of *Doktor Dapertutto*, based upon the life and work of Meyerhold, the famous Russian director; this was supplemented by a workshop demonstration of Meyerhold's famous 'Biomechanics', physical exercises for the actor. To many these Biomechanics are familiar, though little understood, from widely published series of photographs. It was a revelation to see them in the flesh and in motion and really to understand the point and appreciate the beauty.

The third company was the one from Lugoj in Romania which was 'wounded' in 1971. I had maintained contact through occasional correspondence with their director, Dan Radu Ionescu, a leading actor and director in Romania, who had dropped me a hint that an invitation to London might be accepted and approved. Tony decided to take a chance on them unseen; this paid off and we had a quite hilarious and irreverent production of *The Merry Wives of Windsor*. Apart from the delight of seeing what such a foreign company made of a Shakespeare comedy, it was moving to sense the overwhelming gratitude of the members of the company for giving them their once-in-a-lifetime experience of leaving Romania and visiting England.

In sum, we had six marvellous weeks of international theatre, opening windows on what was going on in many other countries, seeing outstanding work from which we had much to learn, and creating or cementing many friendships and relationships.

And if there were some difficulties on the way, well, I said I had asked for it, didn't I?

Chapter 20

An Outward Looking Theatre

by Martin Bowley*

Although the phrase "to be an outward looking theatre" first found a formal place in the Questors vocabulary only in the 1972 Statement of Aims—and thereafter became increasingly central to the theatre's philosophy—it in many ways was no more than a re-statement and redefinition of earlier ideals and concepts. As early as 1947, 'The Quest and What it Means' stated that "we must look beyond our own immediate parochial circle to find our true place in the theatre as a whole, otherwise our work, however worthwhile, would eventually die back on itself." In an article in the brochure published on the occasion of the theatre's fortieth birthday I wrote "the greatest danger I foresee over the next few years is that we may become too inward looking—too involved with our own entertainment and instruction. The effect of such a tendency would be to cut off the inflow of new members with new ideas, and the end result could only be smugness and sterility. We must constantly be looking outwards, constantly relating our own work to the outside world."

Significantly, both 'The Quest' and the 'Statement of Aims' single out the Little Theatre Guild of Great Britain as the prime medium for looking outwards to the mainstream of theatre, and for accepting our responsibilities for extending and developing the art of theatre. Not surprisingly, perhaps, for The Questors has always played a leading part in the work of the Guild and provided much of the impetus for the formation of the Guild in 1946. As early as 1938, together with John Fernald, Alfred Emmet had sponsored a resolution at the British Drama League Conference proposing a special Little Theatre section of the BDL. That resolution was a casualty of the war, but it was during the war years that the need became even greater for

* Martin Bowley QC joined The Questors in 1962 as an acting member. He was Company Secretary from 1963 to 1972 and Chairman from 1972 to 1984. He resumed the Chairmanship in 1988.

some structure to keep Little Theatres in touch with each other, to work together for mutual improvement of standards, and to obtain adequate recognition by outside organisations.

Alfred Emmet has written that "it is not easy now to recall the sense of total isolation when working in an amateur little theatre during the war years. Each little theatre was alone in wrestling with its problems; how to obtain timber licences so that scenery could be made, clothing coupons to buy materials for costumes, petrol coupons for transport of a show to some hospital or ARP centre and, above all, how to get the wise men at Customs and Excise to agree that a particular play was 'educational' and therefore qualified for exemption from entertainments duty."

In 1946, three main factors brought together the nine founder members of the LTG. Firstly, just loneliness and the desire to find friends with common aspirations for the theatre. Secondly, the need for mutual help and co-operation in tackling difficulties and problems. Thirdly, the conviction that the little theatre movement was of importance and that its united voice should be heard in circles of power and influence—and money! The Guild was formed at a meeting at the Waldorf Hotel in London on 18th May 1948, with the inaugural conference the following day at The Questors Theatre.

The Questors served as secretary for the first nine years of the Guild's history, and on its standing committee for a total of 14 years, culminating in the Chairmanship for the year 1960-61. These were the years in which the Guild established contact with, and in some cases representation on, virtually all other national theatre organisations both amateur and professional, registered a satisfactory procedure with Customs and Excise for entertainments duty exemption, agreed percentage royalty terms on behalf of little theatres with 14 play agents, carried through the commissioning of a new play, was the inspiration behind the founding of the Charles Henry Foyle New Play Award, played a substantial role in the British Theatre Conference in 1948 and took an active part in the formation of the International Amateur Theatre Association in 1952.

John English of Highbury Little Theatre—and another founding father of the Guild—has paid tribute to Alfred Emmet's work for the Guild at that time: "He initiated most of the action and held it all together. He bore the brunt of the Guild's successful campaigns for remission of entertainments duty and percentage royalties for Guild members. He was the central pivotal point around which co-operation between the United Kingdom Little Theatres worked throughout those all important ten foundation years.''

In addition to that inaugural conference in 1946, The Questors has hosted no fewer than six other national conferences of the Guild—events which have rightly been described as ''ordeal by hospitality''. In the early years the Guild met at the Theatre in 1947, 1951 and 1959. As soon as possible after the opening of the Playhouse—in fact in June 1965—the Guild was invited to meet once more in Ealing. The theme for the conference was 'New Plays'. In addition to seeing the film ''This is a beginning'' about the planning, building and opening of the new Playhouse, delegates had the opportunity to see two of the productions in the New Plays Festival—Kon Fraser's *The Igloo* and Derek Marlowe's *How I assumed the role of the Popular Dandy: for purposes of seduction and other base matters*, and to take part in a discussion with eight writers—all of whom had had new works produced at The Questors Theatre—on what the amateur theatre can do for the playwright.

In July 1972, the Guild returned again to Ealing for a national conference, this time to discuss 'The Open Stage'. The conference opened with three performances of *The Proposal* by Chekhov by different companies using different stage forms— The Tower Theatre on a proscenium stage, Bradford Playhouse in the round, and The Questors Theatre on a thrust stage. The exercise, entitled ''One into three will go'', was intended to explore the impact of different stage forms on both directors and actors. Thereafter delegates once again had the opportunity to see two of the New Plays Festival productions—James Saunders's *Hans Kohlhaas* in the newly established Stanislavsky Room Studio Theatre, and a double bill of James Hepburn's *Time, Life, Sex and You Know What* with Tony Gariff's *The Timekeeper* in the Playhouse—the Hepburn, like the Marlowe in 1965, a play more memorable for its title than its text! Speakers at the conference on the problems, viability and limitations of open staging included Fred Bentham of Strand Electric, John Reid of Theatre Projects, Colin George then at the Crucible Theatre in Sheffield, Ron Daniels (who had recently worked at the Victoria Theatre, Stoke-on-Trent and now an Associate Artist of the Royal Shakespeare Company) and Michael Billington, theatre critic of *The Guardian*. With 153 delegates, this was the largest conference in the Guild's history—a record which was only broken II years later when, in October 1983, 48 theatres sent a total of 224 delegates to the most recent national conference in Ealing.

The 1983 conference focused on 'Studio Theatre', and delegates saw both *ESP*, an original production devised by the company, in the Stanislavsky Room and Alan Bennett's *Habeas Corpus* in the Playhouse. Speakers at the conference included Michael Billington, Peter Whelan, Bill Wilkinson—financial controller of the Royal Shakespeare Company—and Sam Walters, director of The Orange Tree Theatre in Richmond. It was a chilly weekend—the new heating system had not been commissioned in time!—but nothing could cool the heated debates, both inside and outside the formal sessions, on the rationale for studio theatres, the way in which the work there can or should feed through into the main theatre, the type of work on which a studio should concentrate and the technical facilities which a studio requires.

One aspect of the work of The Questors which would not have happened—in fact could not have happened—had it not been for the Little Theatre Guild is the English Amateur Theatre Week. These Weeks, held in 1977, 1980, 1983, 1987 and 1989, were modelled on the International Amateur Theatre Weeks which were held regularly between 1969 and 1982. Three companies are invited to bring a production to play in repertoire on the Questors stage. The director of the EATWs—myself!—chooses a theme; in 1987 it was 'Anger and After' and in 1989 'Theatre in the 80s'. Companies are selected from the members of the Guild whose work I have seen when attending conferences and seminars at other theatres. These visiting companies are accommodated by Questors members and have the opportunity to see at least one Questors production as well as the productions of their fellow visitors. To provide an element of continuity, we always try to invite back one company from the previous Week. To date, the theatres which have taken part are Bradford Playhouse, the Crescent Theatre from Birmingham, The Tower Theatre, The Talisman Theatre from Kenilworth, Bolton Little Theatre, South London Theatre Centre, the Loft Theatre from Leamington Spa, The People's Theatre from Newcastle-upon-Tyne, Leicester Little Theatre and, a newcomer in 1989, Lewes Little Theatre.

Perhaps the last word should come from 'The Quest':

"On the one hand we must look out to the mainstream of theatre. On the other hand we must look round to other groups and lend a helping hand whenever and wherever we can. It is not enough to be sufficient unto ourselves."

Chapter 21

Now We Are Sixty, 1964–1989

And what of the main body of The Questors' artistic work since 1964 and the opening of the new Playhouse? Up to and including the Playhouse 25th Anniversary in April 1989, a total of 344 plays had been presented in the Playhouse by the main acting group, with a further 137 being Studio productions, making 481 in all. (Student Group productions are excluded from all the statistics presented in this section—they are given in Chapter 23.) Of the total, 99 were new plays or English premières; 406 were full-length plays. Over half of the plays presented were by foreign authors—244—although the most popular author, by some considerable way was, of course, Shakespeare. In the 25 years from 1964 to 1989, The Questors presented no fewer than 34 productions of Shakespeare plays, averaging one every nine months. Joint second in the popularity stakes, in terms of numbers of productions given, come two modern English authors, James Saunders and Harold Pinter (10 apiece), closely followed by Ibsen with nine productions, Ayckbourn with eight, and Chekhov, Brecht and Tennessee Williams each with seven.

Relatively few examples from the English Jacobean and Restoration periods are included in the list—only 18 in all. Nine productions of plays from the classical Greek and Roman theatre (including adaptations) have been presented and seven by Eastern European authors (excluding Brecht and Chekhov). Western Europe, Ibsen aside, accounts for 44 productions in all, but with only eight authors receiving more than a single production—in particular Strindberg, Anouilh, Pirandello and Lorca. Modern American playwrights, having been largely neglected between 1964 and 1974, have subsequently been more popular; 17 plays by US authors, plus a handful of Canadian plays (notably three by Michel Tremblay) have been given productions. And the list of modern English authors is extensive, although few have had more than a couple of exposures.

The list of statistics above is of little interest on its own, although it does indicate that there is truth in The Questors' claim to present "the very best in world drama". Singling out individual productions is obviously fraught with difficulty, being essentially a subjective exercise. However, there are certain productions which stand out on many people's list of 'the best'. In 1974, to mark the tenth birthday of the Playhouse, Martin Bowley wrote the following, under the heading Ten of the Best:

"I asked a number of members who have been active for the past decade to list their ten best productions of the last ten years. It was certainly a difficult task, and that was reflected in many of the replies I received. It was also, I hope, an interesting and worthwhile exercise... For what it is worth, the eleven best—for there was a tie at tenth place—were, in strict chronological order:

1965 Sadou & de Najac's *Let's Get a Divorce* directed by Alan Chambers

1966 Saunders's *A Scent of Flowers* directed by Peter Jeffries

1967 Brecht's *Mother Courage* directed by David Gower

1968 Pinter's *The Homecoming* directed by Stephen Hollis

1968 Chekhov's *Uncle Vanya* directed by Alfred Emmet

1969 Ibsen's *Peer Gynt* directed by David Gower

1970 Lawrence's *A Collier's Friday Night* directed by Michael Custance

1971 Seneca's *Oedipus* directed by David Gower

1972 Saunders's *Hans Kohlhaas* directed by Bill McLaughlin

1972 Orkeny's *Catsplay* directed by Spencer Butler

1973 Shakespeare's *As You Like It* directed by Michael Custance

"If anything I suspect that this list goes some way to supporting my own view that there is a very real Questors style and tradition, based essentially on respect for the text... we are a writers' theatre and... our best work is achieved often by small casts, working closely together, exploring the script and seeking to discover and present the author's intentions."

In the souvenir brochure published to mark the fortieth birthday of the founding of The Questors, Alfred Emmet listed his personal 'Ten to Remember', going right back to 1929 (all ten of these productions have been discussed in earlier chapters). No Playhouse production was included; at the time (1969), Alfred wrote, "we are still so much trying to find our way and learning how to use this marvellous building, that one cannot yet plot a course through the 76 productions presented there and see clearly which are the most significant landmarks, pointing the way to future development." Twenty years later, he was invited to repeat, or rather, to update the exercise, and this forms the penultimate chapter of this book.

Of the more irreverent memories which members have related of individual productions, there are far too many to do other than scratch the surface and give a few of the more quotable examples; most of these have been corroborated by at least two people, so there is a chance that they are actually true...! Understandably, the majority of them refer to The Questors' more 'epic' productions—on the grounds that the longer the play and the bigger the cast, the more opportunity there is for disaster, perhaps, or is it that there are simply more people to remember an occurrence and turn it into a good story in the Grapevine? Related by several people is the famous 'drunken army' of *Mother Courage* (1967), the soldiers who gun down the dumb Kattrin near the end of the play as she desperately bangs her drum to warn the town of its impending doom—a scene once referred to by Kenneth Tynan as the most powerful in the entire dramatic canon. The soldiers in the Questors army, doubling other parts earlier in the evening, generally had time for at least one or two drinks between appearances and on the last night it is widely held that several could not even see Kattrin, let alone point their guns at her!

Tony Shipley remembered the first Shakespeare production in the Playhouse, *A Midsummer Night's Dream* directed by Alan Chambers (November 1964), in *Questopics* in 1983, chiefly for "a technological failure involving Titania's bower... Fred Cann (the construction supremo at the time) tried the experiment of flying the bower on several nylon lines and at first all seemed well—at least it went up and stayed up. Thus encouraged, Fred went on to try it with the added weight of a human body—his own. Again all went well at first. Up went the bower and Fred, and the crew tied off. But the nylon was stretching under the weight and Fred, still in the bower, slowly and sedately descended to the ground, to his great embarrassment and to the great amusement of the stage crew."

The 1966 production of *Macbeth* caused totally different problems. This was directed by Alan Clarke, who was unfortunately ill during much of the rehearsal period, with Alfred Emmet as Associate. Alfred recalls: "Alan had an idiosyncratic approach: everyone was corrupt, including Duncan, Banquo, Macduff and Malcolm. While I did not agree with this interpretation, I worked loyally to give effect to it while Alan was in hospital. He took over when he came out of hospital and seemed reasonably satisfied with what I had done. But then, at the final dress rehearsal, Alan changed his mind about the whole interpretation, which gave Peter Healy (playing Macbeth) something of a problem, one to which he responded nobly. This was the production that prompted Michael Hordern's remark in the Grapevine afterwards (there were several other *Macbeths* knocking around at the time): 'The best *Macbeth* I have seen this week'''.

In 1969, after the last night of the fortieth birthday production, Ibsen's *Peer Gynt*, Alfred Emmet, who had resigned as Honorary Director earlier in the year, was to be presented with a gift from the membership of The Questors, an antique desk. Needless to say, this was to be a complete surprise for Alfred himself, who was appearing in the production—along with practically every other acting member on the books. Roger Kelly, then a very new member and one of the ASMs on the production, recalls that the desk had been secreted, in its three component parts, in the old dimmer room in the prompt side walkway under the auditorium. "We had to get it out of there, up... onto the back of the stage and assembled on a truck during the curtain call and what was the first part of Sir Michael Redgrave's speech...we had to do it in about 45 seconds. And on the night before this, after Alfred had gone home, we had to rehearse this ... until about one in the morning."

1974 was 'The Year of the Streaker' and several sporting events during the year were enlivened by the sight of bare flesh in unexpected places, so to speak. The Questors did not escape this phenomenon. It happened on the first night of one of the productions in the New Plays Festival, *The Owl-Winged Faculty* by John Norman, a play whose theme, appropriately enough, was student protest. In time-honoured Questors tradition, the ASMs were press-ganged to bolster the cast during the crowd scenes, and in this particular performance, one new young ASM decided to add an impromptu touch of rebellion of his own. The audience, fortunately, had no idea that anything unscripted had happened but it was extremely distracting for the rest of the cast, to say the least. Ken Ratcliffe, playing a don who was haranguing his fellow-SCR habitués during the sequence in question, was congratulated afterwards for showing no signs of being thrown at all (he asserts that he did not realise what was happening until the end of the scene, the offending parts being hidden from his view by the other actors).

There was a further exercise in self-parody in 1985 (comparable to the success of **Fratricide Punished** in the Fifties, referred to in an earlier chapter), when the Coarse Acting company was invited to put on its famous Chekhovian spoof **The Cherry Sisters** as a late-night accompaniment to Tony Rushforth's production of **The Cherry Orchard**. With the venom for which the stage is notorious, one character actually based his costume (and some of his performance) on that of Alfred Emmet in the main production. But the Cherry Orchard cast, who came *en bloc* to the show, took it all in good part... fortunately.

In addition to the mainstream of its theatrical activities, The Questors has over the years initiated and encouraged many other artistic endeavours. There is not space to give a detailed history of all these activities, but they deserve mention here since they have contributed not insignificantly to the richness and depth of artistic experience available to members of The Questors. Although music, apart from that incidental to productions, did not feature largely in The Questors life for many years (a lack attributed by several members, somewhat irreverently and, he maintains, totally untruthfully, to Alfred Emmet's being tone deaf!), it did gradually creep in. As mentioned in Chapter 13, concerts of new music were a regular feature of the New Plays Festival 'Fringe' and musical events of one sort or another had been organised for fund-raising purposes since fairly early on. George Benn recalls one particularly disastrous 'Soirée' given by an ensemble of the Palm Court Trio ilk which included a somewhat idiosyncratic cellist who arrived something the worse for drink and who sat throughout the performance distractingly close to the edge of the stage; "that was the first and last time we ever had a soirée". A Music Club, formed in 1963 with the aim of providing a season of concerts each year "of varied character by high level professional performers", proved rather short-lived, being disbanded in 1967 because of lack of support. This was something of a disappointment and a mystery, since the Shaw Room proved an eminently suitable venue for musical events, particularly concerts of chamber music.

More successful was The Questors Young Musicians Group, also formed in 1963 to provide individual classes and group work for local young instrumentalists. By 1967, the Group had 80 members and was running 15 classes in a local school, with six teachers. The Questors Young Musicians continues to operate successfully, although the group is no longer formally connected with The Questors Theatre. The Questors Choir, directed by

Tim Godfrey, was established in 1987 as an independent choir affiliated to The Questors Theatre. The choir sings music of all types and has given regular performances in aid of the Redevelopment Fund; the Christmas carol concerts have proved especially popular.

A film society ran, somewhat fitfully, from 1963 to 1980. Originally an affiliated body, the Ealing Film Society, this was superseded by The Questors' own Film Society in 1968. The Society's chairman, Carla Field, wrote thus in the brochure published to celebrate the fortieth anniversary of the founding of The Questors in 1969: "The first season—made up entirely of silent films for reasons of economy—gave us hope and inspired with the sweet smell of success we launched into an ambitious second season"—a season which included screenings in the Shaw Room of **Lady with the Little Dog**, **Intolerance**, the Russian version of **Hamlet** and **Diary of a Chambermaid**. Administrative difficulties led to these activities being suspended in 1971. After a six-year period of inactivity, the Film Society started up again in 1977; by August 1978, according to the following year's Annual Report, it had a membership of 636 and had shown 12 films during the season. It proved impossible to maintain this momentum, however, largely because of the difficulty of finding a suitable space—not only could the Playhouse not be made available very often, but it was also not really suitable as a cinema. A year later, membership was down to 288 and the Society was finally disbanded in May 1980 having attracted too few members to operate cost-effectively.

Poetry readings have long been associated with The Questors. During the 18-year period of the New Plays Festivals, readings of new poetry formed an important element of the Festival 'Fringe'—see Chapter 13 for a list of poets who read new works at The Questors during that time. In 1986, a regular series of monthly readings was inaugurated under the general title of 'Poets at Questors', including readings from two or three invited poets each time and an opportunity for members to contribute their own readings from the floor. Art exhibitions have also been a regular feature of the 'extra-mural'—or perhaps more appropriately 'super-mural'—activities, arranged during the run of most shows for over 30 years, originally in the Shaw Room and then in the Foyer once this space was available. The artists exhibited over the years are obviously far too numerous to name, but reference must be made to Harold Elvin, regular annual exhibitions of whose ceramics were held for 15 years until his death in 1985—indeed, The Questors gave him his first exhibition of works in this medium, in 1970.

1979 was the Golden Jubilee year of the founding of The Questors. In that year, membership of the club was at an all-time high of just over 4,500, and around 150 performances were staged. Productions during the season included a sequence of five English comedies, one for each decade since 1929, and the 50th Birthday production itself was *The Beggars' Opera*. The celebrations also included an English Amateur Theatre Week, a 'Golden Oldies' party, as the members' reunion organised by Wilf Sharp was irreverently known, and an anniversary Gala. This last was arranged by George and Diana Benn and was attended by a number of local and theatrical dignitaries. Many members have recalled the most special moment of all during the evening, the standing ovation given to the Questors President Sir Michael Redgrave at the end of the performance.

In the decade since then, The Questors has seen an enormous change in theatre in this country, not least in the theatre-going habits of its potential audiences. Television, cinema, the advent of home video and the proliferation of good fringe theatres in London, have all had an impact on membership. Increased work commitments and less leisure time, which have become the hallmarks of many professions, have affected active members' ability to devote effort to The Questors on all levels. The positive aspect of these developments is that they continually force the organisation to address how it may best still fulfil the aims of 'Our Quest'. In pursuit of this aim, a working party on The Questors in the Community reported to the Committee of Management in 1987 and recommended actions for improving the accessibility of the theatre to the local Ealing community. First steps towards implementing these recommendations were the hosting of an Ealing Arts Council Festival in May 1988 and the establishment of a group to run Reminiscence Workshops for local senior citizens in 1989.

A major initiative in relation to new plays, and the first since the New Plays Festivals were abandoned in 1977, was taken in 1986, when the first Questors Student Playwriting Competition, carrying a £1,000 prize thanks to generous commercial sponsorship, open to all students in full time further education in the UK, was held. This was extremely successful, attracting over 100 entries and resulting in two exciting productions, of the winning play, *The Death of Joe Hill* by John Fay, and of the runner-up, *The Brick* by Nigel Swain. The Competition was the brainchild of Michael Green, who organised it for the first year. The success of that first Competition led to its being repeated, with equal success, in 1987 and by 1988, it was well on the way to becoming an annual event.

Another important aspect of The Questors' more recent work has been the staging of large-scale productions that the professional theatre (outside the subsidised sector) can sadly no longer afford to mount. Prime examples of these are Ben Jonson's *Bartholomew Fair*, produced by The Questors in 1986, and *The Bedbug* by Vladimir Mayakovsky, staged in 1988. The former was without doubt the largest undertaking to date; directed by John Davey, assisted by Carol Metcalfe, the production assembled a cast of over 70 on the open Playhouse stage, to most exciting effect. It also gave an opportunity to involve audience members directly in a production for the first time, as the bustle of the 17th Century street fair was recreated.

The years since the opening of the Playhouse have not been without their sad moments. Several loved and loyal members, some of whom had been with The Questors since the very early years, have died. Tribute must be paid to the following in particular: Clifford Webb, actor and director, who served as Treasurer, Vice-Chairman, Chairman and Appeals Officer, and as a member of the Plays and Productions Committee for ten years and the Committee of Management for over 16 years; Laurence Nixon, actor, director and Treasurer for many years; Pat Ferriday, Stage Manager and stalwart of the schools tours, in whose memory the Playhouse SM chair was installed; Cliff Hampton, House Manager and Chairman of the FOH Committee; Graham Heywood (Günter Heilbut), Head of Design for many years, Committee of Management member for 13 years, member of the Plays and Productions Committee and the New Theatre Committee, and Deputy Director, of whom Alfred Emmet wrote in his obituary "Günter had the most marvellous 'feel' for the theatre, more I am sure than anyone else who has ever worked at The Questors"; Archie Cowan, the first-ever House Manager, for 13 years from 1945 to 1958, who secured The Questors' first catering licence and who engineered the introduction to Guinness which resulted in the all-important mortgage in 1952; David Gower, one of The Questors' leading directors and actors in the 1970s, who served as Chairman of the

Plays and Productions Committee, as Plays Adviser, as joint Director of Productions and on the Committee of Management for ten years; Arthur Boyd Taylor, founding Chairman of The Grapevine and who served in that capacity for 22 years; Bill Wall, the first Secretary of the Grapevine, long-serving Grapevine Committee member, fondly remembered for his many original and witty contributions to *Questopics*; Ned Gethings, an acting member of 35 years standing who also wrote several plays which were produced at The Questors, including **The Pharaoh Cassidy** which formed part of the first New Plays Festival,—"one of our most vivid personalities"; Ray Moss, remembered for many fine performances, including the title role in **Brand** in the opening production in the Playhouse; Frank Smith, one of the best character actors at The Questors for over 20 years who also served as Treasurer, Secretary and Chairman, and on the Committee of Management for 16 years; Betty Ogden, remembered for many delightful comedy performances since she joined The Questors in the 1940s and who also served on the Committee of Management for many years; and Hilda Collins, Wardrobe Mistress for 30 years, whose quest for perfection was legendary—"on one occasion she sat up half the night, laboriously unpicking the machine-stitched hems of three very full skirts, returning them the next day, immaculately and invisibly hand-sewn". The links with the earliest days of all have been gradually weakened—*Questopics* has referred to the sad loss of three members named in that original list of 17 in 1929. John Ruck, an outstanding actor and The Questors' first Business Manager died in 1971; a memorial sculpture to him, by Norman Branson, hangs in the Foyer. And in 1985, the deaths within a few weeks of each other were recorded of Phil and Hilda Elliott (née Simpson), both of whom had appeared in the first production of **The Best People** at the Park Theatre.

In 1985, it was particularly sad when the beloved President of 27 years, Sir Michael Redgrave, died. He had been very much more than a figurehead throughout those years, being present at all the key events through the planning, building, inauguration and celebration of the New Theatre, culminating in his attendance, though by then very ill, at the Golden Jubilee gala in 1979. His last visit to The Questors was an occasion which remains vivid in many members' minds—the joint 75th birthday party held for Sir Michael Redgrave and Alfred Emmet on the first night of David Pearson's production of Turgenev's **A Month in** *the Country* in 1982, a play chosen because of Sir Michael's long association with it throughout his career.

Fortunately, The Questors continues to be able to attract influential theatrical professionals to serve in non-executive office. (Dame) Judi Dench, who had been a Vice-President of The Questors since 1981, accepted the invitation to succeed Sir Michael as President. The current Vice-Presidents are former MP for Ealing Sir Brian Batsford, actors Roger Rees and Michael Williams, and Alfred Emmet OBE, who was invited to take up this office when he finally retired from the Committee of Management in 1980—"the end of a Questors era". A bronze portrait head of Alfred, by local sculptor and Questors member Colin Walters, stands in the Foyer; it was unveiled in July 1981 during the run of that year's Student Group production, by Hilda Collins, in a ceremony which included the reading of congratulations from both Sir Michael Redgrave and Judi Dench.

Apart from exceptional occasions such as this, The Questors' only tangible method of recognising its particular gratitude to active members is the awarding of Honorary Life Membership, an honour which is jealously guarded and granted to relatively few. The entire list numbered only 23 at the beginning of 1989; their names were Alfred Emmet, Cyril Nairne (who, during the early years of the company's existence, generously lent The Questors many beautiful period costumes from his extensive private collection), Frank Smith, Archie Cowan, Rena Rice, Dudley Clark (who served as the Questors auditor for many years), George Benn, Hilda Collins, Gordon Caleb (Administrator for nine years from 1967 to 1976, who gave the theatre much-needed continuity through a period of radical administrative changes and who was once described as "the ever-present eye of the hurricane which is The Questors Theatre"), Clifford Webb, Arthur Boyd Taylor, Win Wright (Box Office manager for many years), Gwen Taudevin (who single-handedly organised and prepared the Sunday Teas for casts and crews for over ten years), Kit Emmet, Meg Kirby (whose Foyer Gift Stall, later taken over by Vera Robinson, has over the years raised substantial amounts of money for the Theatre), Tom Boyd, Nell Cruse (for her many years of service in the general office as Membership Secretary), Lister Beck, Diana Benn, Betty Ogden, Iris Phelps (the irreplaceable doyenne of the Properties Department), Martin Bowley and Tony Shipley. Those whose particular contribution is not outlined above have been introduced earlier.

The two chapters which round off this history, look, in a sense, both backwards and forwards. Backwards, in the analysis of productions selected by Alfred Emmet for his 'Founder's Dozen' of the last 20 years. Forwards because the future of The Questors is very much bound up with the Student Group, for it is from there that the actors of the next generation will come. The development and improvement of the artistic standards of The Questors have relied in no small measure on the continuing feedthrough of actors from Student Group to acting membership for over 40 years, and the existence of this training course must rank very highly, possibly highest of all, among those "few drops of water" which The Questors have contrived to add to the mainstream of theatre.

Chapter 22

The Founder's Dozen

by Alfred Emmet

For a brochure published to mark The Questors' Fortieth Birthday in 1969, I listed 10 productions which I thought for one reason or another represented landmarks in the history and development of The Questors. I have been asked to repeat the exercise for subsequent productions. What are the special landmarks of the last 20 years, worth recalling and recording?

In chronological order, I would start with Dannie Abse's *The Dogs of Pavlov*, specially commissioned for and presented in the Tenth Festival of New Plays in 1969. This controversial and gripping play seems an outstanding example illustrating the *raison d'être* of the long series of New Plays Festivals, surely one of the most valuable of The Questors' undertakings.

I recall the 1970 production of *The School for Scandal* rather for what it might have led to than for what it actually achieved. While not in itself a particularly memorable show, it was an interesting experiment in the use of back projection of scenery, an idea that was never followed up or developed. It is something that has too often happened, that one designer's or director's experimental idea is not followed up by others, thus becoming abortive. Back projection might, or might not, have proved a valuable line of development, but we shall never know!

The 1972 New Plays Festival saw James Saunders's *Hans Kohlhaas*, as distinguished as any in the long series of Saunders's plays premièred by The Questors. This one was the result of the unique experience of the author working with the director and actors on the rehearsal room floor before pen was put to paper (to coin an alliterative phrase). It also had a record amount of acclaim in the national press. An indifferent professional production was subsequently a kiss of death as far as the British theatre was concerned, though the play had great success on the Continent, particularly in Germany. We revived it in order to take it to the Edinburgh Festival in 1981, but there is a strange chemistry in the theatre which ensures that a revival nearly always lacks something of the *éclat* of the original production.

On a lighter note, reference should certainly be made to the birth of Coarse Acting as a theatrical genre. In November 1972 we staged The World Coarse Acting Championships. One of the participants was the RSC, with Roger Rees and Anthony Pedley, whose memorable presentation of the death scene from *Julius Caesar* is described elsewhere by Michael Green. Since then Coarse Acting has developed, most notably on the Edinburgh Fringe. Indeed, in many circles The Questors is best known for Coarse Acting!

The design of the new Playhouse when first opened provided for productions in the round. Unfortunately the collapsible seating rostra used on the stage for this purpose proved all too collapsible and soon had to be taken out of use for reasons of safety. When folding seating rostra were designed and acquired for the Stanislavsky Room (the Studio Theatre), it was mistakenly thought that they 'would do' in the main Playhouse, but they were the wrong shape; one or two productions in the round sat uneasily in the space and it began to seem as if that was no longer a staging option. At last, in 1975 the director and designer of Charles Dyer's *Staircase* found a way of successfully unifying the temporary and permanent seating. This showed the way and led to further successful in-the-round productions, though some directors, not knowing how to use the form, still fight shy of it.

The following year, 1976, saw two outstandingly theatrical productions, both by the same director, Michael Moriarty. The first of these was Edward Bond's *Lear*, a play I do not personally much go for, in the Playhouse. This broke fresh ground in its imaginative and intensely theatrical use of the Playhouse. I remember thinking "<u>This</u> is what we built the new theatre for". The second was an enormously powerful *Macbeth* in the Stanislavsky Room. Hardly Shakespearean, but in that small space the show had the concentrated horror of a black mass which was quite mind-bending. It demonstrated how, in a small area, one can achieve an intense theatricality which may become diluted in a larger space.

I remember with much pleasure the set for *Prometheus Bound* in 1977 as an example of how stimulating and exciting the very simplest of settings can be if imaginatively designed. This is a lesson which is a difficult one for designers to learn. Unfortunately, the staging was somewhat spoiled by an ugly block left in the foreground; another little lesson—this detail was simple but not imaginative. Most recollections of spectacular sets at The Questors—and we have had some—are of things fitted into a space where they do not really belong.

The Questors has hosted many foreign companies, often of outstanding quality. The most striking and innovative was Studio K from Hungary, whose production of Büchner's *Woyzeck*, presented as a promenade production in the Stanislavsky Room (1979), was a startling and never-to-be-forgotten theatrical experience. Tony Rushforth's promenade production in the Playhouse of Strindberg's *The Ghost Sonata* (1979), in part inspired by Studio K, was something of a landmark, not least on account of its favourable critical reception at the Edinburgh Festival, and was certainly a rewarding challenge to take part in. These influential productions introduced a new style to The Questors and have been followed by other promenade experiments.

1980 saw another brief but illuminating foreign visit, by the Theatre Academy from Poona in *Gashiram Kotwal*, believed to be the first visit to this country by an Indian theatre (as distinct from dance) company; this was a superb demonstration of the theatrical power of suggestion and imaginative make-believe, particularly in the mimed scenes of violence, which exposed the gory vulgarity of the National Theatre's *The Romans in Britain*, running at the same time.

Our first 'community play', *Lark Rise*, was presented in 1984, a fashion likely to be followed, in which to some extent what we call 'artistic standards' give room to community participation. This is a different kind of theatre which possibly speaks more to those participating in the game of make-believe than to the spectators. The rewards are the greater sense of sharing and the enthusiasm engendered. The Questors Theatre lends itself to this sort of show.

The 1987 production of Pirandello's *Right You Are (If You Think So!)* was an exciting theatrical reinterpretation of a 20th century classic originally written for naturalistic presentation. It signalled the need for further exploration of this field, for other attempts have not been so successful.

Finally, as a postscript, I would like to refer to the 'chamber' production in 1987 of *Lady Susan*, adapted from Jane Austen's novel—a delightful and charming entertainment demonstrating how much can be achieved by actors with so little.

P.P.S Since writing this chapter, I have seen and rejoiced at the outstanding ensemble work of the Student Group in *Fear and Misery of the Third Reich*. It is not only the Students themselves, but The Questors company as a whole that will have

learned   something   about   making   theatre   from   this
demonstration.

Looking to the future, we are still learning—and still have
much to learn!

Chapter 23

On Being a Student

The Student Group was founded in 1946 and, like almost everything else at The Questors, the concept and the drive which achieved it came from Alfred Emmet. When Alfred retired as Director of Studies and First Year Group Tutor in 1984 the mantle was ably assumed by his son David. It has been their personal commitment and enthusiasm, above all else, which has ensured the continuation of the Group.

The Student Group and its success is, arguably, one of the major achievements of The Questors. It has provided a constant flow of young, and occasionally not so young, actors to the main acting group, about one third of whom at any time will have completed the Student Course. Many ex-Students have become directors at The Questors and a fair sprinkling has gone on to take important administrative roles in the Theatre over the years. Student Group members are among the most enthusiastic and loyal Young People's Group leaders. There have also been a number of ex-Students who have gone into the profession, both as actors and directors and some of them have achieved notable success in their chosen careers. The Group's important and lasting achievement, however, remains the committed active membership it provides for The Questors.

The impetus for establishing the Student Group, as detailed in Chapter 3, was the extension of the acting classes for members set up in response to the first five-point policy statement's aim of improving the quality of The Questors' work. For that first year, the course was run by The Questors under its own steam; a group of ten (all girls) attended classes every Saturday afternoon and presented a show in January 1947, the course having been completed in December. However, it was soon clear that to offer the sort of training Alfred Emmet had in mind, it would be necessary to employ professional voice and movement tutors. The Questors therefore negotiated via the then County Drama Adviser, Robert Newton, to get a subsidy for an extended training course from Middlesex County Council.

This duly arranged, the first prospectus was issued, for a one-year, three-term, course starting in September 1947. Fees would be £1/1/= per term. The staff included Alfred Emmet as Director

of Studies and Acting Tutor, Miss Sascha Rares as Speech Tutor
and Miss Anny Boalth as Movement Tutor. On the curriculum
was acting, movement, speech, make-up, theatre history and
stage management, "with opportunities provided for students to
help with the technical work on the theatre's major productions".
The Group, numbering about 15 in all, gave a production at the
end of the Summer term, a tradition that has never varied. It
was made clear in the prospectus, however, that transfer to
acting membership of The Questors at the end of the course
was not automatic.

By 1949/50, the course had been extended to two years; the
1950/51 prospectus noted that "selected students" would be given
the opportunity to do a second year. In that year, there were 16
students in the First Year and 10 in the Second Year and it was
in this year that the February Student Group production, of a
series of one-act plays, was inaugurated, another lasting tradition. A year later, an end-of-course workshop by the First
Year Group, termed then and for many years 'Students at
Work', became a further regular feature of the Questors
programme.

Plans were made, and indeed approved by the County Council
in 1955, for the extension of the Course to a third year, to include
advanced classes in speech and movement, but this never got
off the ground, largely owing to insufficient enrolments. During
the late 1950s, the curriculum, as described in the prospectus,
became more detailed and, apart from occasional changes in
wording, it has remained the same ever since:

> "The first year's training is designed to develop the imaginative
> and creative powers of the student, largely by means of improvisa-
> tion and acting exercises; to teach them an awareness of what
> acting means and what it involves; and to establish the ground-
> work of a technical mastery of an actor's instrument. In the
> second year, while the technical work continues, there will be a
> greater emphasis on applying the principles that have been learned
> in order to bring the script to life, and two productions will be
> given by the Group at The Questors Theatre."

Following the local government reorganisation in 1965, the
Student Group was run under the auspices of the London
Borough of Ealing Education Committee (Ealing Technical
College). By the mid-Sixties, there would be, typically, 50
applicants for the 20 places on the First Year Course; the number
of places in the Second Year remained limited to 10. Many of

the names of Student Group graduates of the Sixties will be familiar to audiences at The Questors, as a large number remain particularly active members—Michael Langridge, John Turner, Jillyann Healy, Gillian Kerswell, David Pearson, Ann Bevan, Robin Ingram, Geoff Webb and John Wilson to name just a few. They were obviously good times to be a student at The Questors, as illustrated by the following account, published in *Questopics* in July 1968 as 'The Testimony of Michael Langridge':

"I turned the wind machine with my left hand, delicately varying the speed of revolution to prevent the contraption sounding too much like a coffee grinder and more like the phenomenon it was intended to create. My right hand had a piece of cotton around one finger which was attached to an insignificant fishing net draped over two poles out on the stage, and by jerking my arm every now and again I could flap the net in full view of the audience in order to convince them that the dreadful sound emanating from the wings was indeed a light-to-moderate gale. Whilst I was attempting to synchronise my grindings with my flappings I had to let forth the muted cry of a man drowning in the sea three miles away, a sound almost impossible to produce when one's arms are flailing around like something possessed.

"This sequence of events occurred during my first year as a Questors student and I was assisting backstage on the second year student group One Act Plays. The contortions described above were part of the sound plot for **Riders to the Sea** by J M Synge and on the second night I over-enthusiastically jerked my arm, resulting in chaos. The fishing net nearly came off its poles and finished in a horizontal position as if it was frozen stiff. To justify this rather sudden freak weather I turned the wind machine like a dervish, furiously trying to hide my mistake, only succeeding in making a noise like ten coffee grinders. At this point in the proceedings the cotton broke from the extreme tension and the net gracefully collapsed on the stage taking two of the cast with it. I had sufficient presence of mind to cease the operation of the wind machine and at the time noticed a distinct sigh of relief from the audience who, I was later to learn, had not heard a single line since the curtain went up...

"The last production I was allowed in during my first year was... a play called **The Children of Saturn** (by Lydia Ragosin)— a title that brings tears to the eyes of many a member even now. One incident from this play that I remember vividly happened during a scene which recreated the storming of the Winter Palace by the peasants during the Russian revolution... For some reason only known to the producer the peasants, of which I was one, had to negotiate armchairs, sofas and tables etc, which remained on stage throughout the play, even in the outdoor scenes. ...The cast of peasants numbered about 25 and before going on we had to line up outside the theatre (there were no wings in the old Theatre), sometimes in the pouring rain... Eventually we got our cue, and we filed on stage; that is to say, some of us. Most of the crowd never got there, because of the size of the stage, and remained in the pouring rain, waving their icons for the duration of the scene.''

Funding the Course has become much more difficult over the years. In 1972 the relationship with the local authority was changed to that which now exists, with the Course under the Department of Adult Education and Community Service of the Ealing Education Committee, rather than the Technical College. Fees were immediately doubled (to £5 a year) and budget cuts in 1973 and 1975 necessitated some juggling of the hours between the Student Group and Questabout, which came under the same local authority budget, to enable the course to be completed. As part of the adult education service, of course, the Student Group competes for funding with adult evening classes and over the years since then, the subsidy awarded has progressively failed to meet the costs of running what is an extremely expensive course compared with the usual evening class. The fees payable by the students themselves have therefore had to be gradually increased, although these are always limited to what it is felt an average young student can afford; for 1987/88, for example, they were £75 for the year, with concessionary rates for full-time students, the unemployed and under-19s. From 1980 to 1985, the local authority awarded The Questors a grant of around £1,500 a year to help defray the cost, but the Theatre has on a few occasions had to meet the balance of the cost of running the course. For 1989/90 the decision was taken to remove the Course from the local authority altogether and for The Questors to run it alone, thus, in a sense, coming full circle.

In 1978, an Introductory Group course for under-18s was established, to run as a one-year course, bridging between the top age Junior Drama Workshop and the Student Group proper. This group has never been part of the Adult Education service and is administered—like the JDWs—voluntarily, by members of The Questors. It has run continuously for ten years and proved invaluable; David Emmet wrote in the 1987/88 Annual

Report: "It is difficult to remember how we ever managed without this vital link between the Young People's Groups and the Student Group".

In the 43 years of the Student Group's existence, the students have presented a total of 81 productions (excluding 'Students at Work')—comprising 40 full-length and well over 100 one-act plays. The choice of play for the Student Group is always challenging and not easy to make, requiring as it does suitable parts for all the members of that particular year's group. That there have been over the years so many interesting and memorable productions is due in no small part to the meticulous play research carried out by the Director of Studies and the Second Year Acting Tutor. As for the tutors themselves, the continuity offered by having the same Director of Studies for nearly 40 years has meant that the style and content of the course has turned out actors of consistent quality despite frequent and inevitable changes of staff. Several Second Year Acting Tutors, who also direct the two Student Group productions, served for many years, however, and brought particular enthusiasm and flair to their students; among these were Pamela Richards, Michael Hoddell and Wyllie Longmore.

The Student Group maintains a particular place in the life of The Questors and has a loyal following. Indeed, there are many among the technical staff who look forward to working on the Student Group productions almost more than any other. Designer John Rolfe, for example, answered his own question, "Why do I work so often with the Student Group?" in *Questopics* in 1968 thus:

"Students' team playing has been mentioned frequently enough for Questors to be tired of hearing about it, but it remains a fact, particularly for those working in the team.

"It would be difficult for any group of people meeting three or more times a week, sharing the same interest and similar experiences not to develop a sense of understanding of each other. With students I feel this understanding is more than a conscious anticipation of each other, it is a response to each other on an intuitive level.

"This is heightened by the fact that students are more or less within the same age group. This gives students an ease of communication among themselves which is the vital spark of drama. I am fascinated as I see a play growing in the imagination of this particular age group. This was one of the most intriguing aspects of **The Crucible** (the 1967 Student Group production)... the selection of newspaper clippings displayed in the Foyer during the run. These had been collected by the cast who were delighted with the parallel between the word 'witch' in the play and 'drugs' in the newspapers. The context was different but the hysterical reaction was the same...

"There is a tremendous enthusiasm about getting the complete show on stage that one sometimes does not find in non-student productions. Students expect to help in other departments. This results in real co-operation backstage. Something of the team spirit spreads into wardrobe and workshop... and one often finds the same Questors working together with the students."

Trying to capture the unique flavour of life and The Questors as a member of the Student Group is well-nigh impossible for anyone who has not experienced it. Therefore, a graduate of the Group in that heady period of the Sixties, when the young believed they could not go wrong, was invited to contribute his memoirs! Roger de Toney, who subsequently served The Questors as Secretary for five years and Chairman for four and a half, gave the following account:

"In compiling a personal recollection of my time in the Student Group and the effect which it had on me, I have also attempted to explore the ingredients of its success. It was late 1964 when, harbouring some ambitions to become an actor, I wrote to The Questors asking to join their number. I met Alfred Emmet on one dark December Monday evening and he explained to me that my limited experience (school productions) meant that the Student Group was the only path open to me to be able to act at The Questors. I duly auditioned and was accepted to join the First Year Group in January, on the understanding that I would be required to complete the whole of the First Year Course commencing the following September. I had thus unwittingly laid myself open to five terms of a three-term course.

"The beginning of any course on any subject anywhere must be much the same. The participants, all tense, carefully eye each other up and do their best not to make an exhibition of themselves. They try to assess the style and content of the course and it takes a little while for them to commence making a contribution. The Student Group is no different, though, because this is a participatory course, one is immediately thrown into acting improvisations, strange contortions of the body in movement classes and equally strange contortions of the vocal cords in speech classes. None of this actually dispels that awful fear of making a fool of yourself in front of a bunch of strangers. Some fall by the wayside in the first few weeks; those who survive have only just begun to explore The Questors. Going through the experience of joining one established Group only to leave them after two terms, by which time I felt part of that Group, to become part of another Group did not in any way help to make the start of my 'second' First Year any easier.

"When I joined the Group my experience of acting had been all about learning lines and standing on a stage to say them. Now I was faced with detailed lectures from Alfred on the preparation for playing a role, establishing units and objectives in the manner identified by Stanislavsky in his writings on the art of acting. We undertook improvisation exercises which, in particular, asked us to display our reactions to emotional situations and, in many ways, bare our souls to the other members of the Group. Such work has of course become much more commonplace in the teaching of drama in recent years. But to me and, I suspect, the generations of students before me it was exposing us to a totally new experience and the culture shock was significant.

"By the end of the first term I had overcome some of my inhibitions and begun to feel a little more at home with the Student Group, but the rest of The Questors and its activities was another world that I had hardly entered. Apart from attending classes on Saturday afternoons and one or two evenings a week, First Year students are expected to work backstage on at least one production in the Theatre. During the earliest years of the Group, continuing into the Sixties and even after the growth in general membership which followed the building of the new Playhouse, there were many opportunities for members of the Student Group to participate in main productions. These ranged from the inevitable walk-ons, through making up the numbers to enable the New Plays Festival to go on, even occasionally to taking a significant role in a major production where younger actors were required. At the same time there were opportunities to work backstage and learn the ways of the new and exciting Theatre; at the time I joined, the Playhouse was less than a year old. I may have been particularly fortunate in being able to appear in four productions, as well as working on props and as Deputy Stage Manager for two others, but I recognise now that it was this experience, combined with my participation in the Student Group which both established and cemented my long involvement at The Questors.

"The overwhelming memory of this period of my personal

development is the great striving to reach higher standards displayed by the people privileged to be able to work in the new theatre. Youthful enthusiasm may, of course, have coloured my judgement at the time but looking back now I am absolutely sure that the 18 months I spent on the First Year of the Course developed in me the commitment to achieving the highest possible standards which is the keystone to the Questors philosophy.

"In the Autumn of 1966 I moved on to the Second Year of the Course. This proved to be a totally different experience, another culture shock, even. The involvement with the mainstream of the Theatre's activities suddenly disappeared and instead we were directed towards total commitment to a group of a dozen or so people, preparing for the two Student Group productions to be presented in the early Spring and the Summer. Every group of people develops its own particular identity and working together to put on a play is an activity which by its very nature invites closeness and intimacy. Even so, I recall that Second Year as an unique period in my life. Maybe it was just that we were the right combination of people, maybe it was the plays we were fortunate enough to be doing, maybe it was the Group Tutor, Michael Hoddell, or, more likely, it was a combination of all three. Many other Groups, although unfortunately not all, have, I understand, achieved the same spirit and the same closeness that our Group enjoyed. It is an environment which enables you to develop a real empathy, a life for your production which in some small part helps to overcome the inexperience of the actors.

"For our final production we presented Arthur Miller's *The Crucible*, not the greatest production this fine play has ever received, maybe, but an experience in theatrical participation I can remember equalling only once and never surpassing. There was no doubt, after that I was hooked on The Questors.

"The running of the Student Group, however, has not been without its traumas and crises. That same environment which can foster the closeness of a group, which I have tried to convey, can also rip it apart. The excitement generated in working on a play, the thrill of an improvisation exercise, which can get the adrenalin flowing and lead to the creation of a piece of theatre can equally turn to dissatisfaction, unhappiness or even rebellion. It is inevitable when groups of young people are brought together that there are occasions when all does not go according to plan. People leave the Group and never return, conflict develops within the Group so that it is unable to achieve its full potential; on one occasion only, however, have the problems been so severe that it looked as if a Second Year production might not take place, and even then the day was saved (by Alfred Emmet reading in the main part).

"There are also problems of integrating a closeknit group of young people with the rest of The Questors' activity. The students tend to be noisier, more extreme in their behaviour and appearance, and always pushing new boundaries; it is of course the privilege of youth. However, 'older' members find these traits difficult to come to terms with and are led down the road of questioning if the group is necessary or relevant. This is typified by the final straw comments like "do we have to put up with all the mess they make in the bar?" Young people's attitudes, aspirations and standards have changed enormously during the life of the Student Group. Clearly the style of the Group has had to evolve with these changes. It is, however, remarkable that the basic theatrical principles which always lay at the heart of the course are still successfully instilled into the current generations of Students.

"Some of the inevitable changes have been disappointing. Less and less in recent years have the students had the opportunity to participate in main productions and this has contributed to some of the divide between them and the main acting group. Far less frequently than was the case 20 years ago do we see young people coming out of the Group and establishing themselves at an early stage in the administrative life of the Theatre. Also, every so often there is the loss of a talented young person who no longer feels a commitment to The Questors and moves on.

"I doubt very much whether there can be a quantifiable assessment of the Student Group and its contribution either to The Questors or to the world of theatre at large; we can only make individual judgments. I believe that the existence of the Student Group has been a major contributor to the status of The Questors in the theatre world, setting as it has a standard for training in its chosen field. It has developed a group of people who have for over 40 years formed the 'hard core' of active members of The Questors. Most importantly it has remained faithful to the basic principles it was founded to foster and has provided the opportunity for hundreds of young aspiring actors to begin to learn their trade (be it amateur or professional). I conclude that the formation and continuation of the Student Group has been one of the most important of The Questors' achievements and it ranks very high on the list of Alfred Emmet's great contributions to theatre."

Appendix I

Productions (in chronological order)

Key
NP—New Play/World Première
EP—English Première
SG—Student Group Production
SP—Studio Production

1929/30

The Best People	David Grey & Avery Hopwood	November
Me and My Diary	Gertrude Jennings	March
I'll Leave it to You	Noël Coward	
Wurzel-Flummery	A A Milne	July
The Play's the Thing	Alan Melville	

1930/31

Three One-Acts		November
Postal Orders	Roland Pertwee	
Two Gentlemen of Soho	A P Herbert	
The Road of Poplars	Vernon Sylvaine	
A Bill of Divorcement	Clemence Dane	April

1931/32

To Meet the King	H C G Stevens	April
The Romantic Young Lady	G Martinez Sierra	
(English version by Helen & Harley Granville Barker)		

1932/33

You Never Can Tell	Bernard Shaw	December
First Annual Drama Festival		April

1933/34

EP

Dragon's Teeth	Shirland Quin	December
The Circle	W Somerset Maugham	March
2nd Annual Drama Festival		April

1934/35

The Witch	John Masefield	November
Dr Knock	Jules Romains	December
(tr. Harley Granville Barker)		
3rd Annual Drama Festival		March
The Taming of the Shrew	William Shakespeare	May

1935/36

Wonderful Zoo	F Sladen Smith	November
Captain Banner	George R Preedy	December
4th Annual Drama Festival		March
Twelfth Night	William Shakespeare	May

1936/37

The Birds	Aristophanes (tr. W H Frere)	November
The Shepherds' Play	from the Wakefield Cycle	December
Everyman	an English version of Hugo von Hofmannsthal's Jedermann	
5th Annual Drama Festival		March
The Jealous Wife	George Colman	April

1937/38

Dandy Dick	Arthur Wing Pinero	November
6th Annual Drama Festival		December
Candida	Bernard Shaw	March
A Bride for the Unicorn	Denis Johnston	April

1938/39

The Worthy Master	Pierre Patelin	October
Macbeth	William Shakespeare	November
7th Annual Drama Festival		December
Double Bill		January
Sunday Costs Five Pesos	Josephine Niggli	
The Waxen Man	Mary Reynolds	
Days Without End	Eugene O'Neill	March
Noah	André Obey	May
(English text by Arthur Wilmurt)		

1939/40

The Questors Revue	William Dann, Alfred Emmet & Lionel Locke	November
Double Bill		December
Villa for Sale	Sacha Guitry	
Marry-go-round	Sydney Box	
She Stoops to Conquer	Oliver Goldsmith	January
Arms and the Man	Bernard Shaw	April
8th Annual Drama Festival		May
Magic Carpet		July
The Happy Journey to Trenton & Camden	Thornton Wilder	
Riders to the Sea	J M Synge	
The Far-away Princess	H M Sudermann	

1940/41

	The Western Chamber (tr. S I Hsuing)	13th Century Chinese Romance	October
	Shilling Shakespeare		January
	Extracts from Romeo & Juliet		
	All's Well that Ends Well		
	A Midsummer Night's Dream		
NP	Icarus Preserved	Michael Kelly	March
	9th Annual Drama Festival		May
	The Fantasticks	Edmond Rostand	July
	(English version by Gordon Fleming)		

1941/42

Uncle Vanya (tr. Constance Garnett)	Anton Chekhov	October
The Playboy of the Western World	J M Synge	December
Squaring the Circle	Valentin Kataev	February
As You Like It	William Shakespeare	April
10th Annual Drama Festival		May
Jonah and the Whale	James Bridie	August

1942/43

	The Man with a Load of Mischief	Ashley Dukes	October
EP	It's a Family Affair (We'll Settle it Ourselves)	Alexander Ostrovsky	January
	11th Annual Drama Festival		February
NP	The Dark River	Rodney Ackland	May
	Double Bill		July
	The Bower of Wandel	Gordon Bottomley	
	The Tinker's Wedding	J M Synge	

1943/44

	Moon in the Yellow River	Denis Johnston	October
	The Cherry Orchard	Anton Chekhov	December
	(tr. Constance Garnett)		
	The Western Chamber	(tr. S I Hsiung)	February
NP	Sea Flood	Michael Kelly	April
	12th Annual Drama Festival		June
	Martine	Jean-Jacques Bernard	August
	(tr. J Leslie Frith)		

1944/45

	The Importance of Being Earnest	Oscar Wilde	October
	Comedy Contrasts		December
	The Proposal	Anton Chekhov	
	(tr. Constance Garnett)		
	Sunday Costs Five Pesos	Josephine Niggli	
	Lima Beans	Alfred Kreymbourg	
	Scenes from A Midsummer	William Shakespeare	
	Night's Dream		
	The Rivals	Richard Brinsley Sheridan	February
	A Doll's House	Henrik Ibsen	May
	(tr. William Archer)		
	13th Annual Drama Festival		June

1945/46

NP	But Now I am Returned	Eric Hutchinson	September
	Heartbreak House	Bernard Shaw	November
	Invitation to a Voyage	Jean-Jacques Bernard	January
	(tr. J Leslie Frith)		
	The Arbitration	Menander	February
	(tr. and conjecturally completed by Gilbert Murray)		
	Thunder Rock	Robert Ardrey	April
	Ghosts	Henrik Ibsen	June
	14th Annual Drama Festival		June

1946/47

NP	Diary of a Scoundrel	Rodney Ackland	September
	(from the original comedy by Alexander Ostrovsky)		
	Children in Uniform	Christa Winsloe	November
	(tr. Barbara Burnham)		
	Much Ado About Nothing	William Shakespeare	December
SG	First Student Group Production		January
	Cranford	adapted by Michael Kelly from the novel by Mrs Gaskell	
	Exercise Letter	training exercise	
	The Cradle Song (Act 1)	Gregorio & Maria Martinez Sierra	
	(English version by J G Underhill)		
	The Seagull	Anton Chekhov	February
	(tr. Constance Garnett)		
	The Playboy of the Western World	J M Synge	April
NP	Final Dividend	Michael Kelly	June

1947/48

	The Discovery	Frances Sheridan	September
	Mr Bolfry	James Bridie	November
	15th Annual Drama Festival		December
	Six Characters in Search of an	Luigi Pirandello	February
	Author		
	The Trojan Women	Euripides	April
	(tr. Gilbert Murray)		
	The Apple Cart	Bernard Shaw	May
SG	The Pleasure Garden	Beatrice Mayor	July

NP	The Pastoral Symphony	Millicent George (based on a story by André Gide)	September
NP	The Tuscan Artist	Michael Kelly	November
	By Request	an original revue by Alfred Emmet, Barbara Hutchins & Wilfrid Sharp	January
	Candida	Bernard Shaw	February
NP	Prophesy to the Wind	Norman Nicholson	April
	The Beaux' Stratagem	George Farquhar	May
	The Thracian Horses	Maurice Valency	July
SG	The City Wives' Confederacy	John Vanbrugh	July

1949/50

	The Little Dry Thorn	Gordon Daviot	September
	Othello	William Shakespeare	November
	Double Bill		January
	The Bear	Anton Chekhov	
	Christmas in the Market-Place	Henri Ghéon	
	Shadow and Substance	Paul Vincent Carroll	February
NP	Paradise Street	Antony Brown	March
	The Gentle People	Irwin Shaw	May
SG	Miss Elizabeth Bennett	A A Milne	July

1950/51

NP	The Tinsel of Athens	Lydia Ragosin	September
	The Winter's Tale	William Shakespeare	November
	By Further Request	an original revue	January
SG	Student Group One-Acts		February
	Queens of France	Thornton Wilder	
	Ladies in Waiting	Wendy St John Maule	
	NP—The Mask	Anne Ridler	
	In Search of Valour	Teresa Deevey	
	The Merchant of Yonkers	Thornton Wilder	March
NP	Poor Man's Miracle	Marian Hemar	May
	The Philanderer	Bernard Shaw	June
SG	Double Bill		July
	Riders to the Sea	J M Synge	
	The Women Have Their Way	Serafin & Joachin Alvarez Quintero (English version by Helen & Harley Granville Barker)	

1951/52

	Asmodée (tr. Basil Bartlett)	François Mauriac	September
	Two Gentlemen of Verona	William Shakespeare	November
	The Hopeful Travellers (tr. Iris Capell)	G M Martens & André Obey	January
SG	One-Acts		February
	Arms and the Man (Act 1)	Bernard Shaw	
	A Midsummer Night's Dream (Act III sc.2)	William Shakespeare	
	Deidre	W B Yeats	
	The Anniversary	Anton Chekhov	
NP	Testament of Cresseid	Alexandra Mikellatos	March
	You Can't Take it With You	Moss Hart & George Kaufman	April
EP	Edge of the World	Norman Latimer	June
SG	Corinth House	Pamela Hansford Johnson	July

	Right You Are (If You Think So) (tr. Frederick May)	Luigi Pirandello	September
	The Merchant of Venice	William Shakespeare	November
	Juno and the Paycock	Sean O'Casey	January
SG	Four One-Acts		February
	NP—Monsieur Bon-Bon	Michael Kelly	
	The Women from the Voe	Gordon Bottomley	
	NP—Tinkers' Idyll	Ned Gethings	
	A Family Comedy (1840)	Marjorie Bowen	
	Thieves' Carnival (tr. Lucienne Hill)	Jean Anouilh	March
	Crime Passionnel (tr. Kitty Black)	Jean-Paul Sartre	April
	Tartuffe	Molière (freely adapted by Miles Malleson)	June
SG/NP	Storm in a Paint-pot	Margaret Gibbs	July

	Major Barbara	Bernard Shaw	September
EP	Clérambard (tr. Norman Denny)	Marcel Aymé	November
	King John	William Shakespeare	January
SG	Four One-Acts		February
	Murder in the Cathedral (Part 1)	T S Eliot	
	The Proposal (tr. Constance Garnett)	Anton Chekhov	
	The Other Son (tr. Frederick May)	Luigi Pirandello	
	Crabbed Youth and Age	Lennox Robinson	
	The Family Reunion	T S Eliot	March
	Double Bill		May
	NP—The Secondary Wife	Dorothy Fisk	
	Happy as Larry	Donagh Macdonagh	
	A Bold Stroke for a Wife	Susannah Centilivre	June
SG	The Old Man of the Mountains	Norman Nicholson	July

EP	A Jig for a Gipsy	Robertson Davies	September
NP	Better a Dead Hero...?	R B Rigby	November
EP	The World's Wonder	Alexander Reid	January
SG	Four One-Acts		February
	Antigone (tr. Carl Wildman)	Jean Cocteau	
	Overruled	Bernard Shaw	
	NP—The Swan	Ned Gethings	
	NP—The Affected Young Ladies	Janet Dunbar	
NP	The English Captain	Lydia Ragosin	March
NP	Fanfaronade	Rodney Diak	April
NP	The Night Before Spring	Richard Whitehall	May
SG	Blood Wedding	Federico García Lorca	July

EP	The Three Honourable Gentlemen (tr.Michael Bullock)	Gunther Weisenborn	September
	Hamlet	William Shakespeare	November
	Fratricide Punished	Anon	December

	Double Bill		January
	ss Tenacity	Charles Vildrac (English version by Harold Bowen)	
	A Phoenix Too Frequent	Christopher Fry	
SG	Four One-Acts		February
	On the High Road (tr. Constance Garnett)	Anton Chekhov	
	The Cave of Salamanca (tr. Geoffrey Grimsey)	Cervantes	
	NP—The Loves of Pegeen Cuaran	Edward Percy	
	La Grammaire (freely tr. Edith Saunders)	Eugene Labiche	
	Getting Married	Bernard Shaw	March
	Penny for a Song	John Whiting	April
	She Stoops to Conquer	Oliver Goldsmith	June
SG	Noah	André Obey (English text by Arthur Wilmurt)	July

1956/57

NP	Gilgamesh	Michael Kelly	September
	The Master Builder (tr. Michael Meyer)	Henrik Ibsen	October
	Sacrifice to the Wind (tr. John Whiting)	André Obey	December
	Sweeney Todd	George Dibdin Pitt	December
	The Government Inspector (tr. D J Campbell)	Nicolai Gogol	January
SG	Three One-Acts		February
	EP—Cavallera Rusticana (tr. Eric Bentley)	Giovanni Verga	
	Holiday in Biarritz	Jean Sarmen (English version Emanuel Wax)	
	The Wedding (tr. Constance Garnett)	Anton Chekhov	
	The Golden Cuckoo	Denis Johnston	March
	Pygmalion	Bernard Shaw	May
SG	The Far-off Hills	Lennox Robinson	July

1957/58

	The River Line	Charles Morgan	September
	Titus Andronicus	William Shakespeare (mutilated)	September
	Henry V	William Shakespeare	October
	The Miser	Molière (adapted by Miles Malleson)	November
	Ten Nights in a Bar-room	William W Pratt	December
NP	The Long Spoon	Alexandra Mikellatos	January
SG	Three One-Acts		February
	The Full Moon	Lady Gregory	
	The House of Bernarda Alba (Act II)	Federico García Lorca	
	Sganarelle	Molière (adapted by Miles Malleson)	
	Summer and Smoke	Tennessee Williams	March
	Euridyce (tr. Lothian Small)	Jean Anouilh	May
SG	Time and the Conways	J B Priestley	July

1958/59

EP	The Voice of Shem	Mary Manning (adapted from Finnegan's Wake by James Joyce)	September

	Julius Caesar	William Shakespeare	October
EP	Everybody Loves Célimare	Eugene Labiche & Delacour	November
	(tr. Lynn & Theodore Hoffmann)		
	Maria Marten or The Murder in the Red Barn	Anon	December
	Marching Song	John Whiting	January
SG	Student One-Acts		February
	Antigone	Sophocles	
	(tr. E F Watling)		
	The Skin of Our Teeth (Act 1)	Thornton Wilder	
	Questrionics	an original revue	April
EP	The Scythe and the Sunset	Denis Johnston	June
SG	The Diary of Anne Frank	dramatised by Frances Goodrich & Albert Hackett	July

1959/60

EP	The Cave Dwellers	William Saroyan	September
	The Knight of the Burning Pestle	Francis Beaumont	October
	The Birthday Party	Harold Pinter	December
	The Drunkard	W H Smith	December
	The Beggars' Opera	John Gay (freely adapted by Barbara Hutchins, Eric Kirby & Vincent McQueen)	January
SG	One Acts		February
	The Crucible (Act 1)	Arthur Miller	
	Under Milk Wood (shortened)	Dylan Thomas	
	Three Sisters	Anton Chekhov	April
	(tr. Constance Garnett)		
NP	First New Plays Festival		June
	The House of Cowards	Dannie Abse	
	The Pharaoh Cassidy	Ned Gethings	
	Ends and Echoes: Committal, Barnstaple & Return to a City	James Saunders	
SG	In Search of Happiness	Viktor Rozov	July
	(tr. Nina Froud)		

1960/61

	Not for Aunt Edna		September
	The Lesson	Eugene Ionesco	
	(tr. Donald Watson)		
	Professor Taranne	Arthur Adamov	
	(tr. Peter Meyer)		
	Christopher Columbus	Michel de Ghelderode	
	(tr.George Hauger)		
	The Tempest	William Shakespeare	October
	The Glass Menagerie	Tennessee Williams	November
	(first Stanislavsky Room production)		
	Misalliance	Bernard Shaw	December
	The Ticket of Leave Man	Tom Taylor	December
	Waiting for Godot	Samuel Beckett	Janaury
	(Stanislavsky Room production)		
	Ghosts	Henrik Ibsen	January
	(tr. Norman Ginsbury)		
SG	Four One-Acts		February
	The Shewing-up of Blanco Posnet	Bernard Shaw	
	The Love of Don Perlimplin	Federico García Lorca	
	(tr. George Leeson)		
	The Lady of Larkspur Lotion	Tennessee Williams	
	Portrait of a Madonna	Tennessee Williams	
	Charley's Aunt	Brandon Thomas	March
	Sergeant Musgrave's Dance	John Arden	April

NP	Second New Plays Festival		June
	A Quiet Clap of Thunder	Peter Philp	
	The Courtyard	Antony Brown	
	(Stanislavsky Room production)		
	The South African	T R Sharpe	
SG	All My Own Work	Romilly Cavan	July

1961/62

	The Living Room	Graham Greene	September
	Epitaph for George Dillon	John Osborne & Anthony Creighton	October
	(Stanislavsky Room production)		
	Henry IV Part 1	William Shakespeare	November
	The Rules of the Game	Luigi Pirandello	December
	(tr. Frederick May)		
	(Stanislavsky Room production)		
	Lady Audley's Secret	J M Hazelwood (with Box and Cox)	December
	A Month in the Country	Ivan Turgenev	January
	(Stanislavsky Room production)		
SG	Four One-Acts		February
	NP—Looking Glass, Looking Glass	Ned Gethings	
	Bedtime Story	Sean O'Casey	
	The Only Jealousy of Emer	W B Yeats	
	Riders to the Sea	J M Synge	
	Lysistrata	Aristophanes	March
	(tr. Patric Dickinson)		
	Death of a Salesman	Arthur Miller	March
	(Stanislavsky Room production)		
	Pygmalion	Bernard Shaw	May
NP	Third New Plays Festival		June
	The Children of Saturn	Lydia Ragosin	
	Next Time I'll Sing to You	James Saunders	
	(Stanislavsky Room production)		
	The Joker & Gone	Dannie Abse	
SG	Liola	Luigi Pirandello	July
	(tr. Frederick May)		
	(Stanislavsky Room production)		

1962/63

	All productions in the Stanislavsky Room		
	Traveller Without Luggage	Jean Anouilh	September
	(tr. John Whiting)		
	Step in the Hollow	Donagh McDonagh	October
	Twelfth Night	William Shakespeare	November
	Bulldog Drummond	Gerald du Maurier & Sapper	December
	The Fire Raisers	Max Frisch	January
	(tr. Michael Bullock)		
SG	Three One-Acts		February
	Night-time for the Birds	Colin Finbow	
	Double-Double	James Saunders	
	A Painting on Wood	Ingmar Bergman	
	(tr. Paul Britten Austin)		
	Long Day's Journey Into Night	Eugene O'Neill	March
	The Comical Lovers	Colley Cibber (from John Dryden)	
NP	Fourth New Plays Festival		June
	The Things	Colin Finbow	
	Who Was Hilary Maconochie	James Saunders	
	Don't Wait for Me	David Campton	
	The Pedagogue	James Saunders	

	The Exhibitionists Are Among Us & Goodness Gracious! Is That Really Me?	William Norfolk	
	The Workout	Albert Bermel	
SG	Double Bill		July
	Antigone (tr. Lewis Galantière)	Jean Anouilh	
	These Cornfields (tr. Eric Bentley)	Georges Courteline	

1963/64

	The Rough and Ready Lot	Alun Owen	September
	The Malcontent	John Marston	October
	The Devil's Disciple	Bernard Shaw	November
	East Lynne	Mrs Henry Wood	December
	Struggle Till Dawn	Ugo Betti (tr. G H Williams)	January
SG	Three One-Acts		February
	The Bald Prima-Donna	Eugene Ionesco	
	Lithuania	Rupert Brooke	
	The Wedding (tr. Constance Garnett)	Anton Chekhov	
	Everything in the Garden	Giles Cooper	March
	Brand (tr. James Forsyth) (First production in Playhouse)	Henrik Ibsen	April
	Dandy Dick	Arthur Wing Pinero	May
NP	Fifth New Plays Festival		June
	One Leg Over the Wrong Wall	Albert Bermel	
	Is the House Shut	Dannie Abse	
	The Surrey Recruit	Fred Watson	
	Pop	late night revue	
SG	Dark of the Moon	Howard Richardson & William Berney	July

1964/65

	Hindle Wakes	Stanley Houghton	September
NP	Double Bill		October
	Neighbours	James Saunders	
	No Quarter	Barry Bermange	
	A Midsummer Night's Dream	William Shakespeare	November
NP	The Other Palace	Rodney Ackland	December
EP	Sweeney Todd	George Dibdin Pitt	December
	Quoat-Quoat (tr. Irving Pfefferblit)	Jacques Audiberti	January
SG	Three One-Acts		February
	Sganarelle (tr. Miles Malleson)	Molière	
	Great Catherine	Bernard Shaw	
	Thor, With Angels	Christopher Fry	
	The Country Wife	William Wycherley	March
	The Confidential Clerk	T S Eliot	April
	Let's Get a Divorce	Victorien Sadou & Emile de Najac (English version Angela & Robert Goldsby)	May
NP	Sixth New Plays Festival		June
	How I Assumed the Role of a Popular Dandy: for Purposes of Seduction and Other Base Matters	Derek Marlowe	
	The Shed	Charles Hatton	
	The Igloo	Kon Fraser	
	Ohh!	late night revue	
SG	Major Barbara	Bernard Shaw	July

	The Cherry Orchard	Anton Chekhov	September
	(tr. Ronald Hingley)		
	Big Soft Nellie	Henry Livings	October
	Three Plays for Moderns		October
	NP—Reflexions	Don Roberts	
	Bad Dreams	François Paliard	
	(tr. Trevor Vibert)		
	A Slight Ache	Harold Pinter	
	The Winter's Tale	William Shakespeare	November
	The Silver King	Henry Arthur Jones & Henry Herman	December
	Hecabe	Euripides	January
	(tr. Philip Vellacott)		
SG	Three One-Acts		February
	A Night Out	Harold Pinter	
	The Other Son	Luigi Pirandello	
	(tr. Frederick May)		
	The Red Velvet Goat	Josephine Niggli	
EP	Hercules and the Augean Stables	Frederick Dürrenmatt	March
	(tr. Alexander Gross)		
	(Henry IV)	Luigi Pirandello	April
	(tr. Frederick May)		
	Arms and the Man	Bernard Shaw	May
NP	Seventh New Plays Festival		June
	What Really Happened to Fidelity Hope?	Malcolm Quantrill	
	The Golden Savage	John Hearne	
	The Guy	Walter Lever	
SG	Ring Round the Moon	Jean Anouilh	July
	(tr. Christopher Fry)		

	Fairy Tales of New York	J P Donleavy	September
	A Scent of Flowers	James Saunders	October
	Macbeth	William Shakespeare	November
	Look Back in Anger	John Osborne	December
	My Poll and My Partner Joe	John Thomas Haines	December
	The Father	August Strindberg	January
	(tr. Michael Meyer)		
SG	Three One-Acts		February
	A Phoenix Too Frequent	Christopher Fry	
	The Damask Drum	Yukio Mishima	
	Poison, Passion and Petrifaction	Bernard Shaw	
NP	The Corruptible Crown	Lydia Ragosin	March
	A Cry of Treason		
	A Crown for the Strong		
	Double Bill	Harold Pinter	April
	The Collection		
	The Lover		
	The Beaux' Stratagem	George Farquhar	May
NP	Eighth New Plays Festival		June
	It Was Never So Merry, My Lord	David Shellan	
	Death in Leicester	Roy Minton	
	Private Fires	Fred Watson	
	Verse & Worse	late night entertainment	
SG	The Crucible	Arthur Miller	July

1967/68

	Phaedra	Racine	September
	(tr. Robert Lowell)		
EP	An Italian Straw Hat	Eugene Labiche	October
	(tr. Barbara Hutchins)		
	Round Holes		November
	The Stronger	August Strindberg	
	(tr. Michael Meyer)		
	EP—Out at Sea	Slawomir Mrozek	
	(tr. Nicholas Bethell)		
	NP—Kill! Kill!	Herb Greer	
	Mother Courage and her Children	Bertolt Brecht	December
	(tr. Eric Bentley)		
	The Flying Dutchman	Edward Fitzball	December
	Hedda Gabler	Henrik Ibsen	January
	(tr. Michael Meyer)		
SG	Three One-Acts		February
	Call Me a Liar	John Mortimer	
	The Mayor of Torontal	Gwynneth Jones	
	NP—The Girl	William Trevor	
	Romeo and Juliet	William Shakespeare	March
	Private Lives	Noël Coward	April
	The Way of the World	William Congreve	May
NP	Ninth New Plays Festival		June
	In Search of a Man	David Yallop	
	The Laughing Willow	Arthur Berry	
	No Camels in Israel	Kon Fraser	
	An Anatomie of Horror	late night entertainment	
SG	The Madwoman of Chaillot	Jean Giraudoux (adapted by Maurice Valency)	July

1968/69

	The Homecoming	Harold Pinter	September
	Edward II	Christopher Marlowe	October
	Triple Bill		November
	EP—Triangle	James Saunders	
	Don't Keep the Vanman Waiting	Malcolm Quantrill	
	The Picture	Eugene Ionesco	
	(tr. Donald Watson)		
	Uncle Vanya	Anton Chekhov	December
	(tr. Ronald Hingley)		
	The Shaughraun	Dion Boucicault	December
	Tango	Slawomir Mrozek	January
	(tr. Nicholas Bethell & Tom Stoppard)		
SG	Three One-Acts		February
	Collect Your Hand Baggage	John Mortimer	
	A Slight Accident	James Saunders	
	The Trojan Women	Euripides	
	(tr. Philip Vellacott)		
	Richard II	William Shakespeare	March
EP	Onkel Onkel	Günther Grass	April
	(tr. Ralph Manheim)		
	Man and Superman	Bernard Shaw	May
NP	Tenth New Plays Festival		June
	The Borage Pigeon Affair	James Saunders	
	The Appointment	Malcolm Quantrill	
	The Dogs of Pavlov	Dannie Abse	
	Pageants Faded	late night entertainment	
SG	The Caucasian Chalk Circle	Bertolt Brecht	July

	The Comedy of Errors	William Shakespeare	September
	First International Amateur		September
	Theatre Week		
	Who's Afraid of Virginia Woolf	Edward Albee	October
	Peer Gynt	Henrik Ibsen	November
	(tr. Michael Meyer)		
	Double Bill	Samuel Beckett	December
	Play		
	Happy Days		
	Black Ey'd Susan	Douglas William Jerrold	December
	The Restoration of Arnold	David Storey	January
	Middleton		
SG	Three One-Acts		February
	The Resurrection	from the Wakefield Cycle of	
		Mystery Plays	
	An Office of Profit	Peter Preston	
	Black Comedy	Peter Shaffer	
	Othello	William Shakespeare	March
	The Fall and Redemption of Man	John Bowen	April
	The School for Scandal	R B Sheridan	May
NP	Eleventh New Plays Festival		June
	The Others	David Mowat	
	All the Lonely People	David Pearson	
	The Life and Death of Almost	David Campton	
	Everybody		
	The Red-Nosed Burglar	late night entertainment	
SG	The Disorderly Women	John Bowen	July

	The Importance of Being Earnest	Oscar Wilde	September
	Conditions of Agreement	John Whiting	October
	Henry IV Part 2	William Shakespeare	November
	A Collier's Friday Night	D H Lawrence	December
	Salad Days	Dorothy Reynolds & Julian Slade	December
	Oedipus	Seneca (adapted by Ted Hughes)	January
SG	Student One-Acts		February
	Press Cuttings	Bernard Shaw	
	The Room	Harold Pinter	
	The Eunuch	Terence	
	(tr. Betty Radice)		
	The Duchess of Malfi	John Webster	March
	Double Bill	Joe Orton	April
	Funeral Games		
	The Good and Faithful Servant		
	The Schoolmistress	Arthur Wing Pinero	May
NP	Twelfth New Plays Festival		June
	The Last Emperors	David Shellan	
	John	David Mowat	
	Bleach	Arnold Meyer	
	Poor Dumb Animals	James Hepburn	
	Steam	late night entertainment	
SG	The Rivals	R B Sheridan	July

	The Italian Girl	James Saunders & Iris Murdoch	September
	Second International Amateur		September
	Theatre Week		
	A Delicate Balance	Edward Albee	October
	Hamlet	William Shakespeare	November

	Triple Bill		December
	Striptease	Slawomir Mrozek	
	(tr. Edward Rothert)		
	Week-end	Iosif Nagihu	
	EP—A Few False Slaps	Paul Everac	
	(tr. Catinca Ralea)		
EP	Ding Dong!	Georges Feydeau	December
	(tr. Alan Chambers)		
	The Strange Case of Martin Richter	Stanley Eveling	January
SG	Student One-Acts		February
	Suddenly Last Summer	Tennessee Williams	
	Rites	Maureen Duffy	
	Electra	Sophocles	
	(tr. E F Watling)		
	The Seagull	Anton Chekhov	March
	(tr. Ann Jellicoe & Ariadne Nicolaeff)		
	The Happy Haven	John Arden	April
	The Provok'd Wife	Sir John Vanbrugh	May
NP	Thirteenth New Plays Festival		June
	Candlelight and Babylon	Don Roberts	
	Time, Life, Sex and You Know What	James Hepburn	
	The Timekeeper	Tony Gariff	
	SP—Hans Kohlhaas	James Saunders	
	Steam	late night entertainment	
SG	Double Bill		July
	The House of Bernarda Alba	Federico García Lorca (tr. James Graham-Lujan & Richard L O'Connell)	
	Resounding Tinkle	N F Simpson	

1972/73

	A Day in the Death of Joe Egg	Peter Nichols	September
	A Doll's House	Henrik Ibsen	October
	(tr. Michael Meyer)		
SP	Narrow Road to the Deep North	Edward Bond	October
	The Alchemist	Ben Jonson	November
EP	Catsplay	Istvan Orkeny	December
	(tr. Mari Kuttna)		
	The Ticket-of-Leave Man	Tom Taylor	December
SP	Double Bill		December
	Playing with Fire	August Strindberg	
	(tr. Michael Meyer)		
	Transcending	David Cregan	
	Time and the Conways	J B Priestley	January
SG	Student One-Acts		February
	Marriage	Nikolai Gogol	
	(tr. Bella Costello)		
	No Why	John Whiting	
	Miss in Her Teens	David Garrick	
	As You Like It	William Shakespeare	March
SP	Slow Dance on the Killing Ground	Hanley	March
	Herr Puntilla and his Man Matti	Bertolt Brecht	April
	(tr. Paul Kriwaczek & Paul Lewis, adapted Jeremy Brooke)		
	Heartbreak House	Bernard Shaw	June
NP	Fourteenth New Plays Festival		June
	My Relationship With Jayne	David Mowat	
	Watch on the Works	Pierre Roudy & Cyril Buhler	
	Crincum Crancum	John Norman	
	Nutty Slack	late night entertainment	

	Title	Author	Month
SG	Double Bill	Harold Brighouse	July
	Hobson's Choice		
	Lonesome-Like		
SP	Triple Bill		July
	Self-Accusation	Peter Handke	
	(tr. Michael Roloff)		
	The Waiting Room	John Bowen	
	Icarus's Mother	Sam Shepard	

1973/74

	Title	Author	Month
	Relatively Speaking	Alan Ayckbourn	September
SP	Lysistrata	Aristophanes	October
	Touch-and-Go	D H Lawrence	October
	Cymbeline	William Shakespeare	November
	The Promise	Aleksei Arbuzov	December
	(tr. Ariadne Nicolaeff)		
SP	Waiting for Godot	Samuel Beckett	December
	The Ghost Train	Arnold Ridley	December
	The Cenci	Antonin Artaud	January
	(tr. S Watson-Taylor)		
	The Beasts of Tiresias	Apollinaire	
	(freely adapted by Alfred Emmet)		
SG	Student One-Acts		February
	The American Dream	Edward Albee	
	The Other Son	Luigi Pirandello	
	(tr. W Murray)		
	The Erpingham Camp	Joe Orton	
	She Stoops to Conquer	Oliver Goldsmith	March
	Rosencrantz and Guildenstern	Tom Stoppard	April
	Are Dead		
	Third International Amateur		April
	Theatre Week		
SP	Double Bill		May
	The Friends of the Friends		
	The Ancestor		
	Six Characters in Search of an	Luigi Pirandello	May
	Author		
	(tr. Frederick May)		
NP	Fifteenth New Plays Festival		June
	The Owl-Winged Faculty	John Norman	
	The Last Analysis	Ronald Bowden	
	A Borderline Case	Harry Barton	
SG	Trelawney of the Wells	Arthur Wing Pinero	July
SP	Light Shining in Buckinghamshire	Caryl Churchill	July

1974/75

	Title	Author	Month
	Forget-Me-Not-Lane	Peter Nichols	September
SP	Bits of Beckett	an anthology	September
SP	Triple Bill		October
	Escurial	Michel de Ghelderode	
	The Late	René de Obaldia	
	The Grand Vizier		
	Old Times	Harold Pinter	October
	The Good Woman of Setzuan	Bertolt Brecht	November
	(tr. Eric Bentley)		
SP	The Architect and the Emperor of	Fernando Arrabal	November
	Assyria		
	(tr. Jean Benedetti)		
SP	Directors' Shop Window		November
	After Magritte	Tom Stoppard	
	Chamber Music	Arthur Kopit	

SP	An Evening with T S Eliot	an anthology	November
	The Cocktail Party	T S Eliot	November
	Slag	David Hare	December
	Dracula	Hamilton Deane & J L Balderstone	December
	Friends	Kobo Abe	January
	Electra (tr. H D F Kitto)	Sophocles	January
SG/SP	Resolutions		February
	Transcending	David Cregan	
	The Lover	Harold Pinter	
	Bye-Bye Blues	James Saunders	
	After Magritte	Tom Stoppard	
SP	Readings from Dorothy Parker	an anthology	February
	King Lear	William Shakespeare	March
	The Price	Arthur Miller	April
SP	Directors' Shop Window		April
	Home Free	Lanford Wilson	
	The Twelve-Pound Look	J M Barrie	
	Aria da Capo	Edna St Vincent Millay	
SP	When We Dead Awaken (tr. Michael Meyer)	Henrik Ibsen	May
	The Recruiting Officer	George Farquhar	May
SP	The King	Stewart Conn	May
NP	Sixteenth New Plays Festival		June
	The Island	James Saunders	
	Funland	Dannie Abse	
	Circuses	James Hepburn	
SG	The Lady From the Sea (tr. Michael Meyer)	Henrik Ibsen	July

1975/76

	All Over	Edward Albee	September
	Present Laughter	Noël Coward	October
SP	As I Like It	an anthology	October
SP	Triple Bill		October
	The Ruffian on the Stairs	Joe Orton	
	Lunch Hour	John Mortimer	
	The Proposal	Anton Chekhov	
	Coriolanus	William Shakespeare	November
	Staircase	Charles Dyer	November
SP	Occupations	Trevor Griffiths	November
	On the Spot	Edgar Wallace	December
SP	Women's Writes		January
	Fall and Conversion of Mary	Roswitha	
	Wedding Day	Mrs Inchbald	
	Gaol Gate	Lady Gregory	
	Trifles	Susan Glaspell	
	Silence	Nathalie Sarraute (tr. Maria Jolas)	
	Lear	Edward Bond	January
SG/SP	Elements		February
	Playing With Fire (tr. Michael Meyer)	August Strindberg	
	Riders to the Sea	J M Synge	
	Lovers on the Underground (tr. Colin Duckworth)	Jean Tardieu	
NP	Seventeenth New Plays Festival		March
	Sanctuary	James Keller	
	Agitator	John Norman	
	Operation Cerberus	Michael Kittermaster	
SP	Double Bill	Federico García Lorca	March
	Dona Rosita, the Spider		
	The Butterfly's Evil Spell		

SP	Triple Bill		March
	Wedding Day	Mrs Inchbald	
	Tests	Paul Abelman	
	The Foursome	E A Whitehead	
	The Hotel in Amsterdam	John Osborne	April
	Fourth International Amateur	April	
	Theatre Week		
	Faustus	Wyllie Longmore (after Marlowe)	May
	Don Juan	Molière	May
	(tr. Christopher Hampton)		
SP	Total Eclipse	Christopher Hampton	June
	The Three Sisters	Anton Chekhov	June
	(English version by Alfred Emmet)		
SG	Pride and Prejudice	Constance Cox	July
	(adapted from Jane Austen)		
SP	Macbeth	William Shakespeare	July

1976/77

	In Celebration	David Storey	September
	A Flea in Her Ear	Georges Feydeau	October
	(tr. John Mortimer)		
	Love's Labour's Lost	William Shakespeare	October
SP	Dimension	devised by John Wilson	November
	Suzanna Andler	Marguerite Duras	November
	(tr. Barbara Bray)		
SP	The Watershed	James Keller	December
	The Colleen Bawn	Dion Boucicault	December
	Prometheus Bound	Robert Lowell (from Aeschylus)	January
SP	Man is Man	Bertolt Brecht	February
	(tr. Steve Gooch)		
	Double Bill	Harold Pinter	February
	Landscape		
	Silence		
SP/SG	The Mark Twain Show	Herbert Moulton	February
NP	Eighteenth New Plays Festival		March
	Seagull Rising	A E Ellis	
	Early Shakespeare and the Late	Michael Moriarty	
	Marlowe		
	Lykos; the Danger in the Maze	Paul Ramsey	
SP/NP	Pay Board	devised by David Fletcher	March
SP	Female Transport	Steve Gooch	April
	Family Reunion	T S Eliot	April
SP	Myths	an anthology	April
SP	MoonshiPt	James Hepburn	May
	What the Butler Saw	Joe Orton	May
	First English Amateur Theatre		May
	Week		
SP	Thurberesque	an anthology	May
SP	Random Moments in a May	James Saunders	June
	Garden		
SP	Man is Man	Bertolt Brecht (tr. Steve Gooch)	June
	Saint Joan	Bernard Shaw	June
SP	Paper Chase	an anthology	June
SG	Double Bill		July
	The Sea	Edward Bond	
	Something Unspoken	Tennessee Williams	
SP	Kennedy's Children	Robert Patrick	July

1977/78

	Small Craft Warnings	Tennessee Williams	September
	Absurd Person Singular	Alan Ayckbourn	October
	The Merchant of Venice	William Shakespeare	October
SP	Into Another Dimension	devised by John Wilson	October
	Home	David Storey	November
	Toad of Toad Hall	A A Milne (after Kenneth Grahame)	December
	A Midsummer Night's Dream	William Shakespeare	January
	Rosmersholm	Henrik Ibsen	January
	(tr. Michael Meyer)		
SG/SP	One-Act Plays		February
	Chamber Music	Arthur Kopit	
	The Tinker's Wedding	J M Synge	
	Barnstaple	James Saunders	
	Family Album	Noël Coward	
	Ashes	David Rudkin	February
	Oh, What a Lovely War!	Creighton and Theatre Workshop	March
	The Ride Across Lake Constance	Peter Handke	April
	(tr. Michael Roloff)		
	Hay Fever	Noel Coward	May
SP	A Mad World, My Masters	Barrie Keeffe	May
	Alphabetical Order	Michael Frayn	June
SP	The Caretaker	Harold Pinter	June
SP	Love for Love	William Congreve	July
SG	Separate Tables	Terence Rattigan	July
SP	Faust	Goethe	July
	(tr. David Emmet)		

1978/79

	The Killing of Sister George	Frank Marcus	September
	Penny for a Song	John Whiting	October
SP	Loop of Time	Nicholas Williams	October
	Antony and Cleopatra	William Shakespeare	November
SP	The Rimers of Eldritch	Lanford Wilson	November
EP	Blood Relations	Istvan Orkeny	December
	(tr. Mari Kuttna)		
SP	Vatslav	Slawomir Mrozek	December
	(tr. Nicholas Bethell)		
	The Thwarting of Baron Bolligrew	Robert Bolt	December
	The Waltz of the Toreadors	Jean Anouilh	January
	(tr. Lucienne Hill)		
	The Ghost Sonata	August Strindberg	February
	(tr. Michael Meyer)		
SG/SP	Diversions		February
	Man's Best Friend	James Saunders	
	Mother Figure	Alan Ayckbourn	
	Between Mouthfuls	Alan Ayckbourn	
	Night	Harold Pinter	
	Gosforth's Fête	Alan Ayckbourn	
	A Man for All Seasons	Robert Bolt	March
	It's All for the Best	Steve Gooch	April
	Fifth International Amateur Theatre Week		April
SP	No Quarter	Barry Bermange	May
	The Entertainer	John Osborne	May
SP	Early Plays	Tennessee Williams	May
	Loot	Joe Orton	June
	Jumpers	Tom Stoppard	June
SG	Crime and Punishment	Rodney Ackland	July
	(from Dostoevsky)		
SP	Light Shining in Buckinghamshire	Caryl Churchill	July

191

1979/80

	Venus Observed	Christopher Fry	September
SP	Dusa, Fish, Stas and Vi	Pam Gems	October
	When We Are Married	J B Priestley	October
SP	The Shrew	Shakespeare/Marowitz	November
	The Beggar's Opera	John Gay	November
SP/NP	Martin Guerre	John Davey & cast	November
	One Flew Over the Cuckoo's Nest	Dale Wasserman	December
	The Vampire	J R Planché	December
SP/NP	Count Cornetto's Creepy	Questabout Company	December
	Christmas		
SP	The Constant Couple	George Farquhar	January
	The Misanthrope	Molière	January
	(English version by Tony Harrison)		
EP	Playground	Douglas Verrall	February
SG/SP	One-Act Plays		February
	The Admirable Bashville	Bernard Shaw	
	The Orchestra	Jean Anouilh	
	(tr. Miriam John)		
	The Billy Club Puppets	Federico García Lorca	
	The Hostage	Brendan Behan	March
	Second English Amateur Theatre		March
	Week		
EP	The Girl in Melanie Klein	James Saunders	April
SP/NP	Questors New Writers		May
	The Old Pier	Norman Tucker	
	The House Warning	Judith Harry	
	Plodding On	Robert Jones	
	Cycles	Phillip Sheahan	
	Medea	Euripides	May
	(tr. Rex Warner)		
SP	Director's Shop Window		May
	The Gift of Friendship	Edward Bond	
	Butley	Simon Gray	May
	Macbeth	William Shakespeare	June
SG	Under Milk Wood	Dylan Thomas	July
SP	Measure for Measure	William Shakespeare	July

1980/81

	A Taste of Honey	Shelagh Delaney	September
	Pygmalion	Bernard Shaw	October
SP/NP	Shoeshop	Sebastian Baczkiewicz	November
SP	Three One-Act Plays	John Norman	November
	The White Devil	John Webster	November
	A View from the Bridge	Arthur Miller	December
	Cinderella	V C Clinton-Baddeley	December
EP	Fact and Fiction	Ferenc Karinthy	January
	(tr. Dr Belajthy Belane)		
NP	The Amazing Dancing Bear	Barry K Hillman	February
SG/SP	One-Act Plays		February
	Find Me	Olwen Wymark	
	A Talk in the Park	Alan Ayckbourn	
	Last to Go	Harold Pinter	
	The Black and White	Harold Pinter	
	They Alone Know	Jean Tardieu	
	(tr. Colin Duckworth)		
SP	Mary Barnes	David Edgar	February
	Othello	William Shakespeare	March
	The Magistrate	Arthur Wing Pinero	April
	No Man's Land	Harold Pinter	April
SP	Oedipus the King	Sophocles	May
	The Boy Friend	Sandy Wilson	May

SP	The Impossible Dream	an anthology	May
SP	This Story of Yours	John Hopkins	June
	Knickers	Carl Sternheim	June
SG	Saturday, Sunday, Monday	Eduardo de Philippo	July
SP	The Oresteia	Aeschylus	July
	(tr. Robert Fagels)		

1981/82

	A Streetcar Named Desire	Tennessee Williams	September
	Forty Years On	Alan Bennett	October
SP	Hans Kohlhaas	James Saunders	October
	The Winter's Tale	William Shakespeare	November
SP	Murder in the Cathedral	T S Eliot	November
	Dimetos	Athol Fugard	December
	Aladdin	Geoff Webb and others	December
SP	Clouds	Michael Frayn	December
	Treats	Christopher Hampton	January
SP/NP	The Whirler	Sebastian Baczkiewicz	January
SP	Directors' Shop Window		February
	Measure for Measure (extracts)	William Shakespeare	
	The Stronger	August Strindberg	
	(tr. Michael Meyer)		
	The Party	Slawomir Mrozek	
	(tr. Nicholas Bethell)		
EP	Sisters	Michel Tremblay	February
	(tr. John Van Burek & Bill Glassco)		
SG/SP	One-Act Plays		February
	Lysistrata (extracts)	Aristophanes	
	The Wedding	Anton Chekhov	
	A Respectable Wedding	Bertolt Brecht	
	Hedda Gabler	Henrik Ibsen	March
	(tr. Michael Meyer)		
	Equus	Peter Shaffer	March
EP	The Crimson Island	Mikhail Bulgakov	April
	(tr. C R & E Proffer)		
SP	Directors' Shop Window		April
	Leonardo's Last Supper	Peter Barnes	
	A Jacobean Christening	from A Chaste Maid in Cheapside by Thomas Middleton	
	Betrayal	Harold Pinter	May
SP	Bacchanalia	late-night entertainment	May
	Twelfth Night	William Shakespeare	June
SP	A Japanese Studio	4 one-act Japanese plays	June
	Sixth International Amateur Theatre Week		June
SP	The Maids	Jean Genet	July
	(tr. Bernard Frechtman)		
SG	The Crucible	Arthur Miller	July
SP	Now You See Him, Now You Don't	J M O'Neill	August

1982/83

	Just Between Ourselves	Alan Ayckbourn	September
SP	End Game	Samuel Beckett	September
	The Relapse	Sir John Vanbrugh	October
SP	You're Gonna Be Alright, Jamie Boy	David Freeman	October
	Happy End	Bertolt Brecht	November
	(tr. and adapted by Michael Feingold)		
EP	Bonjour Là, Bonjour	Michel Tremblay	December
	(tr. John Van Burek & Bill Glassco)		

SP	Anthem for Doomed Youth	an anthology	December
	Arsenic and Old Lace	Joseph Kesselring	December
NP	Wilfred and the Wizard Hunt	Jane Dewey	December
	Exiles	James Joyce	January
SP	Glass Houses	Stephen Lowe	January
	The Accrington Pals	Peter Whelan	February
	Sir Gawain and the Green Knight	Peter Stephens	March
	A Month in the Country	Ivan Turgenev	April
	(tr. Ariadne Nicolaeff)		
NP	The Midnight Sun	David Mowat	April
SP/NP	Questors Première Festival		April
	No Flowers By Request	Phillip Sheahan	
	Critical Daylight	Robert Jones	
	Snooper	Jim O'Connor	
	Eleventh Hour Theatre	late-night show	
	As If...	late-night show	
	Oh for Amuse	an anthology	
	Cabaret	Kander, Masterhoff & Ebb	May
SP	Caligula	Albert Camus	June
	Fourth English Amateur Theatre Week	June	
	A Nightingale Sang	C P Taylor	June
SG	Time and the Conways	J B Priestley	July

1983/84

	Period of Adjustment	Tennessee Williams	September
	Habeas Corpus	Alan Bennett	October
SP	Double Bill		October
	Gotcha!	Barrie Keeffe	
	Leonardo's Last Supper	Peter Barnes	
	Hamlet	William Shakespeare	November
SP	A Dream of Passion	an anthology	November
	Bodies	James Saunders	November
	The Third Great Coarse Acting Show	Michael Green and others	December
NP	Waldo and the Wonderful Web	Jane Dewey	December
SP	Little Eyolf	Henrik Ibsen	December
	(tr. Michael Meyer)		
	The Philanthropist	Christopher Hampton	January
SP	Julius Caesar	William Shakespeare	January
	Princess Ivona	Witold Gombrowicz	February
SG	One-act Plays		February
	The Real Inspector Hound	Tom Stoppard	
	Fumed Oak	Noel Coward	
	A Night Out	Harold Pinter	
SP	Turning Point	Paul Thain	March
	Ring Round the Moon	Jean Anouilh	March
	(tr. Christopher Fry)		
NP	Phoenix	David Storey	April
	Loaves and Fishes	W Somerset Maugham	April
SP/NP	Long Way Away	Geoff Webb and cast	April
	The Master Builder	Henrik Ibsen	May
	(tr. Michael Meyer)		
	Lark Rise	Keith Dewhurst	June
	(adapted from the book by Flora Thompson)		
SP/NP	Dancing Naked	David Pearson	June
SG	The Matchmaker	Thornton Wilder	July
SP	Romeo and Juliet	William Shakespeare	July

1984/85

SP	The Just	Albert Camus	September
NP	Abode of Peace	Ruth Prawer Jhabvala	September
	The Importance of Being Earnest	Oscar Wilde	October
SP	Knackering for All (tr. Watson Taylor)	Boris Vian	October
	Henry IV Part 1	William Shakespeare	November
	Don Juan Comes Back From the War (tr. Christopher Hampton)	Ödön von Horváth	November
SP	The Rape of Lucrece	William Shakespeare	December
	The Fantastic Fairground	Goss, Hamel-Cooke & Bond	December
	Sherlock Holmes	Conan Doyle & Wm. Gillette	December
SP	Double Bill		January
	Chekhov	Keith Miles	
	The Proposal (tr. Elisaveta Fen)	Anton Chekhov	
	Knuckle	David Hare	January
SG	Double Bill		February
	Cage Birds	David Campton	
	The Trial	Steven Berkoff (after Kafka)	
SP/NP	Fair Play	Geoff Webb and cast	March
SP	Questickles	late night entertainment	March
	Bedroom Farce	Alan Ayckbourn	March
	A Life	Hugh Leonard	April
SP/NP	Harry	Sebastian Baczkiewicz	April
	Marat/Sade (English version by Geoffrey Skelton)	Peter Weiss	May
	Tom Jones	Joan Macalpine (after Henry Fielding)	June
	The Cherry Orchard (tr. Michael Frayn)	Anton Chekhov	June
	The Cherry Sisters	Michael Green and others	June
SG	The Good Woman of Setzuan (tr. Eric Bentley)	Bertolt Brecht	July
SP	The Sea	Edward Bond	July
SP	Sexual Perversity in Chicago	David Mamet	August

1985/86

	The Daughter-in-Law	D H Lawrence	September
SP	Shout Across the River	Stephen Poliakoff	September
	The Country Wife	William Wycherley	October
SP	Directors' Showcase		October
	Men and Women (adapted by James Hepburn)	D H Lawrence	
	Double Bill		November
	Lunch Hour	John Mortimer	
	Black Comedy	Peter Shaffer	
	Misalliance	Bernard Shaw	November
SP	Hard Feelings	Doug Lucie	December
SP	Micromania	Jane Dewey	December
	Under the Gaslight	Augustin Daly	December
	Can't Pay? Won't Pay!	Dario Fo	January
SP	Wealth	Aristophanes (adapted by Steve Fitzpatrick)	January
SG	One-act Plays		February
	Agamemnon	Aeschylus (adapted by Steven Berkoff)	
	Lux in Tenebris	Bertolt Brecht	
	The Assembly Women	Aristophanes	

SP	Cloud Nine	Caryl Churchill	March
	Bartholomew Fair	Ben Jonson	March
	Blithe Spirit	Noël Coward	April
	Good	C P Taylor	May
NP	Steadman: In the Mouth of the Lion	John Garforth	May
EP	Spellbound	Louis Nowra	June
	Whose Life is it Anyway?	Brian Clark	June
SP	The Hollow Crown	devised by John Barton	July
SG/NP	Albert, Make Us Laugh	Jimmie Chinn	July
SP/NP	Cold Times	Ödön von Horváth (adapted from The Age of the Fish by Geoff Webb)	August

1986/87

	The Glass Menagerie	Tennessee Williams	September
	Destiny	David Edgar	October
	The Norman Conquests	Alan Ayckbourn	November
	Living Together		
	Round and Round the Garden		
	Table Manners		
	Top Girls	Caryl Churchill	November
SP	Double Bill		November
	Death Watch	Jean Genet	
	(tr. Nigel Williams)		
	One For the Road	Harold Pinter	
	Maria Marten or The Murder in the Red Barn	Anon	December
	Old King Cole	Ken Campbell	December
	Blood Wedding	Federico García Lorca (adapted by Alan Chambers)	January
	Tartuffe	Molière	February
	(tr. Steve Fitzpatrick)		
SP/NP	Lady Susan	Jane Dewey (after Jane Austen)	February
SG/SP	Tomfooleries		March
	The Erpingham Camp	Joe Orton	
	Vinegar Tom	Caryl Churchill	
	Night	Harold Pinter	
	Bye Bye Blues	James Saunders	
	The Two Gentlemen of Verona	William Shakespeare	March
	Two Gentlemen	Kevin Madley	March
	The Coarse Acting Show	Michael Green and others	April
SP/EP	American Dreams	Dorothy Velasco	April
	Miracle at Graceland		
	The Radio Ray Fan Club		
	The Metamorphosis of Woody Allen		
	Brief Lives	John Aubrey (adapted by Patrick Garland)	May
	Fifth English Amateur Theatre Week		May
SP/NP	If Shakespeare Was a Friend of Ours, He really Wouldn't Mind Us Doing This	devised by John Wilson	May
NP	The Death of Joe Hill	John Fay	May
SP/NP	The Brick	Nigel Swain	June
	Animal Farm	George Orwell (adapted by Peter Hall)	June
SG	The Man Who Came to Dinner	Moss Hart & George Kaufman	July
SP	Albertine, in Five Times	Michel Tremblay	July
	(tr. John Van Burek & Bill Glassco)		

	Educating Rita	Willy Russell	September
SP/NP	The Man Who Shot the Tiger	Sebastian Baczkiewicz	September
	Candida	Bernard Shaw	October
	The Lady's Not For Burning	Christopher Fry	October
SP/NP	Somewhere in England	Jean & Gordon Caleb & Vincent McQueen	November
	Right You Are (If You Think So!) (tr. Frederick May)	Luigi Pirnadello	December
SP/NP	The Story of Aesop	Steve Fitzpatrick	December
	Dangerous Corner	J B Priestley	January
SP	A Lovely Sunday for Creve Coeur	Tennessee Williams	January
	The Caucasian Chalk Circle (tr. James & Tania Stern with W H Auden)	Bertolt Brecht	January
	A Midsummer Night's Dream	William Shakespeare	February
SG/SP	One-act Plays		February
	The Shewing-up of Blanco Posnet	Bernard Shaw	
	The Orchestra (tr. Miriam John)	Jean Anouilh	
	The Martyrdom of Peter Ohey (tr. Nicholas Bethell)	Slawomir Mrozek	February
	The Bedbug (tr. Kathleen Cook Horujy)	Vladimir Mayakovsky	March
SP	Futurists	Dusty Hughes	March
	The House of Bernarda Alba (tr. James Graham-Lujan & Richard L O'Connell)	Federico García Lorca	March
SP	Skirmishes	Catherine Hayes	April
	Born in the Gardens	Peter Nichols	May
SP	The Fall of the House of Usher	Steven Berkoff (after E A Poe)	May
NP	State of the Art	B F Herst	June
SP	Making Noise Quietly Being Friends Lost Making Noise Quietly	Robert Holman	June
	The Front Page	Ben Hecht & Charles Macarthur	June
SP	Doctor Faustus	Christopher Marlowe	July
SG	Philistines	Dusty Hughes (after Maxim Gorky)	July

	Benefactors	Michael Frayn	September
SP	Miss Julie (tr. Michael Meyer)	August Strindberg	October
	Taking Steps	Alan Ayckbourn	October
SP	The Hired Man	Melvyn Bragg & Howard Goodall	October
	Love's Sacrifice	John Ford	November
	The Father (tr. Eivor Martinus)	August Strindberg	December
	Charley's Aunt	Brandon Thomas	December
SP	Road	Jim Cartwright	January
SP	The Sulky Fire (tr. John Leslie Frith)	Jean-Jacques Bernard	January
	Woyzeck (tr. Marguerite Minster)	Georg Büchner	January
	Measure for Measure	William Shakespeare	February
SG/SP	Fear and Misery of the Third Reich (tr. John Willett)	Bertolt Brecht	February
	Hobson's Choice	Harold Brighouse	March

SP	Hamlet—What Dreams May Come (adapted by John Wilson)	William Shakespeare	April
	London Assurance	Dion Boucicault	April
SP	White Nights & Dostoevsky	Keith Miles	May
	The Seagull	Anton Chekhov (in a version by Thomas Kilroy)	May
NP	The Almas	David Mowat	June
SP/NP	The Mind Forest	R D Steadman-Jones	June
NP	War Street Serenade	Katy Louise Dean	June
SG	Pride and Prejudice	Constance Cox (after Jane Austen)	July
SP/NP	The Penny Showman	devised by the company	July

Appendix 2

List of Presidents of The Questors Theatre

Among those who accepted an invitation between 1930 and 1944 to serve as The Questors' Presidents were Robert Atkins, Ion Swinley, Ben Webster, Gwen Ffrangcon-Davies and Margaret Webster. Then:

John Burrell	1944—1952
Tyrone Guthrie	1952—1958
Michael Redgrave	1958—1985
Judi Dench	1985—present

List of Chairmen

Margaret Broome	1929—1931	George Benn	1953—1957
Egar Woollcombe	1931—1933	John Clemow	1957—1958
Cyril Thomas	1933—1938	Clifford Webb	1958—1962
Philip Allen	1938—1943	George Benn	1962—1972
Frank Smith	1943—1945	Martin Bowley	1972—1984
Philip Allen	1943—1948	Roger de Toney	1984—1988
Eric Voce	1948—1949	Martin Bowley	1988—present
Alfred Emmet	1950		
Ernest Ives	1950—1953		

List of Artistic Directors

Alfred Emmet	Honorary Director	1948—1969
David Gower	Chairman of Plays and Productions Committee	1969—1971
Nevile Cruttenden	Chairman of plays and Productions Committee	1971—1973
	Director of Productions	1973—1976
Brian Rich	Director of Productions	1976—1977
Alan Chambers, Alfred Emmet & David Gower	Joint Directors of Productions	1977—1978
Alan Chambers	Director of Productions	1978—1981
John Davey	Artistic Director	1981—1986
Geoff Webb	Artistic Director	1986—present

List of Theatre Managers

Betty Mercy	General Manager	1944
Barbara Hutchins		1944—1946
Rena Rice		1946—1963
Owen Surridge	Administrator	1963
Tony Clayton		1963—1964
Clyde Jones		1964—1966
Teresa Collard		1966—1967
Gordon Caleb		1967—1976
David Lawler		1976—1978
Mike Monaghan		1978—1978
Ben O'Mahoney	Theatre Manager	1979—1983
Katharine Lindsay		1983—1984
John Garforth		1984—1987
Elaine Orchard		1987—present

Appendix 3

Our Quest

Part I—The Quest and What it Means (1947)

The purpose of The Questors is stated in our Constitution as being "to further the interests of Dramatic Art". This is not to be dismissed as a mere high sounding phrase; we have always regarded it as very real and very practical indeed.

The Questors is an association of individuals banded together for a common purpose, to serve the art of the theatre. To that end have been devoted the talents and labour of many scores of people, who have contributed in one way or another during the past eighteen years to make The Questors what it is today. To that end we invite the assistance of all who share our ideals and will work with us now and in the years to come.

We believe that the theatre has a vital part to play in this post-war world. More perhaps than any other art, it can serve people by enriching their lives with beauty and inspiration; with laughter and with joy; it can give expression to man's aspirations; it can give opportunities in the richest, fullest sense, for needed recreation. And when, as in the case of a community such as ours, there is opportunity for all who wish to do so, to devote their time and energy to creative work in disinterested service, the value of the theatre's contribution to living is increased manifold.

We believe that the theatre should in the broadest sense serve the people. We are not afraid to assert our belief that part of the function of theatre is educative, ie. to raise the level of popular taste, and to serve the people does not necessarily mean to provide only what the majority of people demand.

We believe that in the spirit of service, allied to a sense of responsibility, lies the ultimate hope of the theatre of our time, to which we may hope to make some contribution.

We believe that in studying first how to serve the theatre, we find the best way to serve our members, for so we will provide them with entertainment which is richer and more abiding than the passing pleasures vended by the Entertainments Industry.

These are our guiding principles. Pursuing them, The Questors has become recognised as one of the leading Little Theatre groups in the country.

This reputation, which we wish to maintain, rests primarily on three things. First and foremost on our standard of choice of plays; secondly on the artistic standard of our work; thirdly on our non-parochial outlook.

While our reputation as such is of secondary importance to the work we do in our theatre, these things on which it depends coincide with the factors which we believe to be of supreme importance in our work if it is to be of the greatest possible value to the community.

The policy we have endeavoured to pursue is, therefore, in broad outline threefold:

    1. To maintain the highest standard of choice of play;

    2. To maintain and improve the artistic standard of our productions;

    3. To contribute in any way open to us to the good of theatre as a whole.

How, in practice, is this to be applied?

CHOICE OF PLAY. Situated where we are, on the doorstep of the West End, it would be false to suppose that visits to The Questors Theatre represent the whole of our audiences' theatre going. Our play-choice policy must take account of our geographical situation. Certain types of play can be seen to advantage in the adjacent commercial theatre, and there is little to be gained by our reproducing such plays.

Our aim, therefore, is to choose plays of high quality which our audience would be unlikely to have an opportunity of seeing elsewhere, or of such classical character as to be deserving of continued repetition or fresh interpretation. It is as well to remember that a particular choice at a particular time depends upon many factors, prominent among which is the question of cast and producer available. If a play cannot be suitably cast, the production standard may inevitably fall.

We do claim, however, that in both general and particular our play choice has always been worthwhile, and we have brought to our audiences a wide range of the finest plays in world theatre.The list of plays produced in our theatre is one in which we may take great pride.

STANDARD OF PRODUCTION. This must be maintained and improved at all costs. It is the hallmark of our work. It entails maintaining the firm principle in casting that the best possible cast must be found from the players available, while giving due regard to the desirability of giving promising players opportunities to develop their parts. A full programme of training is of vital importance. Basically the standard depends upon the ready acceptance by our acting members of the principles involved; upon their willingness to work to develop their own artistic talents; upon the spirit of service already referred to; and the voluntary self-discipline which is essential to the pursuit of any art.

TRIBUTARY FUNCTIONS. We must look beyond our own immediate parochial circle to find our true place in the theatre as a whole, otherwise our work, however worthwhile, would eventually die back on itself. On the one hand we must look out to the mainstream of theatre, accepting our responsibilities and endeavouring to contribute thereto, for instance through the medium of the Little Theatre Guild of Great Britain. On the other hand we must also look round to other groups, perhaps less fortunately placed than ourselves (particularly to the young people who will make the theatre of tomorrow), and lend a helping hand whenever and wherever we can. It is not enough to be sufficient unto ourselves.

What does all this add up to for the ordinary member? To one who participates actively in our work, whether an actor, technician, or in any other capacity, it means an opportunity for a creative contribution to a theatre which will live and which will in turn make a contribution to living.

To one who is an audience member it means quite simply an assurance of the best things in the best manner possible.

That is the meaning of 'The Quest'. Its success depends upon your backing and enthusiasm.

Part 2—Statement of Aims (1972)

It is nearly 25 years since a statement of aims of 'The Quest and What it Means' was first drawn up by The Questors. This policy statement was later reaffirmed by the membership in 1960 when the new Playhouse was in a final planning stage. These principles have guided all our activities to the present time.

The Committee of Management believes that the time has come to re-examine and re-state the aims of our theatre; and following this to consider our present and projected activities in the light of these aims.

We have expressed them as follows:
1. To be an AMATEUR THEATRE
2. To be an INDEPENDENT THEATRE
3. To be a theatre DEVOTED TO THE HIGHEST POSSIBLE ARTISTIC STANDARDS
4. To be an OUTWARD LOOKING THEATRE
5. To be a theatre of ADVENTURE

By re-stating our aims in this form it should not be inferred that we are departing in any material way from our earlier policy statetment. However, the real value of this exercise lies in examining the inter-relation of our aims and the way in which they help to guide the planning and realisation of all our activities. To do this we need to elaborate further on each of the five headings.

1. To be an AMATEUR THEATRE:

There is a considerable and continuing interest in theatre in this country. A great many people like to express this interest by participating in theatre during their spare time. The very existence of amateur theatre enables these people to develop and contribute their talents as actors, technicians, designers, whatever. Given the artistic and physical conditions in which to work, groups like The Questors have shown that amateur theatre can give a considerable and valuable service to the art and development of theatre in general. In fact, the amateur nature of The Questors is the very essence of its character and spirit; without it we do not exist. The only area in which we, The Questors, entertain paid staff is in the sphere of administration where the practical problems offer no alternative.

2. To be an INDEPENDENT THEATRE:

In the context of amateur theatre, independence implies both artistic and financial independence. We need to make a profit because we need financial independence to secure artistic independence. Two main policy decisions serve to balance these conflicting demands. They are:

A. That we operate as a membership theatre. Almost half The Questors income is guaranteed at the start of each financial year through our members' subscriptions. It is precisely this kind of financial security which gives The Questors the freedom to pursue the artistic policy of our choice. We now know that a membership of 3,000 is necessary to support our theatre. There is no indication that the current play policy is inconsistent with our membership targets. Clearly the most popular and profitable part of our programme has a classical base. However, this base allows the independence to explore less familiar and new works, as well as new experimental techniques.

Also that we make the fullest possible use of our premises by letting in so far as this is possible without undue interference with our own activities. At the present time letting of the various parts of our theatre contributes a valuable 10% of our total income.

B. An independent theatre also implies administrative independence. The Questors relies on its active members to maintain this essential part of our character. As the work of the theatre grows, the need for active membership involvement increases. Consequently, it is crtitical that new ways of involving the active members in the decision-making process are sought urgently and continuously. A constant regeneration of people and ideas in the active membership is a major key to our existence—to our independence.

3. To be a theatre DEVOTED TO THE HIGHEST POSSIBLE ARTISTIC STANDARDS:

The expression of our aims with regard to artistic standards is the programme we present, whether the production be a major play in the Playhouse or an experimental workshop in the Stanislavsky Room. Reinforcing our quest for the highest artistic standards are our important policies in such matters as periods of rehearsal, training in all aspects of theatre work, and the encouragement of more experimental work.

Analysis of our audience records and questionnaire results show that the classical base of our programme enjoys the greatest popularity with our audience members. It is this base which enables the maintenance of our constant search for new and young ideas, some of which will be successful and contribute to our achievement of the highest possible artistic standards. In this respect we are convinced of the need to establish some form of workshop theatre where the wildest ideas can be explored in an atmosphere of complete freedom, even to fail. From such work come ideas and techniques which in due course will influence our main theatre programme of plays.

4. To be an OUTWARD LOOKING THEATRE:

One of our main strengths is our willingness to see beyond our own entertainment and amusement, to involve ourselves in the local community in which we exist and in the development of the theatre at large. We believe in the art of theatre and we believe in extending and developing that art in terms of ideas and people.

A. In terms of ideas we believe we have a duty to explore methods of direction, design and writing for the theatre—our social and physical structure gives us an almost unparalleled opportunity to have the freedom we currently enjoy; we must continue to encourage new playwrights, particularly within the context of the New Plays Festival; the establishment of a resident dramatist is another important expression of our interest in new works.

B. Extending and developing the art of theatre in terms of people involves work locally, nationally and internationally. Locally we intend to continue and expand our already significant work with young people, particularly through the Student Group, Young People's Groups, presentation of examination set plays, and through presenting professional children's theatre companies in our Playhouse. Nationally we shall continue to give active support to the Little Theatre Guild of Great Britain and other theatre organisations. Internationally we shall consolidate and extend our overseas links via the International Amateur Theatre Weeks and occasional tours abroad.

In essence our outward looking policy is an important part of our progress. Just as we give a great deal, we also seek to learn and develop from our contacts and experience outside the environment we have created for ourselves. By learning in this way we can increase the contribution we, as an organisation, make to our individual members, the community in general and, most important, the art of theatre.

5. To be a theatre of ADVENTURE:

A very general aim because perhaps it encompasses all that has already been written. The spirit of adventure has been the greatest force behind the success of The Questors so far and must continue to dominate our future. Much of The Questors' reputation, nationally amd internationally, has derived from the adventurous quality of our work in terms of the new Playhouse itself, our play choice, our encouragement of experimentation of all kinds.

It is a spirit of enterprise which has fostered what we represent today. It is a spirit that must be continually regenerated and reinforced.